Affirmative Action
and the University

Kul B. Rai
and John W. Critzer

Affirmative Action and the University

*Race, Ethnicity, and
Gender in Higher Education
Employment*

UNIVERSITY OF NEBRASKA PRESS

LINCOLN AND LONDON

© 2000 by the University of Nebraska
Press. All rights reserved Manufac-
tured in the United States of America.
⊖ Library of Congress Cataloging-in-
Publication Data. Rai, Kul B.
Affirmative action and the university :
race, ethnicity, and gender in higher
education employment / Kul B. Rai
and John W. Critzer.
    p.   cm.   Includes bibliographical
references (p.   ) and index.
ISBN 0-8032-3934-3 (cloth : alk. paper)
1. Discrimination in higher education—
United States. 2. Minority college
teachers—Employment—United States.
3. Minority college administrators—
Employment—United States. 4. Affirmative action programs—United States.
I. Critzer, John W., 1947–   II. TITLE.
LC212.42.R35   2000
378.1'2—DC21   99-30467 CIP

Contents

Tables

APPENDIXES

Acknowledgments

We are grateful to those individuals who provided assistance and encouragement in the writing of this manuscript. To no single individual do we owe a greater debt than to Jean Polka, secretary of the Political Science Department at this university. Jean's word-processing skills were crucial to the successful completion of our project. She worked very hard, far beyond the call of duty, to make sure that the final product was professional and as flawless as possible.

Some of the officials at the U.S. Equal Employment Opportunity Commission and the U.S. Department of Education were generous with their time in making data available to us and helping us in some other ways when they could. In particular, we want to thank Esther Littlejohn and Evelyn Williams of the EEOC and Vance Grant of the National Center for Education Statistics, Department of Education. In addition, we appreciate the assistance of Karl M. Engelbach of the California Postsecondary Education Commission for this project.

Connecticut State University awarded us a research grant; Southern Connecticut State University granted us sabbatical leaves; and Southern Connecticut State University's Faculty Development Office made its resources available whenever we needed them. We thank anonymous reviewers for the University of Nebraska Press, who read our manuscript and made useful suggestions for revisions. We express our gratitude to Jane M. Curran, our copyeditor, who did an outstanding job in preparing the manuscript for publication.

We thank the staff of the University of Nebraska Press for their professional and prompt processing of the manuscript.

Kul B. Rai could not have completed this manuscript without the understanding and support of his wife, Priya.

John Critzer would like to thank Kul B. Rai and the other members of the Political Science Department – Harriet Applewhite, Paul Best, Robert Gelbach, John Iatrides, Arthur Paulson, David Walsh, and Clyde Weed – for providing a supportive work environment filled with scholarly exchange, good humor, and friendship.

He would also like to thank J. Philip Smith, formerly Dean of Arts and Sciences and currently Interim Vice President for Academic Affairs, for providing him with reassigned time for research for two semesters, which greatly facilitated work on this project.

John would like to thank his parents, John L. and Sophie H. Critzer, for their continuing support and encouragement throughout this long process. It will not be forgotten. He also greatly appreciates the words of encouragement and support from his brothers and their families, Bob and Janet, and Rod, Kathy, and Joey.

Introduction

RACE, ETHNICITY, AND GENDER IN AMERICA

The dilemma of providing equal employment opportunities to racial and ethnic minorities and women without promoting a system of new inequalities has become a critical issue in the United States as a result of the implementation of affirmative action. Critics charge that affirmative action has created a preference system, while advocates argue that without such government intervention, racial, ethnic, and gender bias would continue in employment patterns throughout the United States.[1]

Fundamental to those who support affirmative action are the past discriminatory values and practices that have shaped social relations, sex roles, and career opportunities. In terms of employment, prejudice based on race, ethnicity, and gender has promoted barriers that have restricted educational attainment and quality, distorted the employment selection process, and created overt or covert job categories for certain members of society. Up to the 1960s, Anglo-Saxon white males enjoyed preferential treatment in employment, while minority group members and women were generally excluded from high-status, well-paying jobs. The rise of various social movements supporting civil rights, feminism, and racial and ethnic identity during the 1960s produced enormous changes in both society and the workplace. Pressure on the federal government led to the end of the Jim Crow laws that segregated blacks and whites in the South and to the passage of the Civil Rights Act of 1964. In addition, efforts were undertaken to have government protect members of society from nongovernmental forces that inhibited individual rights, whether they be economic, social, or political ones. Such attempts to alter the status quo within the labor market have led to charges of reverse discrimination and allegations of a new preference system as minorities and women have moved into positions once controlled by white males.

RACE RELATIONS

The issue of black-white relations has shaped in great part America and its belief system. W. E. B. Du Bois's often-cited quote, "the color line is the problem
of the twentieth century,"[2] continues to remain true, as the current debate
about affirmative action focuses largely on blacks even though other minorities and women are also the subject of equal employment efforts. Central to
this issue is whether efforts to redress the discriminatory practices of the past
have produced preferential treatment for minorities and women, often called
reverse discrimination for white males.

Contemporary black-white relations rest not only on past interactions but
also on current perceptions, as blacks believe that discrimination continues to
exist and whites feel that such practices have mostly ended. The persistence of
Americans' preoccupation with race means that the core values of equality and
liberty are interwoven with how Americans think about race and also how they
act.

Gunnar Myrdal's massive work published in 1944, *An American Dilemma:
The Negro Problem and Modern Democracy*, found an inherent contradiction
between beliefs – the American Creed – and the day-to-day practices of whites
toward blacks. About the American belief system Myrdal stated: "These ideals
of the essential dignity of the individual human being, of the fundamental
equality of all men, and of certain inalienable rights to freedom, justice, and a
fair opportunity represent to the American people the essential meaning of the
nation's early struggle for independence." Yet, writing in the early 1940s, he
found that, in practice, individual as well as group behavior was shaped by a
wide range of motivations, prejudices, and jealousies. As a result, blacks were
denied the basic rights of liberty and equality in relationship to whites.
Myrdal, however, believed that blacks would gain equality, for Americans
would ultimately adhere to the basic values of the Creed. This optimism was
justified by what Myrdal perceived as the unwillingness of Americans to legal-
ize the existing "caste" system of race relations.[3] Although numerous restrictions had been placed on black behavior by whites, these constraints existed
outside the Constitution and the laws of the United States and would not with-
stand Americans' devotion to the values of liberty and equality. Nevertheless,
Liah Greenfeld's remark that "one wants to be equal to one's superiors, but
does not desire equality with those seen as one's inferiors" serves as a reminder
that status attainment also exists in the minds of those who believe in equality.[4]

Andrew Hacker, in his examination of contemporary race relations, con-
trasts the optimism of Myrdal with the observations of Alexis de Tocqueville,

the nineteenth-century French jurist who, following a tour of America, argued that even after the abolition of slavery blacks would come to learn that they would not be able to enjoy all of the rights available to whites.[5] Whites would continue to consider blacks as inferior in status, and any efforts by blacks to change this perception were destined to fail. As Tocqueville argued, "to induce the whites to abandon the opinion they have conceived of the intellectual and moral inferiority of their former slaves, the Negroes must change, but they cannot so long as this opinion persists."[6] Myrdal was not unaware of Tocqueville's view but found refuge in the American Creed as a means to end racial prejudice.[7] On the other hand, Tocqueville believed that traditional attitudes would remain long after blacks acquired their freedom, and that blacks' efforts to seek redress through the courts would be futile, for they would have to rely on white judges.[8]

Tocqueville's view that whites would continue to block black equality after the end of slavery is echoed in the writings of critical race theorists today. They argue that recent civil rights efforts such as affirmative action are likely to alter only the most extreme examples of discrimination, for day-to-day racial prejudice continues through individual and institutional actions.[9] Thus, obstacles to black equality are not only political and social but cultural and psychological as well. Charles Lawrence argues that racism "is a part of our common historical experience and, therefore, a part of our culture. It arises from the assumptions we have learned to make about the world, ourselves, and others as well as from the patterns of our fundamental social activities."[10] A lack of awareness about the depth of prejudice within society leads to unconscious racism, which Thomas Ross states has led to a reversal of the idea of victimization as whites perceive themselves to be victims of affirmative action and the victim status of blacks is questioned.[11] Thus, while headway appears to be made, newer obstacles emerge that continue to weaken efforts to eliminate racism.[12]

Critical race theorist Derrick Bell argues that a good number of whites have willingly accepted economic inequalities because racial discrimination based on color has given them priority in various economic opportunities and furnished "whites of an unspoken . . . property right in their 'whiteness.' "[13] He goes on to argue that this notion of whiteness as property, which emerged with the development of American slavery, continues to the present day and explains in part the opposition to such programs as affirmative action that alter the status system.[14] Ian F. Haney López argues that whiteness as a social construction based on physical characteristics, which has been reinforced by various legal decisions, is transparent within society and produces an avoidance of the social roots and purposes of such a classification.[15] This argument parallels Tocqueville's conclusion that the legal system controlled by whites would not assist blacks in obtaining their rights. Applying their perspective not only to race but to ethnicity and gender as well, critical race theorists argue that major governmental efforts to redress racial, ethnic, and gender inequalities will be limited by social, cultural, psychological, and institutional forces.[16]

This focus is an effort to call attention to the burden of past and current discriminatory practices that critics of affirmative action rarely consider, as some argue that government intervention through affirmative action programs does less to assist minorities and women and more to stigmatize them as individuals unable to succeed on their own.[17] Yet long before anyone envisioned the current affirmative action program, Myrdal found a general perception, especially in the South, that blacks could not manage without white assistance. For example, Myrdal cites the following quotes: "The whites give them all the jobs"; "Actually they live on us white people"; "They couldn't sustain themselves a day if we gave them up"; "What little they have, they have got from the whites"; "The whites pay all the taxes or don't they?"[18] Overall, there was a belief that southern whites provided for blacks who could not succeed through their own efforts. There seems to be a persistent view that blacks are unable to succeed without assistance from whites or government programs such as affirmative action. Although both examine the context of American race relations, Myrdal's more optimistic view that blacks will in time obtain equality is in sharp contrast to the pessimistic view held by many critical race theorists who see major obstacles confronting black progress.[19] Nevertheless, understanding American values and practices underscores the difficulties facing government in attempting to promote equality, whether it be in the workplace or in the greater society.

ASSIMILATION AND INCLUSION

Of course, blacks are not the only ones to have faced discrimination in America: other racial and ethnic minorities have also experienced discriminatory practices. Hispanics, for example, have faced prejudice in their attempts to become accepted members of American society. Recently, Rodney Hero argued that although Myrdal's moral dilemma has been applied to both blacks and American Indians, this application has not been made for Hispanic Americans.[20] This is due in part to differences in treatment; it also resulted, according to Hero, because an ideology of conquest based on manifest destiny was used to justify the taking of Mexican- or Spanish-held land as an act of liberation for its inhabitants. Following the Mexican War in the 1840s and the Spanish-American War of 1898, the territorial expansion of the United States led to the free movement of certain Hispanic groups within American society.[21] New territorial annexation of these lands was justified on the grounds that it brought freedom and liberty to the inhabitants, yet Hispanics were rarely accepted as full members of society. Language differences as well as the fact that many of the inhabitants were of various racial mixtures led to prejudice and discrimination. In the twentieth century, the immigration of other Hispanic groups has often been closely linked to U.S. foreign policy objectives, such as efforts to combat communism in Cuba and Nicaragua. It is also true that others were motivated by poverty to leave their native countries in hopes of finding a better life. This increased immigration, however, has meant discrimination as some Americans perceive even native-born Hispanic Americans as uwanted or even illegal immigrants.

Asian Americans also face discrimination based on race, and the continuing confusion about the difference between native-born and immigrant Asian Americans continues to delay their full acceptance into American society. Myrdal states that a major part of the American Creed is the assumption that ultimately each new group will become assimilated into the dominant culture, but in practice racism leads to different treatment, especially for blacks but also for those of Chinese and Japanese origin.[22] Although Myrdal takes note of the concern by Americans that groups maintaining their own distinctive identities are perceived as a threat, an exception is made for the separation of racial groups. For example, today while many whites criticize Hispanics for maintaining their language, some whites find it acceptable for blacks and Asians to be separated from the mainstream of American culture.

Although Myrdal found that race played a critical role in excluding blacks and Asians from the opportunity to assimilate into American society, this was not the case for Native Americans.[23] Instead, he argued that the older view questioning the ability of Native Americans to assimilate had been replaced by a new view that held out the prospect for their future incorporation into American society. This contradiction in terms of how blacks and Native Americans should be treated can be found in the writings of Thomas Jefferson, who speculated on the inferiority of blacks as a separate race but who considered Native Americans as the equals of whites and approved of intermarriage between the two races.[24]

Although Myrdal pointed to the American Creed with its emphasis on equality, it is also true that Americans have perceived various racial and ethnic groups differently in terms of assimilation and inclusion. This paradox has only heightened the problems of promoting a color-blind society and providing equality of opportunity in the workplace.

THE ISSUE OF GENDER

Just as race is used to divide groups within society, so is gender. Gender discrimination, which is based on perceived physical differences between men and women, cuts across racial and ethnic lines and has generated a division of duties and rights within society based on gender. These perceptions have been reinforced through societal and familial structures and have played a major role in shaping the opportunities available to women in the work force.

Myrdal also commented on the issue of gender, noting that both women and children were just as likely to be treated like blacks in all societies. He argued that women and children "are characterized by high social visibility expressed in physical appearance, dress, and patterns of behavior, and have been 'suppressed.' " Like blacks, women and children in the early history of the United States were under patriarchal rule. In addition, women, similar to blacks, were considered to lack certain physical and mental capabilities. Women were thought to have certain strengths and thus were channeled into certain types of employment. Myrdal found reference to woman as "an ornament" in the antebellum South and stated that men in societies throughout the world often sought "a pet woman" to marry.[25] The idea that patriarchal society promotes women as objects is one of the arguments made by feminist Betty Friedan.[26] She asserts that female subordination leads women to be seen visibly as sex objects, but their lack of equality makes them invisible within society. Friedan states that the dependent status of woman as wife and mother creates repercussions within marriage that are injurious to both husband and child. She calls for giving women greater educational and employment opportunities so that they might become ministers, politicians, or business executives and thus alter the traditional role of women as wives and mothers.

Tocqueville in his examination of early-nineteenth-century America, however, states that an element of free choice existed in a woman's decision to marry: she "suffers her new state bravely, for she has chosen it."[27] He argued that the early education of a woman assisted her in moving from a state of relative freedom to the more restricted role of wife. Such an education gave a woman the spirit necessary to find happiness within the confines of the home. Tocqueville believed that democracy would lead to greater social equality between men and women, but that economic considerations would require them to perform very different functions within society.

Within all societies economic as well as social roles have been determined by gender, usually placing women in positions with less power and lower pay. The difficulties women faced in the nineteenth and early twentieth centuries in gaining the vote and later in the 1960s in raising the issue that women could perform the same tasks as men demonstrate the problem of inclusion not only for minorities but for women as well. The emphasis on changing societal and individual perceptions about female roles in the workplace is rather recent, and many point to affirmative action as the means to make such changes.

There is a long history of exclusion of minorities and women in the workplace that raises serious questions about whether equality of opportunity can be established in only a few short years. More importantly, it demonstrates the persistence of inequality within American society. Now with steps to redress this inequality, white males who are seeing their opportunities diminish argue that a preference system has been created that excludes them. Thus, those who look at affirmative action see it from two very different vantage points: one finding equality, the other discovering discriminatory preference. Affirmative action has divided America over questions about equality and rights and has at its center the issue of race.

AFFIRMATIVE ACTION

The origins of affirmative action stem from the Civil Rights Act of 1964, especially Title VII, which was an effort to promote equality in the workplace. Building on a number of executive orders, bureaucratic rules, and court decisions, the controversial program known as affirmative action was created. Many argue that it has replaced equality with a system of preferences. This program developed in the 1960s and 1970s, first as a response to the civil rights movement and later to the feminist movement. The period of the 1960s was a time of increased federal involvement in numerous social problems, and the drive was led by President Lyndon Baines Johnson. Stating that blacks needed to be provided with "equality as a result," Johnson shifted the widely accepted American concept of equality of opportunity to one that for many meant government would guarantee opportunities through preferential policies for blacks and, later, other minorities and women.

Research by Paul M. Sniderman and Thomas Piazza shows that resentment toward affirmative action has produced hostility toward blacks. They go on to argue that efforts to provide equality for blacks have focused on preferential treatment, which in turn has heightened racial feelings. This dislike for preferential treatment is rooted in the American Creed, with its emphasis on equality. Sniderman and Piazza state that affirmative action, when viewed as preferential treatment, runs counter to the American Creed.[28] Thus, while Americans favor equality and equal opportunity, government policies to ensure practices that promote such values may create what is considered a system of preferences in opposition to basic American values.

Thomas Sowell defines preferential policies as "government-mandated preferences for government-designated groups." He also notes that such policies as the Jim Crow laws and the current affirmative action program fit this definition.[29] Sowell argues that the benefits from such programs tend to go to the more advantaged within the designated groups, while the costs tend to be born by those at the bottom of the nondesignated groups. In addition, perceived losses rather than real losses increase negative reactions to preferential policies and contribute to group friction.

Although Americans have become more aware of racial discrimination, they tend not to favor such programs as affirmative action.[30] For those opposed to affirmative action, its implementation has come to mean preferential treatment for specific groups – blacks, Hispanics, Asians, Native Americans, and women. This concern about preferential treatment has fueled growing resentment toward affirmative action, which many consider to have produced discrimination against white men.

As minorities and women have moved into the workplace, white males perceive that affirmative action has limited their own opportunities for both job positions and promotions by creating reverse discrimination. Compounding this problem is the decline in economic growth, which in the past led to greater job creation.[31] Thus as jobs become scarcer, many white males come to believe that governmental policies restrict their opportunities while assisting minorities and women in obtaining employment. In addition, even though there is no U.S. law that specifically requires the use of goals or timetables in employment practices to compensate minorities and women for past job discrimination, they have been introduced to increase minority and female employment. Critics view such goals and timetables as lowering employment standards and injuring white males. Given this atmosphere of declining job formation and resentment toward affirmative action, there is rising demand to end this program.

In this book we examine the extent to which minorities and women have made the strides that critics charge have led to reverse discrimination. We focus on higher education due to its symbolic nature. Higher education represents in America the manner in which individuals can attain, among other things, economic well-being based upon achievement. Further, public higher education as a responsibility of state government affords students, their families, and the general public an opportunity to visibly determine how their governments are enforcing affirmative action to increase the number of minority and female faculty members as well as professionals, executives, and other employees on campus.

This symbolism of greater equity in employment is an important component of the theory of representative bureaucracy.[32] Given the increased role of the government in public policymaking as well as a concern for greater representation of the diversity of the U.S. population, some scholars argue that the composition of the civil service should be more reflective of the makeup of the country. This idea of representative bureaucracy is closely tied to affirmative action efforts to bring more minorities and women into government employment. We argue that given the pressures for a more representative bureaucracy, public higher education as an arm of state government is more likely than private higher education to provide opportunities for minorities and women. We examine the representativeness of both public and private institutions to see if this hypothesis is correct.

Our study focuses on data made available by the U.S. Equal Employment Opportunity Commission (EEOC). The EEOC requires that each public and private college or university report its employment by race and gender for the following categories – faculty; executive, administrative, and managerial; professional nonfaculty; secretarial/clerical; technical/para-professional; skilled crafts; and service/maintenance. Data provided by the EEOC, however, are summarized by state and are not broken down by individual institutions in order to meet the confidentiality requirements of Title VII of the Civil Rights Act of 1964, amended by the Equal Employment Opportunity Act of 1972.

We analyze EEOC employment data for the years 1979, 1983, and 1991. Affirmative action is generally perceived to have made progress in the late 1960s and 1970s and then suffered a setback during the Reagan and Bush administrations (1981-92). Ideally, we would have liked to study the data for the years 1980 (since Ronald Reagan's presidency started the following year), 1985 (the first year of Reagan's second term), and 1992 (the last year of George Bush's term). We had to make some adjustment in our years of study because of the constraints of EEOC data availability.

In addition, we have access to a recently published survey by the Department of Education's National Center for Education Statistics (NCES), which now has sole responsibility for collecting higher education employment data. Prior to 1993, the EEOC was responsible for collecting data for postsecondary institutions that employed fifteen or more full-time faculty members, while the NCES collected data for other schools as well as sampled less-than-two-year schools of higher education. Starting in 1993, the NCES became the sole collector of data concerning higher education employment. However, as noted in the NCES study, caution must be used when comparing NCES survey data with EEOC data for a number of reasons. Initially we had excluded data for the District of Columbia since the focus of our study was on the American states; also, the data for Hawaii were not available. In addition, the NCES survey, which includes all fifty states and the District of Columbia, utilized imputation methods to account for missing data, which was not the case with the EEOC data.[33] Despite these data collection differences, we believe that a comparison of the two data sets is useful to see if the patterns we discovered have continued into 1995. In order to gain such an overall view, we examine the participation rates for faculty and administrative employment, as our major concern is with how minorities and women have done in obtaining these positions of higher status and pay.

We examine each employment category in the EEOC data to see if minorities and women have indeed made gains within each state in proportion to their share of the state's population. First, we wish to know what is the current status of each category in terms of race and gender. Second, we examine recent hiring practices to understand what steps have been taken to implement affirmative action policies.

If, as Sowell argues, "preferential benefits tend to be concentrated on more lucrative or prestigious things," thus benefiting only those at the top of a preferred group, it would be expected that the greatest gains to be made by minorities and women in higher education employment are in faculty and administrative positions.[34] In contrast to Sowell, we argue that we can divide university employment into two groups: minorities and women tend to find their employment opportunities in lower-status positions, whereas white males hold the higher-status positions. Although minorities and women would make inroads into faculty and administrative positions, we expected that women would continue to do best in lower positions such as secretarial jobs. On the other hand, we expected that minorities would make more gains in service/maintenance positions, since prior to affirmative action this was often their primary opportunity for employment.

After exploring this aspect of affirmative action, we examine the political and socioeconomic determinants of affirmative action in the American states. A number of variables, including measures for political ideology, urbanization, industrialization, and income, were developed to understand their relationship with minority and female employment in faculty and administrative positions. We suspected that minorities and women would do best in states with a liberal political ideology and that minorities would also do well in states where their numbers are relatively large.

In addition to four chapters analyzing higher education employment data, the study includes chapters on the history of affirmative action, inequality and bureaucratic representation in government employment, and minority and female doctorates. Chapter 8 employs multiple linear regression to analyze employment data for faculty and administrative positions in the American States. The ninth and final chapter is a summary of our findings and conclusions. The purpose of this study is to determine whether gains for minorities and women have occurred, and at what levels within higher education institutions, and to examine if indeed a system of preferences has replaced equality in higher education employment.

Affirmative Action
and the University

1

A History of Affirmative Action

The first major or, rather, revolutionary act to end discrimination against blacks, which is one of the foremost goals of affirmative action, was the proscription of slavery in 1865 by the Thirteenth Amendment to the Constitution. The Thirteenth Amendment was an extension of liberal political thought, incorporated in the Bill of Rights (the first ten amendments). The Bill of Rights had provided American citizens with such civil liberties as the freedom of speech and religion and had included safeguards against the federal government's arbitrary use of power in matters of arrest and trial and in other areas of the individual's freedom. It was based on the liberalism of the seventeenth and eighteenth centuries, as expounded by John Locke and, to a lesser extent, by Jean Jacques Rousseau and Thomas Jefferson. Such liberalism, however, implicitly accepted discrimination against minorities and women.[1] The Thirteenth Amendment started the process of changing that thinking, and changes in how minorities and women are viewed continue today.

From a historical perspective, the Fourteenth (1868) and Fifteenth (1870) Amendments also prevented discrimination against blacks. The Fourteenth Amendment made blacks citizens of the United States and of the states in which they resided, and it forbade states from encroaching upon their rights as citizens. The Fifteenth Amendment granted blacks the right to vote. (Women, however, had to wait another fifty years to win that right.) Congress reiterated its intent to decrease discrimination against blacks by passing civil rights laws in 1866 and 1875.[2] Although those laws had the appearance of bringing equality to blacks in areas such as making contracts, filing lawsuits, and even access to hotels, theaters, and railroads, neither the Republicans, who had the majority in Congress and who were responsible for passing the Reconstruction era laws, nor the public were ready for a major change in race relations. Gideon Welles, Abraham Lincoln's secretary of the navy, spoke for virtually all white Americans in 1871 when he said: "Thank God slavery is abolished, but the Negro is not, and never can be the equal of the White. He is of an inferior race and must always remain so."[3]

The U.S. Supreme Court declared the legality of the inferior status of blacks by its decisions in the Civil Rights Cases (1883) and *Plessy v. Ferguson* (1896). "Equal protection of the laws" incorporated in the Fourteenth Amendment, said the Court in 1883, "did not . . . preclude race discrimination by private owners or managers of restaurants, theaters, hotels, and other public accommodations."[4] The Court's rationale was described by Justice Joseph Bradley: "Congress had the power to remedy a discriminatory state law [in order to enforce the Fourteenth Amendment], but could not take affirmative steps to protect blacks from other forms of prejudice."[5] Even that position was watered down in the *Plessy v. Ferguson* case when separate railroad carriages for blacks and whites were sanctioned by the Court under its "separate but equal" doctrine. In the meantime, the southern states had passed their Jim Crow laws, and "by the early twentieth century with the approval of the national government, they had effectively disenfranchised and denied the civil rights of black citizens."[6] Although the National Association for the Advancement of Colored People (NAACP), founded in 1909, made efforts to gain equality for blacks, little progress was made in this area until the 1930s.

RUDIMENTARY BEGINNINGS OF AFFIRMATIVE ACTION

Charles V. Hamilton, a prominent black political scientist, credits Interior Secretary Harold Ickes for utilizing "employment quotas [for black workers] from 1935 to 1937 in the Public Works Administration." He states that "this emphasis on specificity, on spelling out exactly what is meant and intended, is an important part of the African-American political experience."[7] The federal government, however, was not rushing into establishing and enforcing equality for blacks in the workplace. George T. Felkenes and Peter Charles Unsinger opine that "in American law, affirmative action first appeared within the contours of the Wagner Act in 1935. . . . The phrase affirmative action enjoined merely employers to take positive steps to alleviate conflict regarding labor unions in the 1930s."[8] Discrimination against black workers in the 1930s was overt and widespread, and affirmative action, as understood today, had little relevance in employment at that time. Unions openly gave preference to white workers, and the law of 1935 did not bring about any change in this area. Herman Belz argues that "in effect, the NLRA [National Labor Relations Act, also called the Wagner Act] legalized and made the federal government a party to the discrimination practiced by the union movement."[9]

Despite a highly publicized American belief in equality, denial of equality to minorities and women by the government continued until these groups were able to organize themselves and put effective pressure on public leaders for change. The value of such pressure became evident in 1941, when on June 25 President Franklin Delano Roosevelt issued his now famous Executive Order 8802 that is often considered a major milestone in the history of affirmative action.[10] This executive order forbade discrimination in employment in defense industries and government on the basis of "race, creed, color or national origin." Women were not included in the categories against which discrimination was prohibited. Black, Mexican-American, and Jewish workers were the major groups targeted by the executive order. Roosevelt's concern was more with the war effort of the country than with uplifting blacks or any other minorities. Blatant discrimination by unions had excluded blacks from working in the defense industries, and since many potential white workers were fighting in the war, there was a shortage of labor. Roosevelt, however, did express his belief in "the democratic way of life in the Nation," for which he felt the support of all groups was necessary. Internationally, the United States was fighting a war against Nazism and discrimination. Justification of discrimination within the United States, therefore, had become rather untenable. Most important, blacks were beginning to learn the value of organization and large-scale protest in the democratic process. Black leaders had planned a massive march on Washington to protest discrimination against black workers. The idea for such a protest came from A. Philip Randolph, the founder and leader of the Brotherhood of Sleeping Car Porters. President Roosevelt was aware of the protest and was concerned about its negative impact on the U.S. image abroad at the time when the country purportedly was fighting on the side of democracy and justice. By issuing his executive order just a few days before the planned march, he was able to forestall it.

Executive Order 8802 established a five-member Fair Employment Practice Committee (FEPC) to hear complaints of discrimination and suggest measures to redress them. This committee was also to advise the president and the executive departments and agencies in implementing the executive order. The committee "was empowered to investigate and recommend, it lacked real power; enforcement was impossible, because Executive Order 8802 did not specify any sanctions for noncompliance."[11] It was discontinued in the middle of 1946 due to the opposition of conservative members of Congress from the South and also because the country was not yet ready to seriously consider ending discrimination against blacks. Hugh David Graham comments, "During the five stormy years that the tiny, courageous FEPC tried to enforce nondiscrimination in defense contracts, employers, the American Federation of Labor Unions, the Armed Forces, Congress, and public opinion were inhospitable."[12] Yet the FEPC did make a significant contribution to the evolution of affirmative action. It started a process of investigation, documentation, and re-dress of complaints.[13] That process contributed to the formulation of detailed regulations on affirmative action programs and on their implementation and enforcement. The executive order itself "inaugurated the idea of contract com-pliance [on nondiscrimination] which has remained in a variety of forms the principal arena for the practice of affirmative action to the present day."[14]

Two years after the issuance of Executive Order 8802, President Roosevelt signed Executive Order 9346 on May 29, 1943. The 1943 executive order reiter-ated the principle of nondiscrimination in war industries and government, in-creased funding for the FEPC, enabling it to establish field offices, and "extended the reach of the nondiscrimination covenant to all government con-tracts, defense or otherwise, entered into the War and Navy Departments and the Maritime Commission."[15] Presidents Harry Truman and Dwight Eisen-hower continued the practice of issuing executive orders and establishing advi-sory committees for bringing nondiscrimination in employment, because Congress was not yet ready to pass a statute on this issue.[16] These actions changed few hearts and did little to integrate the work force. Nijole V. Benokraitis and Joe R. Feagin comment, "A review of executive orders regard-ing fair employment practices which followed orders 8802 and 9346 indicates that until the early 1960s, although nondiscriminatory prohibitions were ex-panded, federal equal employment policies focused on passive nondiscrimina-tion and were generally ineffective."[17]

Of course, there was some progress in reducing discrimination against blacks and other minorities. In July 1948, President Truman had ordered the integration of the armed forces. Ronald D. Sylvia calls it "perhaps the biggest leap forward in this period."[18] Six years later, *Brown v. The Board of Education* declared the racist doctrine of "separate but equal" of *Plessy v. Ferguson* (1896) unconstitutional and thereby propelled forward the civil rights movement. Congress also started changing its attitude and passed two rather weak civil rights laws, one in 1957 and the other in 1960. It was during President John F. Kennedy's term of office that progress toward affirmative action and civil rights began to accelerate.

The growing civil rights movement and President Kennedy's personal con-cern for the downtrodden were responsible for the next major step in the his-tory of affirmative action. Less than two months after taking office, on March 6, 1961, President Kennedy issued Executive Order 10925, which for the first time used the phrase *affirmative action* in the sense of nondiscrimination in employment. The use of this phrase in the Wagner Act of 1935, where it first appeared in the political lexicon, was intended to resolve labor conflicts.

Kennedy's 4,500-word executive order included the following often-quoted sentence: "The contractor will take *affirmative action* to ensure that applicants are employed, and employees are treated during their employment, without regard to their race, creed, color or national origin" (emphasis added). This directive to federal contractors clearly stipulated that the government would take a more active role in reducing discrimination against minorities (women were ignored in this executive order also). Indeed, "for the first time, the government ordered its contractors not only to avoid discrimination, but to take positive steps to redress the effects of societal discrimination."[19] Even more important was the government's message that it would now enforce compliance of the nondiscrimination policy of the executive order. The executive order established a President's Committee on Equal Employment Opportunity for this purpose. This committee, chaired by Vice President Lyndon Baines Johnson, required annual employment statistics reports on the work force from the government contractors, and although several government agencies were given responsibility for the implementation of the executive order, the committee was ultimately responsible for its compliance and enforcement. Its rules included a contract cancellation penalty for noncompliance. The penalty could also extend to the debarment of the offending contractor from future government grants or work.

It is often argued that President Kennedy's executive order merely reiterated the principle of nondiscrimination in employment and had a race- and color-neutral character. Some scholars relate it to the tenets of classical liberalism that espoused nondiscrimination.[20] It is true that minorities were not mentioned as the target groups of the executive order, and that women were clearly excluded from the purview of the government's nondiscrimination policy. Preferential treatment for minorities or women was perhaps not even implied in the order. One study calls the use of the phrase *affirmative action* in it "probably . . . no more than a flourish of a drafter's pen in Washington."[21] Regardless of the intentions of President Kennedy and his writers, the phrase *affirmative action* stuck and came to mean much more than what classical liberalism implied for nondiscrimination in employment. As Felkenes and Unsinger state: "In spite of the fact that E.O. 10925 in context attempts to lay foundation for affirmative action by not allowing discrimination against anyone on the basis of race, creed, or color [or national origin], in the opinion of vast segments of society, affirmative action begins to emerge as a governmental program granting preferential treatment."[22]

President Kennedy's executive order did not apply to construction contracts. That omission was corrected by another of his executive orders, signed in 1963. Far more important, the president also addressed the issue of gender equality in employment by appointing in 1961 a President's Commission on the Status of Women. Two years later, also under Kennedy's administration, Congress passed the Equal Pay Act, which required equal pay for men and women for the same work. In June 1963, a few months before his assassination, Kennedy proposed the first major civil rights bill of this century. An expanded version of that bill became the famed Civil Rights Act of 1964.

THE CIVIL RIGHTS ACT OF 1964

Kennedy's civil rights proposal was aimed at ending discrimination in voting, public accommodations, public education, and federally assisted programs.[23] Before Kennedy's assassination, Congress, with the administration's support, added nondiscrimination in private employment to the bill. Discrimination in employment on the basis of race, religion, or national origin was to be banned by Congress. The ban on sex discrimination was included in the bill soon after Lyndon Johnson became president. The expanded version of the bill faced a long and difficult debate in Congress, especially in the Senate, where Southern Democrats tried to kill it with a filibuster. A compromise was finally reached, and the bill was signed into the Civil Rights Act in July 1964.[24]

The civil rights laws of 1957 and 1960 were meek in comparison to the 1964 law. Perhaps the most noteworthy sections of the two laws (1957 and 1960) were those concerning voting rights, but even in this area Congress was in no mood to grant equality to blacks. Senator Paul H. Douglas, a strong supporter of civil rights legislation, had commented on the 1960 law: "Like the mountain that labored and brought a mouse, the United States Congress, after eight weeks of Senate debate and weeks of House debate, passed what can only by courtesy be called a civil rights bill."[25]

As a result, despite *Brown v. Board of Education*, the debates in Congress, and the efforts of the civil rights movement, discrimination against and segregation of blacks had continued almost unabated. The changes that brought down the walls of apartheid and conveyed some equality to blacks as well as women essentially began with the Civil Rights Act of 1964. Charles and Barbara Whalen cite "five forces" responsible for the passing of the Civil Rights Act, 1964:

> First, by 1963 blacks throughout America, as Martin Luther King explained, decided the time for effective civil rights legislation had finally arrived. . . . Second, protest, which had been localized in the past, was widespread. . . . Third, the protestors' cause was abetted by the excesses of those who opposed their demands. . . . Fourth, civil rights leaders suc-

cessfully exploited these grisly incidents [reflecting callousness of the civil rights opponents] to attract support to their cause. . . . Fifth, the decision of the Leadership Conference on Civil Rights to frame H.R. 7152 [the bill originally introduced under John F. Kennedy's administration] in moral terms and to activate religious leaders in states with small black populations was critical to the success of the bill, especially in the Senate.[26]

The most important part of the Civil Rights Act of 1964 concerning affirmative action was Title VII, which was amended by the Equal Employment Opportunity Act of 1972. The 1964 law had prohibited discrimination by private employers with twenty-five or more workers on the basis of race, color, religion, sex, or national origin. To start with, employers (and unions) with one hundred or more employees (or members) were covered. This number was to be reduced to twenty-five or more in stages over three years. The 1972 amendments made the nondiscrimination provision applicable to employers with fifteen or more workers. Nondiscrimination by unions also now became applicable in unions with fifteen or more members. The 1964 law and the 1972 amendments were also applicable to employment agencies. More important, in 1972, for the first time, federal, state, and local governments as well as educational institutions were required by law not to discriminate against minorities or women. Furthermore, the 1972 law strengthened the Equal Employment Opportunity Commission (EEOC), which the 1964 law had created for the implementation of Title VII. The EEOC's initial charge was to investigate and conciliate and also to file *amicus curiae* briefs, which meant that it could not be a party to an employment discrimination suit in court for correcting such discrimination, but it could instead volunteer advice to the court. The 1972 act empowered the EEOC to file a suit directly against an employer in violation of the nondiscrimination provisions of the law.

Although the phrase *affirmative action* was included in the 1964 act, its usage was in a different context from that of President Kennedy's executive order. Instead of giving a directive to federal contractors to take affirmative action in order to ensure nondiscrimination to applicants and employees, the 1964 act required that if the court were to find an intentional unlawful employment practice, it could order *affirmative action* of a remedial nature, such as reinstatement or hiring of employees or any other equitable relief. In addition to court-ordered remedies to correct employment discrimination, employers were required to practice nondiscrimination by voluntary measures. Voluntary affirmative action by employers became an essential part of the federal regulations issued to implement Title VII.

An important part of Title VII of the 1964 act was that preferential treat-

ment was not to be granted to any racial or other group. A categorical statement declaring the intent of Congress not "to grant preferential treatment to
any group because of race, color, religion, sex, or national origin" was crucial to
win the support of minority leader Senator Everett Dirksen in order to break
the filibuster in the Senate and pass the bill. Several proponents of the bill said
in the Senate that the bill would not permit such preferential treatment. Hu-
bert Humphrey, the Majority Whip in the Senate and a strong supporter and
sponsor of the bill, unequivocally declared: "The title does not provide that any
preferential treatment in employment shall be given to Negroes or to any other
persons or groups. . . . In fact, the title would prohibit preferential treatment
for any particular group."[27]

The statements made by some black leaders at the time of the consideration
of the civil rights legislation reflected an acceptance of nonpreferential treatment in employment. Roy Wilkins, executive director of the National Association for the Advancement of Colored People (NAACP), expressed his views
against a quota system (which clearly accepts preferential treatment) at Congressional hearings: "Our association has never been in favor of a quota system. . . . We believe the quota system is unfair whether it is used for Negroes or
against Negroes."[28] Color blindness in employment and other areas was also a
major theme in the statements of white as well as black civil rights leaders of
that time. In an argument before the Supreme Court in *Anderson v. Martin*,
Jack Greenberg, then director counsel of the NAACP Legal Defense Fund, said:
"The state has a duty under the Fifteenth Amendment and the Fourteenth
Amendment to be color blind and not to act so as to encourage racial discrimination . . . against any racial group."[29] Such statements later provided fuel for
the arguments opposing affirmative action, since a form of quota system ig-
noring color blindness did indeed develop in the 1970s and 1980s.

EXECUTIVE ORDERS AND BUREAUCRATIC RULES

Although the Civil Rights Act of 1964 provided the statutory basis of affirmative action, federal departments and agencies developed the presidential
executive orders and bureaucratic rules that formulated this program, including compliance and enforcement procedures. In September 1965, President
Lyndon Baines Johnson issued Executive Order 11246, reaffirming equal opportunity in federal employment and directing federal contractors not to discriminate against any job applicant or employee on the basis of race, color,
religion, or national origin. Two years later Johnson included women in his
Executive Order 11375 and also prohibited separate seniority rosters for men
and women, separate want ads, and discrimination against women on the basis

of marriage or childbearing status. These orders regarding nondiscrimination echoed President Kennedy's executive order on affirmative action and the Civil Rights Act of 1964. The real contribution of President Johnson in the area of affirmative action was his insistence on compliance and enforcement. In other words, the federal government, in addition to prescribing nondiscrimination, required evidence of it by federal contractors. The executive order of 1965 assigned the primary responsibility for enforcing compliance to the Labor Department, which established the Office of Federal Contract Compliance (OFCC), renamed the Office of Federal Contract Compliance Programs (OFCC) in 1975. OFCC was given the overall authority for enforcing compliance with Executive Order 11246. Under this executive order, the Labor Department could also delegate investigative and compliance responsibilities to other federal agencies or departments. As a result, several agencies and departments, such as EEOC and the Justice Department, have participated in enforcing affirmative action.

Three months before issuing Executive Order 11246, President Johnson delivered a commencement speech at Howard University in Washington DC. In that speech he advocated "equality as a result" and "not just legal equality." Johnson was speaking on the eve of the passing of the Voting Rights Act of 1965. The civil rights lobby by that time had become strong and assertive. President Johnson may have wanted to placate this lobby by his Howard speech, which sounded like a logically constructed, passionate plea for uplifting blacks from centuries of discrimination. Hugh Davis Graham, however, argues: "Despite the Howard speech, affirmative action played no role in the planning for this order [Executive Order 11246]. Johnson's overarching concerns were interagency coordination and the avoidance of politically damaging battles between enforcement officials in Washington and Democratic organizations in the major cities, like Mayor Richard Daley's Chicago."[30]

The passing of the 1964 Civil Rights Act and the issuance of the 1965 and 1967 executive orders by President Johnson led to a system of detailed bureaucratic rules and procedures on affirmative action, endless compliance forms, and the establishment of contract-compliance offices in federal agencies and affirmative action units in state and local governments, colleges and universities, private businesses, and nonprofit institutions. These compliance offices and affirmative action units have emerged as institutional interest groups advocating the continuation of affirmative action.

The OFCC and the EEOC were largely responsible for initiating the growth of the bureaucratic rules, procedures, and forms concerning affirmative action. One of the first such forms, which in a modified form is still used by employers, was developed in 1966 and required reporting of employees by race/ethnicity (and later sex) in designated occupational categories.[31] In the same year, the concept of "bid responsiveness" in contracts was introduced by the OFCC. This concept started pre-award reviews of the prospective contractors' affirmative action obligations. In order to procure business, the contractor with the lowest bid was required to show that it could meet the affirmative action guidelines of nondiscrimination. With pre-award evaluation of a contractor's affirmative action obligations, the federal government did not need to wait for the courts to find unlawful discrimination before taking action.[32]

The 1967 executive order had required contractors to prepare written affirmative action plans in order to ensure nondiscrimination in employment. Detailed affirmative action guidelines were, however, formulated by the OFCC in 1968. These guidelines were later revised and issued by the Labor Department as Order No. 4 in 1970 and Revised Order No. 4 in 1971.[33] The revised order required the application of affirmative action guidelines not only to minorities but also to women. Federal contractors or subcontractors that received contracts of $50,000 or more and employed fifty or more workers were required by these guidelines to develop affirmative action programs. For the first time, an affirmative action program was defined as "a set of specific and result-oriented procedures." Contractors were required to determine, on the basis of careful analysis, the areas of underutilization of minorities and women and then to develop "goals and timetables," which the contractors were to realize by applying "good-faith efforts" in order to correct deficiencies in their affirmative action programs. Contractors were also required to disseminate their affirmative action programs to their employees and to evaluate the programs. These programs were to apply not only to recruitment but to all other facets of employment as well, including training, promotion, fringe benefits, and job termination.

Result-oriented affirmative action does not apply only to the private sector. In 1971 the Civil Service Commission also accepted the concept of *goals and timetables* in employment in federal agencies.[34] Critics charge that such affirmative action guidelines, incorporated in bureaucratic regulations, violate the nonpreferential intent of Title VII of the Civil Rights Act and Executive Order 11246, and that they helped create reverse discrimination and a quota system in employment. George T. Felkenes and Peter Charles Unsinger argue:

> In effect, the meaning and attitudes surrounding E.O. 11246 and the 1964 Civil Rights Act have taken on new character. Where the Labor Department set out to expunge any semblance of discrimination based on race, color, sex, or national origin, which occurred primarily when employers

accorded preferential treatment to white males, Order No. 4, Section 60-2.10 of the Code of Federal Regulations chose instead to legitimatize a preferential treatment policy. It prompted employers to take notice of an applicant's race, color, sex, or national origin and discriminate accordingly.[35]

The development of affirmative action in the 1970s and 1980s was based on its progress during the Johnson administration, notably the 1964 Civil Rights Act, the two executive orders, and the guidelines formulated by the OFCC. A white backlash, however, had already set in against the affirmative action measures. At the same time, black frustration and anger because of inadequate economic gains had erupted into riots in some cities. It was under these conditions that in 1967 OFCC proposed a Philadelphia Plan, which required federal construction contractors to prepare schedules for hiring minorities. Such schedules were to be prepared before a contract was granted. This test for exploring the "pre-award policy" was initiated a year earlier and faced vehement opposition from the white-controlled construction industry and unions. Questions were also raised regarding the legality of the plan, since it appeared to be creating preferential treatment for some groups. By the time Lyndon Johnson's term ended, the Philadelphia Plan seemed all but dead. It was revived by President Richard Nixon – or, rather, by Labor Secretary George Schulz. Ironically, Nixon had campaigned against Johnson's Great Society Program and was not considered a supporter of affirmative action.

In June 1969, the Department of Labor issued the revised Philadelphia Plan, which was "no watered-down version of its predecessor . . . [and] made tough demands on the Philadelphia construction industry."[36] The goal of this plan was to increase minority hiring in the construction industry so that it eventually would reach proportional representation. Prospective federal contractors were required to submit with their bids their minority hiring targets within a range. If any contractors, after being awarded a bid, were unable to meet the minority hiring goal, they had to give evidence of having made a good-faith effort toward the realization of the goal. The preferential treatment of minorities in employment implied by this plan, in particular its proportional hiring feature, offended many members of Congress and some influential interest groups that wanted to preserve privileges for whites. President Nixon, however, was able to overcome these criticisms. Some scholars believe Nixon was, in fact, a supporter of civil rights, his conservative image notwithstanding. Herman Belz notes, "Far from being an opponent of civil rights, Richard Nixon was a strong supporter of them."[37]

A majority of the analysts, however, consider Nixon's civil rights or affirmative action policy to have been guided largely by political expediency. Nixon's attack on the liberal programs of Lyndon Johnson in the 1968 campaign had offended civil rights activists whom he perhaps wanted to appease by decisions such as the Philadelphia Plan. It is also possible that "Nixon hoped to expand the black middle class and to split the Democrats' black-labor alliance."[38] Two months after the Department of Labor's announcement of the Philadelphia Plan, President Nixon issued Executive Order 11478, establishing "a continuing affirmative program" for employment in the federal service. He then expanded preferential treatment of minorities in employment in Order No. 4 and Revised Order No. 4, considered above.

By the end of Richard Nixon's first term as president, administrative rules on affirmative action, clearly stipulating preferential treatment of minorities and women in employment, were in place. Presidential support for affirmative action continued during the Ford and Carter administrations but halted for twelve years when Ronald Reagan became president in 1981. Despite Reagan's and his successor George Bush's opposition to affirmative action, however, this program continued. Influential interest groups within the bureaucracy at the federal level as well as at the state and local levels had already developed that strongly supported affirmative action; civil rights groups outside the government also continued to favor its continuation. The federal government, however, had to keep revising its regulations on affirmative action as court decisions on this issue were made.

COURT DECISIONS

The first affirmative action suit was initiated by the Justice Department in 1966. It succeeded in challenging the hiring rules of a New Orleans craft union that excluded minorities from the trade. A federal court, starting a precedent of racial balance, required that "the union must seek out and invite minorities to use the services of its hiring hall, and for a time it must name job referrals on an equal basis one-for-one, minority and white. The requirements would cease when the evidence showed that the excluded minorities had been afforded a fair chance to obtain work experience and qualify for union membership."[39] In 1970, a federal court ruled that the Philadelphia Plan, which also had sought racial balance in employment, was valid under Executive Order 11246 and that goals and timetables did not violate Title VII.[40] In the meantime, several court cases had interpreted the Equal Pay Act in favor of women.[41]

One of the most important Supreme Court cases supporting affirmative action was *Griggs v. Duke Power Company* (1971). In this case the Court ruled that the Duke Power Company had discriminated against black workers and thereby violated Title VII of the 1964 Civil Rights Act by requiring a high school diploma or satisfactory scores on standardized tests for jobs except those involving manual labor. The plaintiffs, all black workers who believed that they were discriminated against by the power company, had argued that the job performance had no relationship to the high school diploma or the test scores.

In the early years of the enforcement of Title VII, specific goals were also set in some court cases.[42] Such a relatively unequivocal position of the federal courts did not last long. In the controversial *Regents of the University of California v. Bakke* (1978) case, on which the Supreme Court was almost evenly split and Justice Lewis Powell helped the Court arrive at a 5–4 decision, the 16 percent quota for the admission of disadvantaged minorities into the University of California Medical School at Davis was declared invalid. However, the Court also ruled that race could be considered as one of the factors in university admissions. A year later the Supreme Court gave up this ambivalent attitude toward affirmative action in *United Steel Workers of America v. Weber* (1979). In this case the Court supported a quota system in training programs for black workers in skilled-craft positions until these workers reached their proportion in the local work force. In 1980 in *Fullilove v. Klutznick*, the Supreme Court continued its pro–affirmative action position by upholding the Public Works Employment Act of 1977 according to which 10 percent of the federal funds for local public works projects were to be spent on contracts to be awarded to businesses owned by designated minorities.

During the Reagan-Bush era the Supreme Court began shifting its position on affirmative action, due in part to its changed personnel makeup and in part to the conservative political mood in the country. A legal expert, however, argues: "During the 'Reagan revolution' conservative Republicans railed that affirmative action was nothing but a quota system in mild disguise, fanning the flames of racial division with the scary cliche of 'reverse discrimination.' Fortunately, the federal courts would not be stampeded and repeatedly rejected invitations to throw out effective remedies because they were inconsistent with someone's pet philosophy."[43] There is little doubt that the federal courts during the 1980s helped weaken affirmative action. Two cases in particular, *Watson v. Fort* (1988) and *Ward's Cove Packing v. Atonio* (1989), had adverse impact on minorities and women in employment. Nicholas Mills notes, "Contradicting its 1971 *Griggs v. Duke Power Company* decision, which made employers ultimately responsible for showing the 'business necessity' of any employment practice that had discriminatory impact, the Court declared in *Watson* that 'the ultimate burden of proving that discrimination against a protected group has been caused by a specific employment practice rests with the plaintiff at all times.' "[44] John Edwards sums up the key features of the Ward's Cove case: "In essence, *Ward's Cove* shifted the burden of proof of discrimination from the employer to the employees; it required that precise and particular discriminatory practices be identified (rather than statistical disparate impact) and it made employer-justification of disparate impact practices much easier by abandoning the 'business necessity' requirement and substituting the much looser 'serving legitimate employer goals.' "[45]

In some other cases the Supreme Court specifically restricted the rights of women employees in filing bias suits and extended white males' rights to file reverse discrimination suits.[46] It was to counteract the effect of such cases on affirmative action that the Civil Rights Bill of 1990 was introduced. President Bush called it a "quota bill" and, despite the bill's overwhelming support in Congress, vetoed it (in the House there was over two-thirds support for the bill, but in the Senate there was one vote less than two-thirds). In the following year the compromise Civil Rights Act of 1991 was passed. The 1991 law shifted back the burden of proof in disparate-impact discrimination cases to the employer, but not without giving leeway to the employer to demonstrate that such impact or presumed discrimination was due to the nature of a job and business necessity. In other words, what appeared to be discrimination was permissible or unavoidable in certain circumstances. The law also provided relief to minority and female workers in cases where discrimination or harassment could be demonstrated. On the crucial issues of affirmative action and discrimination, however, the 1991 law remained vague and subject to different interpretations in future lawsuits.

The 1991 Civil Rights Act did little to further promote affirmative action for minorities and women. The conservatism of the 1980s strengthened with Republican control of both the House and the Senate in 1994. The Supreme Court reflected that mood. It supported reverse discrimination claims of white males and required stringent criteria for affirmative action benefits for minorities and women. One of the most important cases decided by the Supreme Court in the 1990s was *Adarand Constructors v. Pena* in 1995, in which the claims of a white contractor against a federal set-aside program were upheld. The case arose because of the congressional requirement that at least 10 percent of the federal funds spent on highway projects be allocated in contracts to businesses owned by "disadvantaged individuals," presumably minorities and women. In making its 5–4 decision, the Supreme Court not only returned the case to the Federal District Court in Denver, Colorado, where the case had originated, but, more importantly, it required that such programs, which classify people by race or similar criteria, must be "narrowly tailored" and serve "a compelling government interest." Furthermore, the *Adarand Constructors* case reversed the Supreme Court's own ruling in *Metro Broadcasting v. F.C.C.* five years earlier, in which the Court had supported giving preference to minority applicants for broadcast licenses. The 1995 decision "also cast grave doubt on the continued validity of a 1980 decision, *Fullilove v. Klutznick*," which had upheld the 10 percent rule for minority contracts.[47] Echoing similar doubts about affirmative action, the United States Court of Appeals for the District of Columbia Circuit ruled in April 1998 against a Federal Communications Commission decision that required special efforts by radio and television stations to recruit minorities, on the grounds that such efforts did not serve a compelling public interest.

Similar doubts about affirmative action in higher education were raised by the Supreme Court. In July 1996, by refusing to hear an appeal by the State of Texas, which challenged a decision made by the United States Court of Appeals for the Fifth Circuit, the Supreme Court, in *Cheryl Hopwood v. State of Texas*, let stand a ruling that invalidated consideration of race as a factor in admissions into the University of Texas Law School.[48] A month later, in *U.S. v. Board of Education, Piscataway*, the United States Court of Appeals for the Third Circuit struck down the layoff of a white school teacher in New Jersey. In the Texas case, in refusing to hear the appeal, the Supreme Court had used a technicality regarding a change in the admissions policy of the University of Texas Law School. In the New Jersey case, the appeals court had argued that the Piscataway Board of Education's policy was not aimed at correcting past discrimination, which was the intention of Title VII of the Civil Rights Act of 1964.[49] The Supreme Court, before its summer recess in 1997, announced that it would hear this case in its next term. However, in November 1997, a few weeks before the scheduled hearing, the parties agreed to a settlement of over four hundred thousand dollars to be paid to the laid-off white teacher. About 70 percent of this amount was put up by a coalition of civil rights groups that clearly perceived the Supreme Court to be unsympathetic to affirmative action and feared a precedent-setting decision that would prove harmful to this program.

THE POLITICAL DEBATE ON AFFIRMATIVE ACTION IN THE 1990S

Few political issues are so controversial in the 1990s as affirmative action. A majority of voters appear to be opposed to the program, although many more whites than blacks or Hispanics favor dismantling it altogether.[50] Although poll results differ, depending to a considerable degree on the questions asked, there is little doubt that the number of people with reservations about affirmative action is increasing. According to a news story published in the *New York Times* in July 1995, "most polls indicate that 60 percent of all voters have deep reservations about the fairness of affirmative action."[51] A Connecticut poll, reported in the *Hartford Courant*, captured the mood of the country. Connecticut residents, according to the poll, "are unwilling to endorse programs that set quotas or that give preference to people because they are female, black or Hispanic. But they do believe the programs as originally structured were good ones, and that some kind of government action is needed to guard against discrimination."[52]

Public opinion on affirmative action is not based only on generalities. A growing impression has been that upper- and middle-class minorities and women have benefited from affirmative action and that those who have really needed the program have been left out. In an op-ed article, we have argued that upper- and middle-class minorities and women should be excluded from affirmative action and that it is possible to develop a list of categories based on economic and social factors.[53] The privileged do not need special considerations from affirmative action programs, since they have resources and connections that ordinary folks lack.[54]

Another argument against affirmative action is that it has divided American society and pitted groups against one another without eliminating bias.[55] Some critics maintain that it is demeaning to minorities and women. Shelby Steele, a black writer, spoke of "the indignity and Faustian bargain it presents to minorities" and "the hypocrisy and shameless self-congratulation it brings out to its white supporters."[56] Many women and minority members complain that even when they succeed without any assistance from affirmative action programs, they are not considered equal in merit to their white male counterparts.

On the other hand, arguments in support of affirmative action are also quite compelling. A common theme in such arguments is that discrimination against women and minorities, particularly in the job market, is still pervasive and that affirmative action is needed to eliminate it. It is true that blacks have made gains in entering the middle class and occupations that previously were dominated by whites.[57] However, their entry is generally into the lower rungs of the economic ladder, and the top positions continue to be controlled by whites, especially males. A U.S. Labor Department report indicated that the percentage of white male managers declined from 65 percent in 1980 to 51 percent in 1990 and the percentage of white female, minority male, and minority female managers showed increases.[58] If we consider only senior management positions, we find the white grip over the economy continuing. According to the bipartisan Federal Glass Ceiling Commission report released in early 1995, 95 percent of the senior corporate management positions are held by white men.[59] It also appears true that white women have benefited more from affirmative action programs than minorities. For example, "white women hold close to 40 percent of the jobs in middle management, but black women hold only 5 percent and black men even less."[60]

Another Labor Department report, published in 1995, buttresses the argument that affirmative action has not caused any hardship or reverse discrimination to whites. Analyzing more than three thousand discrimination rulings of the federal district and appeals courts from 1990 to 1994, the Labor Department concluded that fewer than one hundred of these cases concerned reverse discrimination.[61] A law professor, however, disputed this report and maintained that the reason for so few reverse-discrimination cases was that affirmative action had been made legal and that the Supreme Court had "given employers broad latitude to use race and sex preferences to hire and promote women and minorities over white males with superior qualifications."[62]

The congressional election held in 1994, which resulted in Republican control of both the House and the Senate, worked as a catalyst in fueling the affirmative action debate. Polls revealed that over 60 percent of white males had voted for the Republican candidates. This, according to political pundits, reflected white male anger against federal government policies, including affirmative action. An anti–affirmative action movement emerged in California. In June 1995, California's governor, Pete Wilson, issued an executive order dismantling some of the affirmative action programs in the state. The following month the University of California Board of Regents voted to do away with affirmative action hiring policies and to phase them out in admissions and contracts. The anti–affirmative action movement gathered enough public support to place a "Civil Rights Initiative" on the ballot in the November 1996 election. The California Civil Rights Initiative, called Proposition 209, states:

> The state will not use race, sex, color, ethnicity or national origin as a criterion for either discriminating against, or granting preferential treatment to, any individual or group in the operation of the state's system of public employment, education, or public contracting.

Proposition 209 was approved in California by a vote of 54 percent to 46 percent. However, its constitutionality was immediately challenged in a federal district court by the groups opposed to it. The district court prevented enforcement of Proposition 209 by issuing a temporary restraining order. The United States Court of Appeals for the Ninth Circuit, however, overruled that decision. By refusing to hear a challenge to the appeals court's decision, the Supreme Court, in November 1997, let stand that court's decision, essentially leaving unresolved the issue of race- or sex-based preferences in public employment, contracting, and education. A year later, in the November 1998 election, Washington State's voters endorsed by a 58 percent "yes" vote Proposition 200, which would prohibit the state government from "discriminating or granting preferential treatment based on race, sex, color, ethnicity, or national origin" in public employment, education, and contracting.

In the meantime, "white male anger" prompted President Bill Clinton to cast doubts on the continuation of federal affirmative action programs. When he realized such a move might cost him more minority and female votes than his gain from white males in the 1996 presidential election, he changed his position and came out in July 1995 strongly in support of affirmative action. Clinton's stand was supported by a review of the federal affirmative action programs, which he had ordered, and which concluded that "most hiring and other preferences based on race or sex are justified in employment and education."[63] In order to placate opponents of affirmative action, Clinton said that "affirmative action has not always been perfect, and affirmative action should not go forever. It should be changed now to take care of those things that are wrong, and it should be retired when its job is done."[64] After Clinton's reelection, his administration threw its support on the side of the groups challenging the constitutionality of Proposition 209. The administration further watered down its stand on affirmative action by declaring a shift in its position on the *Piscataway* case in August 1997. It continued to follow a politically expedient policy of reducing affirmative action while defending it.

Also keeping his eyes on the 1996 presidential election, Senator Majority Leader Robert Dole introduced the Equal Opportunity Act of 1995 in the Senate in July 1995 in order to end federal affirmative action programs. Representative Charles Canady of Florida introduced the same bill in the House. This bill, according to a newspaper account, "would end the use of 'racial and gender preferences' in federal contracting, hiring and other federally conducted activities. It would not ban the government from engaging in 'outreach' and recruitment, the new GOP buzzwords for affirmative action. . . . The bill would prohibit timetables and goals for achieving racial and gender balance in the federal government equating such methods with quotas."[65]

Although the debate on affirmative action will continue, and some major revisions to it are probable, the program is not likely to be abandoned altogether. The interest groups in support of affirmative action are strong enough to prevent its demise, and the country's mood is not entirely against it. Al-

though polls reveal public opposition to the inequities brought about by affirmative action, they also indicate support for the concept. Affirmative action in
the future, therefore, will perhaps focus more on nondiscrimination than on
preferential treatment for designated groups.

In the following chapters we examine the impact of affirmative action and
the controversy surrounding it on higher education employment in the period
1979–91. We also provide an analysis of the 1995 data, the latest available at the
time of this writing. In chapter 2 we expound the theory of representative bureaucracy and argue that this theory can be applied to higher education employment. We develop hypotheses based on this theory that concern the
progress of minorities and women in various job categories in higher education. In formulating our hypotheses we make a distinction between public and
private higher education and thus prepare a framework for the comparison of
affirmative action's influence on employment in these two types of institutions.

2

Inequality and Bureaucratic Representation in Government Employment

Discrimination against minorities and women has existed not only in the private sector but in the public sector as well. Focusing on the public sector raises important questions about the prospects for removing public employment barriers and also about the role of minorities and women as citizens and the degree to which government represents them as well as the white majority. The institutionalization of a representative bureaucracy is considered by some to be a means to ensure that the various groups making up the nation are represented in government. Bureaucratic representativeness carries both symbolic and policy implications for the majority and for minority groups. Affirmative action in government is both a measure of government responsiveness to its own laws and policies and its willingness to ensure representative bureaucracy for all.

DISCRIMINATION IN GOVERNMENT EMPLOYMENT

Race, ethnicity, and gender have shaped to a significant extent opportunities for government employment. Various minority groups and women have faced exclusion or have been relegated to lower positions due to physical characteristics or ethnic backgrounds. Rather than being in the forefront of promoting equality, government has often mirrored the discriminatory practices found in the private sector and society. For those who wish to see equality of opportunity in government employment, affirmative action efforts have become necessary in order to ensure that minorities and women have greater access to government positions.

Blacks

Blacks have faced exclusionary policies toward service in government, with public officials erecting numerous barriers to deny them access or limit their presence throughout most of American history. Initially, blacks were denied the opportunity to serve in the military during the American Revolution. Later, Congress in 1792 made service in the militia open only to white men.

While affirmative action programs are often criticized for promoting those who lack the proper training, it is government that has often placed stumbling blocks before blacks in acquiring such knowledge. For example, in 1802 Postmaster General Gideon Granger supported a law barring blacks from delivering the mail, for he wished to avoid "everything which tends to increase their knowledge of natural rights, of men and things, or that affords them an opportunity of associating, acquiring and commuting sentiments, and of establishing a chain or line of intelligence." After the Civil War, some blacks were able to find government employment in the federal government and in state and local governments, primarily in the South, but such employment was halted with the end of the Reconstruction era. The passage of the Pendleton Act in 1883 setting up the federal civil service system did bring about a major increase in black federal employment; early in the twentieth century, however, President Woodrow Wilson's efforts to ensure racial segregation within the federal service once again limited black employment in the federal government.[1] Presidential efforts by Harry Truman to desegregate the military after World War II and John Kennedy's call for affirmative action in federal employment ultimately led to a greater concern for equal employment opportunities within the federal government.

Initially, however, affirmative action did little to assist blacks in obtaining federal employment. Some studies have shown that affirmative action for the period 1962–80 had a relatively small impact on black federal employment.[2] In addition, agency variations existed; the Equal Employment Opportunity Commission (EEOC) had the highest percentage of blacks and the National Aeronautics and Space Administration (NASA) the lowest.[3] Some progress occurred by the mid-1980s, but gender has also played a role in shaping outcomes for blacks. For example, between 1976 and 1986, Gregory B. Lewis found that black women made the greatest gains in white-collar positions, while black males had the lowest growth.[4] On the other hand, in comparison with average white male salaries for federal white-collar employment in 1986, black females received 41.3 percent less and black males received 25.8 percent less. Research on the federal executive branch shows that although blacks represented roughly 12.1 percent of the U.S. population in 1990, they held 16.7 percent of these positions in 1991 (of which 71 percent were held by black women).[5] This positive finding, however, is offset by the fact that blacks are more likely to be found in the lower ranks and that they hold only 4.5 percent of the positions in the Senior Executive Service – the managerial elite of the federal government.

For state and local governments, research demonstrated that blacks did make gains in the 1970s. For example, it was discovered that blacks had made greater overall employment progress as well as greater inroads in managerial positions in state and local governments than in the private sector.[6] Nevertheless, in municipal governments for this period, blacks were more likely to be found in maintenance and service employment rather than in managerial, professional, or protective service positions.[7]

In terms of earnings, our examination of EEOC data for 1991, which combines information for both state and local governments, showed that the median salary for full-time employment (excluding jobs in education) for black males was $24,117 and for black females was $21,672 in comparison to $29,269 for white males.[8] One job category in which the median salary for black males ($43,256) nearly had parity with the median salary for white males ($43,654) was officials and administrators, but there was a wider difference for black females ($39,502).

Entry into government service has historically been quite difficult for blacks. Even with the implementation of affirmative action programs, blacks in the federal government are more likely to be employed in the EEOC than in other agencies. Although there has been some movement into the federal government, blacks still tend to be found in the lower ranks, which is generally the case for state and local governments as well.

White Women

Women have faced a long tradition of exclusion and discrimination in the public sector. Marital status was often used to limit female opportunities. For example, federal postal regulations in 1913 excluded married women from working in post offices.[9] In addition, women were also denied access to certain positions based on their physical characteristics. It is only with the implementation of affirmative action that women have been able to make major inroads into government service, often with a considerable degree of resistance.

Although women often lag behind white males in employment opportunities and earnings, they have made great strides in federal employment. Their greatest opportunities tend to be found in such agencies as the Department of Health and Human Services (64.9 percent of all employees) and the Selective Service System (64.7 percent) rather than in the Federal Mediation and Conciliation Service (25.0 percent) or the Department of Transportation (23.9 percent).[10] Nevertheless, although minorities have moved into the federal bureaucracy, white males (41.77 percent) and white females (33.68 percent) dominate white-collar positions as white females replace white males.[11] White women, however, continue to earn considerably less than white males. Lewis found that in 1986, white women earned 36.7 percent less than white males in federal white-collar positions.[12] Gains, however, have been made as women begin to move into policymaking positions. During the period 1974–90, the percentage of women of all races in the Senior Executive Service increased from 2 to 11 percent.[13] This increase, however, is offset by the fact that women continue to dominate clerical and secretarial positions. Thus, while white women have done well in federal employment as they replace white males, they continue to receive lower salaries and face difficulties in moving into the top positions within the federal bureaucracy.

A study of state and local government employment during the 1970s found that women were overrepresented in financial administration, public welfare, hospital and sanitarium, health, and economic security positions and were especially underrepresented in such positions as police and fire.[14] Although white women made up 42.7 percent of the population in 1980, they held 31.2 percent of all positions in state and local governments and 20.0 percent of the managerial positions.[15] Another more recent study of state employment found evidence that there are better opportunities for promotion for women in state government than in the federal government and that pay equity is becoming less of a problem.[16]

Examining data from the EEOC for state and local government median salaries for 1991, we found that the widest gap between median salaries for white females ($36,443) and white males ($43,654) was in the officials/administrators category.[17] All gender and racial/ethnic groups except Native American females had higher median salaries than white females in this category. The narrowest gap in median salaries between white females ($19,382) and white males ($21,336) was in the administrative support category. All groups except Native American males and females had higher median salaries than white females for these positions. While white females are being hired in greater numbers, their salaries have not kept pace with their increased presence in government service. One possible explanation is that state and local governments have sought to attract and retain minorities by paying them higher salaries than for white females in some categories.

White women have done well in finding employment in federal, state, and local governments. Increasingly, they are moving into administrative and policymaking positions once dominated by white males. White females, who were not the initial target of affirmative action programs, have benefited greatly from efforts to promote equal employment opportunity, as their employment patterns come in line with those of white males. Nevertheless, salary parity and promotions to the highest levels continue to be elusive.

Hispanics

Historically, Hispanics have not faced the same intensity of discrimination as have blacks in finding employment in the public sector; nevertheless, discrimination has meant that Hispanics have not done as well as expected had they been treated as equals. Antonio Sisneros cites a 1988 EEOC report indicating that federal employment for Hispanic Americans lagged behind the private sector.[18] Discrepancies also exist within the federal government; J. Edward Kellough noted that federal agencies with the highest percentages of Hispanics included the EEOC (9.9 percent) and the Department of Justice (9.3 percent), while the lowest percentages were to be found in the Federal Home Loan Bank Board (0.9 percent) and the International Trade Commission (0.8 percent).[19] Pan Suk Kim found that the number of Hispanics in the federal service fell behind their proportion of the population.[20] Nevertheless, Hispanics are more likely to hold administrative and professional positions in the federal government than in the private sector.[21] In terms of earnings, Lewis found that Hispanic females received 43.2 percent less and Hispanic males received 22.9 percent less than white males in federal white-collar positions.[22]

Sisneros notes that even in states and local areas where there is a significant number of Hispanics, they tend to do less well than others in the public sector.[23] Hispanics are overrepresented in maintenance and service positions and are underrepresented in managerial and professional positions.[24] Still, just as in federal employment, Hispanics find greater opportunities in managerial and professional positions in state and local governments than in the private sector.[25] In terms of earnings in state and local governments for 1991, we found that in the officials/administrators category, the median salary for Hispanic males ($43,705) was slightly higher than that for white males ($43,654).[26] This edge was also apparent in the skilled crafts: Hispanic males ($26,648) and white males ($25,926). A wider difference was found in protective services: Hispanic males ($32,280) and white males ($29,640). Hispanic females ($29,317) almost had parity with white males in protective services. The widest gap in median salary for Hispanic females ($37,039) and white males ($43,640) was in the officials/administrators category. These high earnings may point to a major effort by state and local governments to attract and retain Hispanics in order to comply with affirmative action guidelines.

Hispanics are more likely to be employed in the private sector rather than in the public sector. However, they are more successful in holding managerial and professional positions in the federal government and in state and local governments than in the private sector. In addition, their salaries at the state and local level are in many cases equal to or higher than those of white males. Nevertheless, the past history of discrimination in and outside of government has meant fewer opportunities for Hispanics.

Asians

Exclusion has played a primary role in shaping the employment patterns of Asian Americans. However, with increased efforts to open up immigration as well as greater pressure for equal opportunity, Asian-American employment has improved. Another major factor that has enhanced the employment opportunities for Asians is their professional training and skills. Nevertheless, despite their educational backgrounds and the increased efforts to promote their employment, Asian females and members of certain Asian groups are less likely to be employed in the public sector.

In 1983, while Asians represented 2.1 percent of the U.S. population, their participation in federal employment was 2.6 percent and for white-collar federal employment 2.3 percent.[27] By 1989, the Asian population had increased to 2.8 percent, and their share of federal employment to 3.7 percent and white-collar employment to 3.2 percent. Whereas other minority groups tend to be employed in the lower ranks of the federal government, Asians are more likely to hold mid-level management positions. For the Senior Executive Service, Asians held 0.8 percent of these positions in 1989. In terms of federal agencies, Asians had their largest percentages in the Navy, Veteran Affairs, NASA, and the Environment Protection Agency. Their small percentages were to be found in Defense Logistics, Agriculture, Justice, and Interior. In comparison with other Asian Americans for 1980, Filipino males and females and Japanese males had the highest percentages in the federal work force, while Asian-Indian females and Vietnamese males and females had the lowest percentages.[28]

In examining the salaries of federal white-collar employees, Lewis found that Asian males earned more than white males in 1976, but by 1986 their salaries were 5.7 percent below the average white male salary.[29] On the other hand, Asian females earned 33.3 percent less than white males in 1986. Controlling for education and other criteria, he found that Asian males with similar characteristics to white males still earned 5.9 percent less and Asian women earned 20.8 percent less in 1986. Although Asians are extremely well educated, they have not been able to maintain earnings parity with white males. More recently, Pan Suk Kim and Gregory B. Lewis found a decline in the percentage of Asian males and females holding managerial positions.[30] For Asian males, the authors suggest that low communication skills for immigrants might be a factor. For Asian females, they argue that affirmative action may have helped them in relationship to white males but not as extensively as it has assisted white females.

Asian males made up roughly 0.2 percent of the population in 1970, but in state and local government employment they held 0.3 percent of the positions in 1975, with females having similar percentages.[31] Asian employment in state and local governments varies by group; for example, in 1980, Asian-Indian males and females and Japanese females were more likely to hold positions in state governments than Filipino males, Korean females, and Vietnamese males.[32] In local governments, Asian-Indian females, Filipino females, and Japanese females had higher employment percentages, while Chinese males and Korean males and females had the lowest percentages.

In comparison with the median white male salary ($11,631) in the state and local government sector for 1975, Asian males ($14,496) did extremely well, although Asian females ($10,353) did less well.[33] Our examination of EEOC data for 1991 demonstrated that both Asian males and females in most job categories had median salaries above those for white males.[34] The median salary for Asian females ($28,284) is below parity for white males ($29,301) in the technician category, which is also the case for Asian females ($19,904) in comparison with white males ($21,481) in the service/maintenance category. However, in all other categories Asians have higher median incomes than all the other groups based on race, ethnicity, and sex.

Asian Americans, especially males, have done relatively well in finding employment in the public sector and in their earnings pattern. Asian females have done less well, but in most cases they have done better than other groups. Their high education levels are one reason for this difference. Nevertheless, one recent study has shown that Asians are beginning to lose ground in federal employment.[35] Group competition may be one explanation for this decline, as white females increasingly move into government service, replacing white males.

Native Americans

Government has played a significant role in shaping the lives and employment of Native Americans. Given the unique relationship between the federal government and Native Americans, efforts have been made to promote Native American self-sufficiency, thereby increasing their employment opportunities.[36] Such efforts to assist those living on reservations have generally failed to promote economic well-being. During the 1950s, the policy of termination developed by Congress to promote self-sufficiency had great impact on certain designated tribes: the demise of reservations, the denial of their previously held treaty and legal rights, and the destruction of functioning economic and social communities. Unfortunately, the relationship between Native Americans and the federal government continues to be one in which federal efforts rarely provide assistance and often create new problems.

In terms of federal employment, a preference policy was established under the Indian Reorganization Act of 1934 to employ Native Americans in the Bureau of Indian Affairs (BIA). This attempt, perhaps the first to implement a policy of affirmative action in government, was described by the chair of the House Indian Committee, Representative Edgar Howard of Nebraska, who cosponsored the act, in this manner: "This provision in no way signifies a disregard of the true merit system, but it adapts the merit system to Indian temperament, training, and capacity."[37] He was concerned that Native Americans were being denied the opportunity to play a role in shaping the very policies that affected their lives. In practice, although Native Americans were given preference over more qualified whites in entry-level positions, advancement has been difficult.[38] In 1972, efforts undertaken to increase promotions for Native Americans in the BIA led to court challenges that upheld the preference policy for Native Americans.[39] Nevertheless, Walter C. Fleming, writing in 1989, noted that the lower ranks continued to be staffed primarily by Native Americans and that no Native American women had held positions in the top ranks.[40] In a comparison of federal white-collar employees, Lewis found that Native American males earned 16.6 percent less and Native American females earned 46.4 percent less than white males.[41] Kim pointed out that for 1989 data, Native Americans represented 0.7 percent of the population and held 1.1 percent of the positions in the federal government. However, he also noted that 57.6 percent of Native Americans continued to hold lower-level white-collar positions, although in terms of average grade level they ranked second to whites for managerial positions.[42] In addition to employment at the federal level, Native Americans tend to be found more often in local governments rather than state governments, which is related to reservation governance.[43]

According to EEOC data, median salaries in 1991 for Native American males were near parity with white males in a number of job categories in state and local governments.[44] In the skilled crafts, Native American males ($26,597) earned more than white males ($25,926). The widest gap between median earnings for Native American males ($32,574) and white males ($36,214) was in the professional category. For Native American females, there was a wider gap between their earnings and those of white males. In the officials/administrators category, Native American females ($34,696) did very poorly in relationship to white males ($43,654), although this was not the case for Native American males ($41,850). It appears that efforts at the state and local level to attract Native Americans have resulted in rather high salaries, but Native American males are the primary beneficiaries, with Native American females continuing to lag in both earnings and employment.

The unique status of Native Americans in American society has led to a number of laws that have attempted to redress their losses and their current conditions. However, these efforts have rarely been successful and often have been counterproductive for Native Americans. Although a preference policy for employment exists within the BIA, rarely have Native Americans been able to move to the key positions that shape the policies affecting their lives. The implementation of affirmative action has increased their numbers in government employment, but as a group they tend to hold lower-level positions, and Native American females continue to be underrepresented and underpaid.

BUREAUCRATIC REPRESENTATION

In this book, we examine the impact of affirmative action on positions in higher education and its implications for bureaucratic representation in state governments. While faculty members would be the first to complain about the bureaucratic nature of modern universities, they along with university police, maintenance and service workers, and many other higher education employees would also question the application of the term *bureaucrats* to their positions. For those in higher education and for most Americans in general, the terms *bureaucrats* and *bureaucracy* imply inefficiency, "red tape," ineptness, and routine.[45] In addition, it is argued that since bureaucrats have enormous power today, they should be more reflective of the nation's diverse population and policy preferences.[46] Why consider faculty members and other nonadministrative and nonclerical employees as bureaucrats? Why should the concept of representative bureaucracy be applied to higher education? These questions are central to determining if minorities and women have gained greater access to equal employment opportunities in higher education.

Bureaucracy

While the term *bureaucracy* is usually applied to government, business organizations also fall under this category. Max Weber, the most significant scholar of bureaucracy, used the term to refer to "organizations with a pyramidal structure of authority, which utilize the enforcement of universal and impersonal rules to maintain the structure of authority, and which emphasize the nondiscretionary aspects of administration."[47] Bureaucracy is considered by Weber to be the most efficient and effective means known to organize and maintain modern society.[48] Central to this process is a reliance on knowledge and technical skill that is directed by a hierarchical order as rules are determined through reason. Thus, access to bureaucracy is provided to all, without preference or privilege.

Central to the workings of bureaucracy are its employees – the bureaucrats who are simply "individuals who are employed in large-scale formal organizations." Thus, accountants and public relations executives in a large business firm and college professors and university administrators in public higher education institutions are considered bureaucrats. But more importantly, bureaucrats have come to acquire discretionary powers.[49] Given the need to deal with a multitude of individuals and problems, various bureaucrats, usually trained professionals, have acquired the power to make decisions without constant reference to rules and hierarchy. Commonly referred to as "street-level bureaucrats," teachers, police officers, and social workers make day-to-day decisions about which grades students should receive, who has violated the law, and who is eligible for welfare benefits. College professors, as members of a large organization, are responsible for determining the contents of their courses, grading procedures, and the type of examinations to be given. University security officers, service and maintenance workers, clerks, and administrators within universities also have discretion and function within a large organization. Bureaucratic discretion has come to play an important part in how bureaucracy functions, which has led to questions about the representative nature of bureaucracy. Should those with such power be representative of all segments of society? If so, how should they be selected? Such questions are directly related to efforts to promote equal employment opportunity through affirmative action.

Representative Bureaucracy

During the twentieth century, government responsibilities have expanded to include the environment, the economy, educational funding, health care, welfare, and nuclear weapons, but many of the policy choices about these issues have been shaped by bureaucrats rather than elected officials. This growth in power has led some to refer to bureaucracy as the fourth branch of government and others to consider it the most dominant one.[50] Although democratic representation throughout American history has centered on the voice of the people through their elected officials, some scholars of bureaucracy have raised important questions about the need for representation within the bureaucracy, given its policymaking powers.

British scholar J. Donald Kingsley is given credit for first using the concept of representative bureaucracy, although he was primarily concerned with one aspect of representation within the British civil service – class.[51] In the United

States, actions were taken during the nineteenth century by Presidents Jefferson and Jackson to provide representativeness through government service.[52]
Thomas Jefferson brought in members of his party to initially balance the previous administration's hold on government appointments but continued
bringing in his people even after this level had been reached. Andrew Jackson
moved to alter the upper-class hold on positions by opening up access to all.
Although Jackson is usually credited with introducing the corrupt spoils system, rotation of office, and the ideal of egalitarian government service, he nevertheless drew on educated men and did not remove as many officeholders as
his speeches suggest.[53] Their efforts, however, benefited white males, although
the development of the spoils system in urban politics did assist certain white
ethnic groups in finding government employment.

The ideal of making government service more democratic by opening up
positions to non-elites serves to raise the issue of what type of representation
should be found within the bureaucracy. Frederick C. Mosher argues that two
types of representativeness exist: active representation and passive representation.[54] With active representation, bureaucrats may represent the interests of
the public or a specific interest. Mosher cautions that such representativeness,
if extensive, would be disruptive to democracy since the sum total of special
interests does not represent the public interest. In addition, given the unequal
power and influence of some groups, little could be done to create equality
among the various interests. Passive representation, on the other hand, is based
on family and social makeup and could be statistically measured in terms of
such characteristics as education, race, or class. However, Mosher noted that
little research had been done on the impact of the backgrounds of individuals
on their official duties. Some studies, however, have shown that those in the
higher policymaking positions tend to be more liberal than the general public
and that government agency rather than background is a better predictor of
attitudes toward public policy.[55] Passive representation symbolizes, according
to Mosher, two important American values: an open civil service and equality
of opportunity.[56] Such symbolism is clearly related to government's position
toward a particular group, for Samuel Krislov argues that visible acceptance or
rejection of a group by government has implications for the group's power as
well as for its position within society.[57] In turn, it is also true that government
is more likely to recognize a group with power. Just as important, however, is
the point made by Krislov that "[i]f the elimination of prejudice cannot be
achieved in the public bureaucracy it is unlikely that it will be achieved any-
where."[58] Thus passive representation based upon family or social origins can

carry important symbolic weight based upon the actions of government that can expand or contract a group's status and its fortunes within society.

What are the proper means for producing such a representative bureaucracy? V. Subramaniam argues that Kingsley's discussion of representative bureaucracy created some confusion about its composition. Kingsley's primary concern was to see that the values of the dominant class in Britain, the middle class, were reflected in the makeup of the bureaucracy rather than representation for all groups. Subramaniam states that a literal definition of representative bureaucracy would mean that *"every* economic class, caste, region, or religion in a country is represented in exact proportion to its numbers in the population."[59] He goes on to argue that advocates for this form of representative bureaucracy in the United States favor selection from the various groups within American society based on merit rather than adherence to strict proportionality.

Although for some people representative bureaucracy serves as a means for promoting greater representation of the various social groups within bureaucracy, a number of critics have questioned its basic assumptions. One major criticism is the assumption that family and social origins are linked to values. As Kenneth John Meier notes, socialization is a lifetime process, and bureaucrats may be directly influenced by their experience within a government agency.[60] In addition, top-level bureaucrats who have experienced upper mobility may hold different values. Finally, Meier argues that the most important decisions are made at the top rather than through the entire bureaucracy. Thus, it is not necessary that representativeness occur throughout the bureaucracy. Subramaniam raises the important point that a representative bureaucracy might lead to factionalization and ineffectiveness due to competing interests.[61] However, he believes that the American bureaucracy has avoided this problem because bureaucrats tend to share a consensus of values based on equality. Subramaniam's view, however, was formulated prior to the explosion of interest groups in the United States in the 1960s and more recent efforts to scale back government programs. Reductions in government programs and spending, coupled with heightened interest group activity, could create pressures for bureaucrats and their particular agencies to become more vocal advocates.

Despite these criticisms, representative bureaucracy remains an important issue, especially with the increased attention given to affirmative action.[62] For example, Dennis Daley argues that affirmative action is one possible means for implementing the theory of representative bureaucracy.[63] Affirmative action also highlights the numerical imbalance in the composition of bureaucracy and serves to assist those who have been excluded for reasons other than merit. Nevertheless, steps to implement affirmative action have led to charges of preference and a devaluation of merit. David Rosenbloom states that merit and representative bureaucracy could exist side by side but only in a middle-class society.[64] However, he then goes on to argue that a number of problems do exist within American society. He notes that those who seek entry and advancement within the civil service may lack, due to poverty, the needed educational skills and values that recruiters seek. In addition, he argues that while the overwhelming number of federal government jobs are based on merit, political appointment is used for many of the senior policymaking positions and is determined by the power that groups have within the political process, something minorities and women often lack. Bringing representative bureaucracy to fruition is a difficult task, given that not everyone has had equal access to educational opportunities that might open doors for entry into and advancement in the civil service system. The relationship of representative bureaucracy to education, especially higher education, is crucial if previous patterns of discrimination are to be overturned.

Representativeness and Higher Education

The implementation of affirmative action is relevant to higher education, especially public colleges and universities, for the employment of minority and female faculty members, administrators, and other key employees offers a clear message to students, their families, and the public about the willingness of these organizations to support the goals of equal employment opportunity. At state public higher education institutions, increasing the number of minority and female faculty members in highly visible and important positions demonstrates the commitment of state governments to affirmative action. The greater presence of minority and female faculty may also serve to encourage minority and female students to pursue such a career goal. The visibility of minorities and women in important positions on college campuses serves as an important symbol to students and the larger society about the commitment of state governments to equality.

But can state governments influence the presence of minorities and women in state higher education employment? Although state officials do not play a direct role in day-to-day employment decisions, they can shape the employment environment so that a clear message is sent to personnel directors and others involved in the employment process that equal employment opportunity is a significant goal to be achieved at state-supported institutions. In terms of the implementation of affirmative action, Daley argues that it is state political and administrative officials who play the pivotal role.[65] We believe that this is especially true for the period 1979 through 1991, with the transfer of the presidency of Jimmy Carter to Ronald Reagan and then to George Bush, which resulted in a decline in the commitment of the federal government to affirmative action. Judith J. Hendricks found that the support of the governor and other high-ranking officials is critical for the development of a sound policy for implementing affirmative action at the state level.[66] Thus, we expect state public officials to be able to influence affirmative action outcomes by creating an environment more conductive to the employment of minorities and women. We examine our hypothesis about the role of state governments in promoting representative bureaucracy in two ways. First, we explore the extent to which public higher education institutions provide greater employment opportunities for minorities and women than private institutions. Second, a set of political and socioeconomic factors is developed and analyzed in order to measure the association of these factors with minority and female faculty and administrative positions in public and private colleges and universities.

In addition, we evaluate Thomas Sowell's argument that "preferential benefits tend to be concentrated on more lucrative or prestigious things," indicating that only those at the top of a targeted group benefit from affirmative action policies.[67] We suspect, contrary to this argument, that minorities and women continue to be employed in positions with less pay and status, such as secretarial positions for women and maintenance and service positions for minorities. Although we expect to find that there have been some inroads by women and minorities into higher-status positions, we believe that higher education employment can be divided into two groups, with white males continuing to dominate the better positions and minorities and women holding the lesser positions. We base our argument on the scholarly literature on labor markets, which demonstrates that race and gender can play a significant role in shaping employment outcomes.[68] These findings are based on research concerning dual labor market theory. The basic theory emphasizes two labor markets: one with well-paying employment and with benefits and opportunities for advancement, and the second made up of low-paying jobs with poor working conditions and with no opportunity for advancement.[69] The original scholarship focused on discrete industry differences; however, more recent work posits that differences can exist within firms and organizations rather than just across industries.[70] Justifications for dual labor markets focus on the ability of employers to limit their labor costs and avoid unionization. Race and gender are significant features of this model, for minorities and women are more likely to be found in secondary market employment. For example, Gordon

Lafer argues that employers, who may act without racial bias, seek to minimize their labor costs by drawing on blacks who have faced a long history of exploitation, little political influence, and social stigma.[71] Given this literature, we believe that minorities and women are more likely to hold lower-status positions within the "other" occupational categories in higher education employment.

Throughout American history various practices have made access to employment in the public sector difficult for minorities and women. Affirmative action efforts at the federal, state, and local levels have produced positive outcomes for these groups; however, discrepancies continue to exist. The goal of representative bureaucracy has been advanced as one means of promoting the various interests within society. This goal is clearly linked to affirmative action efforts to make the workplace more reflective of the diversity within American society. Developing a representative bureaucracy is not without difficulties since issues about merit and educational qualifications are sure to emerge. Examining higher education institutions, especially public ones, offers a unique view of how state governments are addressing the problems of discrimination and meeting the goals of equal employment opportunity in an increasingly diverse America.

3

Blacks in Higher Education Employment

The education of blacks has always been a major and controversial issue throughout American history. During the slavery era, many laws existed to restrict their ability to receive an education. After the Reconstruction Era, numerous laws were passed in the South to restrict black access to education by providing "separate but equal" schools, resulting in the segregation of blacks. The *Brown v. Board of Education* decision in 1954 officially ended state-supported segregation in educational facilities, but numerous court decisions and court challenges to busing showed that this issue was not to be easily surmounted through the legal system.

Prior to *Brown*, various court challenges had been made by the National Association for the Advancement of Colored People (NAACP) to overturn the Jim Crow laws that had maintained the segregation system in the South. In the area of higher education, one significant early step in 1938 was *Missouri ex rel. Gaines v. Canada*, in which the Supreme Court ruled in favor of the admission of a black student, who had been denied equal protection under the law, into the state's law school.[1] Nevertheless, such decisions did not end segregation in colleges and universities, as efforts to inhibit and obstruct black educational opportunities continued. While historically black colleges and universities (HBCUs) offered blacks an opportunity to receive a college education, public HBCUs were often established by states to maintain segregation in higher education. As Julian B. Roebuck and Komanduri S. Murty note, "public HBCUs were created by the southern state governments for three reasons: to get millions of dollars in federal funds for the development of white land-grant universities, to limit black education to vocational training, and to prevent blacks from attending white land-grant colleges."[2] Later efforts such as the Higher Education Act of 1965, which made available a number of grants to students who were severely disadvantaged, provided many black students with the opportunity to attend higher education institutions; nevertheless, segregation still existed in the late 1960s.

In 1970, the NAACP Legal Defense and Educational Fund went to court to open up educational facilities by arguing that the Department of Health, Education, and Welfare (HEW) had failed to constrain state-supported segregation by not discontinuing funding to segregated colleges and universities as required by Title VI of the Civil Rights Act of 1964.[3] The *Adams v. Richardson* (1970) case was a response to a report made by HEW that had found segregated colleges and universities in ten states and had attempted to secure voluntary compliance to end higher education segregation. In 1974, Judge John H. Pratt of the U.S. District Court for the District of Columbia ordered that action be taken against any of the ten states that did not develop desegregation plans. However, the same justice dismissed the case in 1987, stating that the Department of Education was not directly responsible for the problem and that the withdrawal of federal funding was not an adequate step for redressing the injuries. Pratt's decision was reversed by the U.S. Court of Appeals for the District of Columbia in 1989. This case, which involved numerous attempts to develop desegregation plans, would be overshadowed by a more important Supreme Court decision in 1992. The latter case, which began in 1975, concerned the role of the state of Mississippi in ensuring equal higher education institutions and reached the Supreme Court in 1992 as *U.S. v. Fordice*. The Court ruled that "even after a State dismantles its segregative *admissions* policy, there may still be state action that is traceable to the State's prior *de jure* segregation and that continues to foster segregation."[4] Thus, efforts must be made to eliminate any policy that is a product of past discrimination. The difficulties in eliminating segregation in higher education remain, as suggested by the extensive time required for both the *Adams* and *Fordice* cases to work their way through the legal system.

Only recently have black faculty established a foothold in white institutions. Such a notable as W. E. B. Du Bois was unable to find employment in a prominent university, except for a brief stay at the University of Pennsylvania in the late 1890s, and ultimately he was employed by a black institution, Atlanta University.[5] There were a few past examples of blacks finding employment in white institutions, such as Charles L. Reason, who taught at the abolitionist New York Central College in the 1850s, and Father Patrick Healey, who became president of Georgetown University in 1873. But the experience of William A. Hinton, who after twenty-nine years as an instructor and lecturer at Harvard University was promoted to full professor in 1929, demonstrated the difficulties blacks faced in employment and promotion decisions in white higher education institutions for most of the twentieth century. Only with the coming of World War II and the resulting labor shortages were blacks able to move to white campuses as faculty members. Foreshadowing the current sentiment that affirmative action efforts lead to reverse discrimination for whites, Herbert G. Espy, president of State Teachers College of Geneseo, New York, responded to a request to open up faculty positions to blacks in 1945 by noting his concern that department chairs might question "that the needs of our students now warrant making any special effort to employ Negro teachers or to discriminate against white applicants."[6]

Restrictions placed on data collection on minority faculty prior to the 1970s by higher education institutions and various levels of government meant that little was known about minorities on college campuses.[7] The few studies that were completed by researchers showed that by 1938, of the two hundred black faculty members employed, only six held positions in white colleges and universities.[8] By 1961, slightly fewer than three hundred blacks held positions in white institutions. In 1961, blacks held 3 percent of all faculty positions, rising to 4.4 percent in 1976. Between 1976 and 1985, black faculty increased by 1.9 percent in contrast to an earlier growth rate of 126 percent between 1961 and 1976. Thus, while blacks represented 3 percent of all faculty positions in the early 1960s, there was a drop to 2.2 percent in the early 1970s, and an increase to 4 percent in the early 1980s.

BLACK FACULTY

To examine the progress of blacks in both public and private higher education, we use EEOC data available for the years 1979, 1983, and 1991. Based on the theory of representative bureaucracy, we expect state governments to attempt to implement affirmative action in order to ensure more representativeness within state government employment as well as to comply with federal guidelines. Thus, we hypothesize that blacks are more likely to have made progress in public higher education institutions than in private institutions.

The data available from the EEOC provide us with a number of opportunities for examining minority and female employment in higher education. Separate data were available for 1983 and 1991 for public and private higher education but not for 1979, for which combined data are given. Participation rates are provided, which indicate the percentage of faculty members based on race, ethnicity, and sex. For example, for the state of Alabama, data for 1983 show that in public higher education, black males held 3.7 percent of the faculty positions. This percentage can be compared to a nonsouthern state with a large black population such as New York, in which black males held 2.3 percent of the faculty positions in the same year. A comparison with 1991 shows that the participation rate for black males increased from 3.7 percent to 4.5 percent in Alabama, while in New York the rate increased from 2.3 percent to 2.9 percent. Examining these rates will give us some sense of minority and female progress at the macrolevel; nevertheless, we are aware that at the microlevel a variety of factors can influence hiring practices, such as credentials, candidates' regional preference, departmental needs, and even prejudice.

In addition, we are not only concerned with the progress made by minorities and women in individual states but with the representative nature of employment practices as well. One way to examine that feature is to use representation ratios, which are determined by dividing the participation rate by the percentage of each racial or ethnic group for each sex in a state's population. For example, in 1980, black males represented 11.89 percent of the population in Alabama. Using that percentage to give us an estimate of the black male population in 1983, we divide that percentage of the population into the participation rate of 3.7 percent, yielding a representation ratio of 0.31. The closer this ratio is to 1.0, the more this particular racial/ethnic group by sex is employed according to its distribution within the state's population. (A representation ratio exceeding 1.0 indicates overrepresentation of a group.) For the state of New York, we divide the black male proportion of the state's population, 6.23 percent, into the participation rate of 2.3 percent, producing a representation ratio of 0.37. Thus, by a small margin, black males in New York are more likely to be employed according to their distribution within the state than in Alabama. Of course, this means that in a state with a low proportion of black males, their ratio will be quite high. For example, the percentage of black males in Maine in 1980 was 0.17, and the participation rate for black male faculty members was 0.3, resulting in a representation ratio of 1.77. As a result, black males who are faculty members exceed their share of the population in that state. On the other hand, an examination of white females shows that their representation ratio for faculty positions in public higher education in Maine is 0.44. Clearly, white females were underrepresented in terms of their numbers in that state. While this ratio is far from perfect, it does give us an indication about the representative nature of higher education. As we are concerned about the extent to which states have made an effort to make higher education institutions, especially public ones, more like their state's population, representation ratios serve an important purpose. Needless to say, it is also useful to examine participation rates in order to understand the progress of minorities and females in higher education. As a result, we present both numbers.

Data for the participation rates are available for forty-nine of the fifty states, with the exception being Hawaii. Both participation rates and representation ratios are presented in the appendixes; however, as some state data are missing or unavailable, we discuss in the text only those states for which there are complete data.

Examining the participation rates for black faculty in all colleges and universities in the relatively short period 1979 to 1983, we find a decline from 4.5 percent to 4.2 percent (table 1). By 1991, however, black participation in faculty positions had risen to 4.9 percent. Thus, for blacks to acquire and maintain faculty employment remains tenuous. The existence of affirmative action is no guarantee that employment levels will always remain stable for blacks. Although blacks made up 11.8 percent of the U.S. population in 1990, they did not have parity with their share of the population, for they held only 4.9 percent of faculty positions in 1991. The representation ratios show that blacks holding faculty positions in terms of their share of the population moved from only 0.39 in 1979 to 0.42 by 1991. We also found in 1983 that blacks were more likely to be employed in public institutions rather than private institutions, although by 1991 this difference had narrowed. Why is this change taking place? Perhaps private higher education institutions have become more aggressive in recruiting blacks, and perhaps public institutions, in an attempt to be more representative, are bringing in other minorities and white women rather than blacks. It is apparent from the data in table 1 that black males do somewhat better than black females in obtaining faculty positions. Being black and female does not benefit black women but instead can produce what Cynthia Fuchs Epstein refers to as "the multiple negative."[9] While Epstein found that in some cases, especially in the professions, the multiple negative could assist black women, this is not the case when we look at overall numbers for faculty appointments. Problems facing women in general concerning social and family influences on career choices and the lack of mentors in graduate school may explain why women face difficulties in achieving a successful academic career.[10] We speculate that black women may have greater difficulties in finding mentors as students and later as faculty members, which may explain our findings.

The data for newly hired tenure-track faculty in table 2 show that private institutions had a slight edge over public institutions in 1983, but by 1991 this edge had shifted to public institutions by half a percentage point. Overall, in 1991 we find that 3.8 percent of the newly hired tenure-track positions in all colleges and universities were held by black males, who represented 5.6 percent of the U.S. population in 1990, and that 3.2 percent of these positions were held by black females, who made up 6.2 percent of the U.S. population in 1990; in both cases their percentage of these positions is considerably less than their share of the total population.

Achieving the rank of full professor represents an important recognition of one's ability within academia. The data in table 3 show that in 1983 only a very small percentage of blacks (2.2 percent) held this rank, but by 1991 that percentage had doubled in public institutions to 4.4 percent. Major differences existed due to gender. In both public and private institutions, less than 1.0 percent of full professors were black females in 1983, while black males represented 1.6 percent of the total. In 1991 black female professors increased to 1.9 percent, with public institutions providing greater opportunities than private schools. For black males, we find that they had a better chance for promotion to full professor in private institutions than public institutions in 1983, but by 1991 this had been reversed by a slight margin.

Blacks were more likely to find faculty employment in the period 1979–91 in some states than in others. The data for 1979 (a combination of both public and private higher education institutions) show that participation rates range from 0 to 7.7 percent for black males (appendix 1) and from 0 to 6.8 percent for black females (appendix 2). Only in the states of Alabama and Louisiana do the participation rates for black males and black females equal or exceed their proportion of the national population (5.4 percent for black males in 1980, 6.1 percent for black females). The states of Georgia, Maryland, Mississippi, and Tennessee have participation rates for black male faculty that range from 4.6 to 5.2 percent, and for black females, the states of Delaware, Georgia, Mississippi, Tennessee, and Virginia have rates that range from 4.1 to 5.3 percent, so their percentages nearly reach the proportion of blacks in the national population. There are eighteen states that fall below 1.0 percent for black males and twenty-two states for black females, which only confirms that black males do better than black females in obtaining faculty positions.

An examination of the representation ratios for black males (appendix 21) and black females (appendix 22) shows that in only five states do black male faculty positions exceed the black male population: Maine, Montana, New Hampshire, South Dakota, and Vermont. Black female representation ratios that exceed their share of the state population were found in Montana, North Dakota, South Dakota, and Vermont. These states have low percentages of blacks in the total population, which increase the ratios. (This demonstrates one limitation of the use of representation ratios, so we use participation rates as well to provide a clearer frame of reference.)

Does having large numbers of blacks within a state guarantee that there will be a greater proportion of blacks in faculty positions? In order to explore this question, we examine the states with the largest percentages of blacks based on 1980 data: Alabama (25.59 percent), Georgia (26.82 percent), Louisiana (29.44 percent), Mississippi (35.20 percent), and South Carolina (30.39 percent). The participation rates for black females (appendix 2) show that the two states with the highest percentages of blacks in their populations, Mississippi (with a participation rate of 4.1 percent) and South Carolina (3.6 percent), have lower participation rates in 1979 than Delaware (4.4 percent) and Tennessee (4.5 percent). This is also true for black males (appendix 1) in South Carolina (with a participation rate of 3.8 percent) in comparison with Delaware (3.9 percent) and Tennessee (4.6 percent). Given that South Carolina has a black population of 30.39 percent, nearly twice that of Delaware (16.13 percent) and Tennessee (15.81 percent), large numbers of blacks do not necessarily ensure more black faculty members. This is not to say that blacks do not do well in the South, but it does appear that in addition to the size of the black population, political and socioeconomic factors also need to be considered. It should also be noted that the HBCUS, both public and private, exist primarily in the southern states and in such border states as Delaware, which may explain why blacks do better in these states. Unfortunately, due to government privacy restrictions, the EEOC data give aggregate data for states, but not for individual colleges and universities. (Our efforts to obtain such information have been mixed. Some states have been willing to provide this information, whereas others have referred us back to the EEOC).

Next we examine the data for 1983 in public higher education. Looking at the southern states, which have both the largest black populations and more black faculty members, we find that for black males only, the southern states of Louisiana, Mississippi, and North Carolina have participation rates above their proportion of the national population of 5.4 percent for 1980 (appendix 1). For black females, the states with participation rates above their national figure of 6.1 percent for 1980 are Louisiana and Mississippi (appendix 2). There are twenty states with rates below 1.0 for black males and for black females. The representation ratios reveal that black males have ratios above 1.0 in the states of Maine, Massachusetts, Minnesota, Montana, New Hampshire, South Dakota, and Vermont (appendix 21). Five of these states have black populations below 1.0 percent; Minnesota has a black population of 1.31 percent and Massachusetts has 3.86 percent. For black females, only in the states of Idaho, Montana, and Vermont, which have black populations below 1.0 percent, do the ratios exceed 1.0 (appendix 22). Of the states with high black populations, Mississippi has the highest representation ratios for both black males (0.47)

and females (0.38), and Georgia has the lowest (0.29 for males, 0.32 for females). In Georgia, black females have a slight edge over black males among
the five states with the largest number of blacks. The border state of Delaware
has a ratio of 0.49 for black males and 0.70 for black females. Delaware is the
second smallest state in the Union and the site of one of the historically black
land-grant colleges and universities, which may explain the ratios we have
found.

In private higher education for 1983, the states of Georgia, Louisiana, and
Mississippi have participation rates for black males that are above their share
of the national population (appendix 1). For black females, the states of Georgia, Louisiana, Mississippi, and Virginia have rates equal to or above their proportion of the national population (appendix 2). Twenty-three states have
participation rates below 1.0 percent for black males, and thirty states have
rates below 1.0 for black females. For the representation ratios we find that
only Maine, New Hampshire, and North Dakota have ratios above 1.0 for black
males and that there are ratios of zero for the states of Delaware, Idaho, Montana, South Dakota, Utah, and Vermont (appendix 21). All of these states except Delaware have very low percentages of blacks in their populations. For
black females, ratios above 1.0 are found in the states of Maine, New Hampshire, and South Dakota (appendix 22), while ratios of zero are found in
Delaware, Idaho, Montana, North Dakota, and Vermont. Thus, while South
Dakota and Vermont have ratios above 1.0 for black males, both have ratios of
zero for black females. Delaware again stands out as a case in which its strong
ratios for public higher education evaporate for private higher education,
which is probably due to the presence of a public HBCU. For the states with the
highest black populations, we do find that some of the ratios are close to 1.0 in
the states of Georgia (0.73 for black males, 0.66 for black females) and
Louisiana (0.87 for black males, 0.76 for black females). However, South Carolina, with the second largest black population in 1980, has ratios of 0.31 for
black males and 0.24 for black females.

Next we examine the participation rates for 1991 in public institutions. The
states of Louisiana, Mississippi, and North Carolina have participation rates
above their proportion in the national population (5.6 percent) for black males
in 1990 (appendix 1). In some southern states, we find that the participation
rates declined, as in Mississippi (from 7.8 percent to 7.3 percent) and in South
Carolina (from 4.6 percent to 3.9 percent). We do see an increase in the state of
Georgia, as the participation rate for black males rose from 3.6 percent to 5.4
percent. The states of Alabama, Louisiana, and Mississippi have rates that
equal or exceed their proportion in the national population (6.2 percent) for

black females in 1990 (appendix 2). In comparing the states for 1983 and 1991 with representation ratios at or above 1.0 for black males, we find that Maine, Massachusetts, Minnesota, New Hampshire, and South Dakota were replaced by Idaho, Iowa, and West Virginia and that Montana and Vermont were above 1.0 in both years (appendix 21). For black females, however, Vermont remains the only state with a ratio above 1.0, as Idaho and Montana slipped below 1.0 in 1991 (appendix 22). Overall, black females continue to fall behind black males, as in the previous years.

For private higher education, we find that the participation rates for 1991 in the states of Alabama, Georgia, Louisiana, and Mississippi exceed their proportion in the national population for black males in 1990 (appendix 1). In private higher education in 1991, the states of Arizona, Louisiana, Maine, Nevada, and New Hampshire have representation ratios above 1.0, with the states of Alaska, Idaho, Montana, North Dakota, South Dakota, Texas, Vermont, Virginia, and West Virginia with ratios at zero (appendix 21). For black females, the states of Alabama, Georgia, Louisiana, Mississippi, and Nevada, a nonsouthern state, had rates above their proportion in the national population for 1990 (appendix 2). For black females, ratios above 1.0 were found for the states of Arizona, Louisiana, Maine, and Nevada (appendix 22). However, the following states had ratios above zero but below 0.20: Connecticut, Illinois, Indiana, Kansas, Nebraska, New Jersey, New York, Pennsylvania, and Tennessee.

In general, blacks are more likely to find faculty employment in public higher education institutions rather than private institutions located in the southern or border states. However, as noted earlier, the EEOC data do not provide for an examination of individual colleges and universities to see if such employment is taking place primarily at public HBCUs. Nonetheless, a recent study by the Southern Education Foundation does examine this issue. Of the nineteen states that once had *de jure* segregation, this study focused on twelve primarily southern states but also including Maryland and Pennsylvania. It was found that blacks were more likely to be employed in HBCUs rather than in flagship state universities. Maryland stood out as having 4.9 percent of black faculty members at the University of Maryland, while the other states ranged from 2 to 4 percent at the state universities (data by gender was not available.)[11] On the other hand, blacks made up on average 58 percent of the faculty at HBCUs, while whites represented 91 percent of the faculty at flagship institutions. Thus, much of the growth in black faculty employment may be taking place in the public HBCUs. Unfortunately, the EEOC data do not provide information on individual colleges and universities.

To examine the progress of blacks since 1991, we utilized the most recent higher education survey conducted in 1995 by the Department of Education's National Center for Education Statistics (NCES). As noted in the introduction, while there are differences in data collection from the EEOC, this survey does provide some sense of the recent course of affirmative action in higher education employment. A comparison of the NCES data for 1995 with our results shows that for faculty positions, black males now have only a slight edge in finding positions in public rather than private higher education, while for black females the small lead in public rather than private institutions has grown considerably. The NCES data also suggest that black males in both public and private institutions are beginning to see their share of newly hired tenure-track positions decline, while the share for black females is increasing slightly. (The 1995 NCES data for newly hired tenure-track positions should be viewed with even greater caution, for we found decreases for most groups since 1991.) In addition, the data indicate that the rate for black males and females achieving full professorships appears to be declining.[12] While problems of comparison must be considered, these findings suggest that blacks may be losing the gains made earlier, as opposition to affirmative action and competition for a scarce number of faculty positions increase.

BLACK ADMINISTRATORS

The progress of blacks in landing administrative positions in higher education is quite different from those seeking faculty positions. One major difference is that a doctoral degree is not always a requirement for obtaining these administrative positions. An examination of the total participation rates shows a doubling of the growth of blacks in these positions (table 4). However, this increase is not shared equally by both sexes. For black males in all higher education institutions during the period 1979 to 1983, there was a slight decline in obtaining positions, with the participation rate returning to its previous level by 1991. In 1983, public higher education colleges and universities provided greater opportunities to black males, but by 1991 the difference between public and private institutions had almost disappeared. Initially in 1979, black females were at a considerable disadvantage in comparison with black males, for their participation rate was only 0.1 percent; by 1991, it had increased to 4.5 percent, giving the edge to black females over black males. In 1983 and 1991, black female administrators found their greatest opportunities in private institutions rather than public higher education. We find mixed support for our hypothesis that blacks would do better in public institutions rather than private higher education. The gap between public and private higher education is narrowing for black males, while black females find private higher education institutions more hospitable than public schools.

An examination of the representation ratios shows that although there has been a decline for black males between 1979 and 1991, the ratios are closer to 1.0 than those for faculty positions (tables 1 and 4). Why have administrative positions been a better source of employment for blacks, especially black females, in comparison with faculty positions? W. Lee Hansen and Thomas F. Guidugli found for the period 1975 to 1983 a growth rate of 15 percent for executive, administrative, and managerial positions in comparison with a growth rate of 9 percent for faculty positions in higher education.[13] However, the largest gain during that period was for nonfaculty professionals. Examining public colleges and universities, Hansen and Guidugli found a decline of 2 percent for faculty positions versus a 6 percent increase for administrative employment and an 11 percent increase for nonfaculty employment. In private higher education, faculty positions grew by 37 percent, administrators by 29 percent, and nonfaculty positions by 30 percent. Reasons for the growth in administrative positions, according to the authors, include the need for new administrators to respond to governmental policies, numerous student services, and the demand for a variety of professionals such as computer experts. Using the data made available to us by the EEOC, we find that during the period 1979 to 1991, overall faculty employment increased by 12.5 percent while administrative employment rose 25.2 percent and nonfaculty employment (excluding both faculty and administrators) grew by 25.4 percent (table 5). An examination of table 5 shows that faculty and administrative positions grew in public colleges and universities, while in private institutions there was a decline in faculty positions during the period 1983–91.

Next we turn to the state data for 1979, which show that the participation rates for black males were above 5.0 percent in a number of southern states as well as in the two border states of Delaware and Maryland and in New Jersey, which also have relatively high percentages of blacks (appendix 3). An examination of the representation ratios for 1979 shows that twenty-four states, mostly southern and border states, have ratios above 1.0 and that only Wyoming has a ratio of zero (appendix 23). For black females, the participation rates support an earlier assessment that few if any opportunities existed in administrative positions for black females (appendix 4). There is an extremely high number of states with rates of zero, and only Delaware (0.8 percent) and Illinois (0.5 percent) have participation rates that stand out from the rest.

Looking at 1983 data, we find the participation rates for black males in public higher education quite high, as there was an overall increase in the participation rates for this year (appendix 3). Once again most of the southern states have high rates above 5.0 percent, as do the states of Delaware, Illinois, Maryland, Massachusetts, New Jersey, Pennsylvania, and Rhode Island. An examination of the representation ratios shows that twenty-one states have ratios above 1.0 (appendix 23). Only the states of New Hampshire and North Dakota have ratios of zero. For black females, the representation ratios show positive movement from the bleak opportunities available in 1979 (appendix 24). The four states of Maine, Massachusetts, Minnesota, and Washington have ratios above 1.0, while eight states with low percentages of blacks have ratios of zero.

For private higher education institutions in 1983, we find that black males have participation rates above 10.0 percent in Alabama, Louisiana, and Mississippi (appendix 3). In terms of representation ratios, black males have ratios above 1.0 in eleven states (appendix 23). These states include the southern states of Mississippi and Tennessee as well as states with relatively low percentages of blacks, such as Maine and Vermont. Ratios of zero are found in the states of Idaho, Montana, North Dakota, South Dakota, and Utah, which also have low percentages of blacks. For black females in private higher education institutions, the states of New Hampshire, South Dakota, Tennessee, and Vermont have representation ratios above 1.0, while eight states have ratios of zero (appendix 24). An examination of the participation rates shows that black females have rates above 10.0 percent in Georgia, Louisiana, and Mississippi (appendix 4).

A comparison of the overall participation rates in administration for public higher education in 1983 and 1991 shows a slight decline in positions for black males (appendix 3) and a large increase for black females (appendix 4). States such as Delaware, Illinois, New Jersey, and New York have rates that are within the range of the southern states of Alabama, Georgia, Louisiana, Mississippi, North Carolina, South Carolina, and Virginia. Low or zero ratios tend to be found in those states that have low percentages of blacks. Nevertheless, for black males, the representation ratios for administrative positions have dropped, for in 1991 only fifteen states have representation ratios above 1.0 (appendix 23). We suspect that this decline is the result of other groups, including white females, filling these positions. On the other hand, for black females, nine states have ratios above 1.0, and only three states have ratios of zero (appendix 24). An examination of the participation rates shows that black females do well in the southern states of Alabama, Georgia, Louisiana, Mississippi, North Carolina, and Virginia but not in South Carolina (appendix 4). States outside the South where black females do better include Illinois, New Jersey, and New York.

Overall participation rates in administration for private higher education institutions showed a marked increase for both black males (appendix 3) and females (appendix 4) in 1991. For example, state data show that black males have participation rates above 10.0 percent in Alabama, Georgia, and Mississippi, while black females have rates above 10.0 percent in those states as well as Louisiana. Nevertheless, low or zero rates continue to be found in states with few blacks. What is especially significant for black females is that their overall representation ratio for private institutions, 0.85, is closer to 1.0 than the ratio of 0.73 for black males. Although we have found increases for black females in both public and private higher education institutions, and in private higher education institutions for black males, it is necessary to view these data with caution. Given the restrictions for the EEOC data, the growth in administrative positions for blacks may be occurring primarily in the HBCUs.

Comparing our findings based on EEOC data with the NCES survey, it appears that our earlier finding that black males did better in public institutions rather than private higher education held in the mid-1990s and that the gap between the two types of institutions, which was narrowing, has instead widened.[14] On the other hand, for black females, the gap that favored them in private schools rather than public institutions has become quite small. It also appears that there might be a slight growth in the share of positions going to blacks in public higher education, while there is a similar decline in private institutions. In addition, blacks continue to do better in finding employment in administrative positions rather than faculty positions. Such findings suggest that public institutions continue to do more to enhance employment opportunities for blacks than private institutions.

BLACKS IN OTHER OCCUPATIONS

We also examined the extent to which blacks have made progress in the other occupations within higher education, which include professional non-faculty, secretarial/clerical, technical/para-professional, skilled crafts, and service/maintenance positions.[15] Based on our previous discussion of dual labor market theory (see chapter 2), we expected that blacks are more likely to be employed in the lower-status and lower-paying positions such as secretarial and maintenance than in the professional non-faculty and technical/para-professional categories. Black males during the period 1979 to 1991 were more likely to be employed in service/maintenance positions or the skilled crafts than in the other three categories (table 6). Black males were overrepresented in terms of their proportion of the population in these two categories, especially service/maintenance. They were less likely to be employed in professional positions and secretarial/clerical positions. For professional positions there was a small increase from 1979 to 1983 but then a slight decline by 1991. For service/maintenance positions, there was a minor increase from 1979 to 1983, but by 1991 there was a decline to below the rate for 1979. This probably occurred as other minorities and white females were competing for these positions. For the other categories there were some increases, especially in the skilled crafts and to a less extent in the technical/para-professional category. Black males were better represented in all the job categories except skilled crafts in private institutions in both 1983 and 1991 than in public higher education institutions (table 7).

Black females were more likely to be employed in service/maintenance, secretarial/clerical, and technical/para-professional positions than in either of the other two categories in 1979. While there was an increase for black females in secretarial/clerical positions by 1991, there was a drop from 11.5 percent to 10.9 percent in technical/para-professional positions, and a drop from 17.5 percent to 14.8 percent in service/maintenance positions (table 6). There also was an increase in professional positions for black females from 4.8 percent to 5.9 percent between 1979 and 1991. It appears that there was some movement as black females were able to obtain more desirable positions such as those in the professional category, but they continued to be overrepresented in secretarial/clerical and service/maintenance positions, and there was no progress toward greater employment in the skilled craft positions.

In 1983 as well as in 1991, black females were more likely to find employment in private higher education institutions rather than public institutions in all employment categories except the skilled crafts, where there was no difference between the two types of institutions (table 7). Especially noteworthy is an increase in professional positions for black females in private higher education, which produced a representation ratio of 1.13 in comparison to a ratio of 0.87 in public higher education. Between 1983 and 1991, there was a drop in the participation rates for black females in private higher education for the service/maintenance and technical/para-professional categories, but they continued to have representation ratios above 1.00 in private higher education in all categories except for the skilled crafts. This evidence provides little support for our argument that greater representativeness for blacks would occur in public institutions rather than private higher education.

Considering the state data is important for understanding variations in employment patterns.[16] In general, blacks did especially well in the South, but we also need to note that for each employment category there are other states with participation rates equal to or exceeding those of the southern states. For example, in 1979, black males and females did well in professional positions in the southern states but also in such states as Delaware, Illinois, and New Jersey. Examining the lowest employment level, service/maintenance positions, we found that blacks did well in the southern states but had very low participation rates (below 1.0 percent) in states with extremely small percentages of blacks, such as Idaho, Maine, and New Hampshire as well as Minnesota and Utah. Thus, although efforts were made in states with low percentages of blacks to fill faculty and administrative positions, this was not the case for service/maintenance positions. No doubt this was due to the need to hire based on proximity, since these are low-paying jobs and lack opportunities for advancement.

The separate data for public higher education employment showed that blacks did well in the South relative to other regions, with certain nonsouthern states standing out. Thus, for 1983, blacks in professional positions did well in the South but also in Delaware, a border state, and New Jersey – a trend that continued into 1991. Noteworthy was the state of New Jersey, which continued to have a higher participation rate than Alabama, Georgia, and South Carolina but not Louisiana and Mississippi (the five states with the largest black populations). Black females had their strongest rates for professional positions outside the South in Delaware, Illinois, Maryland, New Jersey, New York, and Pennsylvania in 1983. By 1991, this trend in these nonsouthern states continued, although there was a decline for New Jersey, and the state of Ohio is added to the list. Outside of the South, the states of Illinois and New Jersey tended to have better participation rates for both black males and females in the secretarial/clerical and technical/para-professional fields than other states. New Jersey was also a state where black males did well in the skilled crafts. This was also true for black females in the skilled crafts for 1991, although the rates remained relatively low in all other states. In service/maintenance positions, black males had high rates in the southern states and in New Jersey, with a rate of 20.0 percent in 1991. Black females had high participation rates outside the South, especially in New Jersey and Ohio. But this was the lowest of all the categories, and thus high numbers did not necessarily mean progress for blacks.

For private higher education, blacks did better in the South, with some exceptions. Illinois stood out as a state where blacks did relatively well in comparison with other states for nearly all the "other" categories for both 1983 and 1991. However, black females continued to have participation rates of zero in the skilled crafts for a number of states in private higher education, which was also the case for public higher education. In 1991, it was only in the states of Georgia, Louisiana, Mississippi, Missouri, and Virginia that participation rates were above 2.0 percent. In the service/maintenance category, black males had high rates in such states as Alabama and Mississippi but rates of zero in a number of states including Idaho, New Hampshire, and Wisconsin. Participation rates for black males and females outside the South also remained relatively high for service/maintenance positions in comparison with the other categories.

Are blacks more likely to be employed in lower-status positions than in higher-status positions within the other occupations? Black males were more often to be found in service/maintenance positions than in professional positions. Black males made up 17.2 percent of those in service/maintenance positions and only 2.8 percent of those in professional positions in 1991 (table 6), so there does seem to be some evidence supporting our argument that blacks tend to be found in lower-status positions. Black females were more likely to be found in service/maintenance, secretarial/clerical, and technical/para-professional positions than in professional positions or the skilled crafts. Their participation rate in the traditionally male-dominated field of the skilled crafts (1.1 percent in 1991) was quite low. Thus "the double negative" of being both black and female does seem to persist. Nevertheless, some progress has been made, as black males are to be found in the skilled crafts, a relatively high-paying field, and black females are increasing their numbers in the professional category, which has higher status and better pay. Thus, while it does appear that blacks continue to be found in lower-status positions and that gender does play a role in limiting the success of black females, affirmative action is assisting blacks in making inroads into higher-status positions.

We have found that blacks as a group do poorly in faculty positions as a percentage of their share of the U.S. population. We did find some support for our hypothesis that blacks are more likely to be employed in public institutions rather than private institutions. By 1991 that difference had begun to narrow, although the 1995 NCES survey showed this gap for black females was widening. Blacks do best in the South, but their strong presence in the southern states does not always guarantee that there will be large numbers holding faculty positions. In addition, we suspect that much of this progress is in the HBCUS. We find that blacks do better in administrative positions than faculty ones, which is probably due to the recent growth in higher education administration and better opportunities in HBCUS. As with faculty positions, blacks do best in the South. Black females did better in private rather than public higher education until the gap was nearly closed by 1995. The edge for black males in public higher education had widened, according to the recent NCES data. For the other occupations, we found support for our argument that blacks tend to be employed in lower-status positions. In addition, there is some evidence showing that blacks are moving into higher-status positions. The implementation of affirmative action has meant progress for blacks; nevertheless, their success in finding employment in higher education institutions has been mixed, as variations exist across occupations and regions of the country.

4

White Women in Higher Education Employment

To become a faculty member and to a lesser extent to be an administrator in higher education, a doctorate is normally required. Other positions in academic institutions often require some type of advanced training or skills, yet women of any race or ethnic background historically faced numerous obstacles in obtaining such education or training. Most of these barriers were social ones reinforced by colleges and universities that restricted access to the campus or, for those admitted to colleges and universities, that limited their choice of majors. In addition, admission to graduate school was difficult, for women were viewed as future mothers rather than as possible educators or scholars in higher education. Nevertheless, opportunities did open up as social change led to both administrators and faculty members coming to accept, begrudgingly in many cases, women as students and colleagues.

Historically, a young girl's relationship to her family and her future role as mother shaped her early educational experiences. Some educational opportunities were provided for girls in the colonial era. Barbara Miller Solomon states that positive attitudes toward education for girls grew during the colonial period, as education was increasingly recognized as being useful to society.[1] In the first half of the nineteenth century, some women attended various academies, usually to prepare to become school teachers or to acquire the proper training for upper-class society. A few colleges for women were founded during the 1850s but failed. Nevertheless, Vassar College, founded in 1865, and both Smith College and Wellesley College, established in 1875, did survive. Women were admitted to state universities beginning in 1855 but often faced restrictions such as a state residence requirement. A failed attempt to have women enter Harvard University led to the establishment of Radcliffe College in 1894. Harvard ultimately admitted women with the coming of World War II. Other Ivy League institutions such as Yale University did not admit women as undergraduates until the early 1970s.

Access to graduate school was often limited. It was not until 1877 that Boston University granted a Ph.D. degree to a woman, fifteen years after the awarding of the first doctorate to a white male by Yale. The case of Mary Calkins, in which Harvard refused to award her a Ph.D. degree in 1895 despite her passing a doctoral examination, showed the difficulties women faced in acquiring academic credentials in the late nineteenth century.[2] A major concern (which continued into the twentieth century) was the utility of a higher education degree if the woman should marry. Writing in the early 1960s, Betty Friedan noted the need for women not only "to cook the church supper, but to preach the sermon; not just to look up the zip codes to address the envelopes, but to make the political decisions."[3] Thus while inroads into higher education had been made in the twentieth century, women continued to have few opportunities to become ministers, politicians, or college professors until the 1960s. Efforts to bring down these barriers began to be made in the late 1960s and continued into the 1970s and beyond.

But, in 1975, Peggy Elder could still argue that despite changes produced by the women's movement, women in higher education had made little progress in the past one hundred years as students, faculty, and administrators due to cultural barriers that in some cases might make a woman reluctant to seek success. Institutional barriers also continued to be a problem, as Elder cites the following comment by a department chair: "We interviewed a black man and a white woman we knew were poorly qualified from their credentials. When we finally brought in the outstanding man we wanted all along, everyone was so relieved that we hired him on the spot."[4] Barriers to women's employment remained despite efforts to the contrary.

Helen S. Astin and Mary Beth Snyder, in their analysis of affirmative action in the 1972–82 period, found skepticism among male faculty and administrators toward affirmative action programs in terms of costs, mobility, and their perception of a "limited availability of qualified women for faculty and administrative positions."[5] Women in academia, on the other hand, felt that change was not as rapid as it should be and that they remained in the lower faculty positions or were provided with few opportunities to make important policy decisions.

The data for faculty positions showed that women in 1929 made up 29 percent of faculty positions; this figure dropped to 22.3 percent in 1972 and grew to 27.5 percent by 1985.[6] Women continue to teach in such departments as education, languages, nursing, and library science rather than in the sciences and engineering, although there has been some movement into these fields. Women also tend to serve as faculty members in community colleges and four-year colleges rather than universities, especially research institutions.

Martin J. Finkelstein found that although women had made gains in higher education during the early 1980s, such progress was tempered with the fact that employment was in the "traditional female" departments, their ranks and salaries were lower than males', promotions usually took longer for women, and they were less likely to be employed at the more prominent universities. He goes on to argue that affirmative action has increased the chances for women to be considered for faculty positions but has not led to a major step toward greater employment in these slots.[7] Shirley Clark and Mary Corcoran argue that a "triple penalty" exists for women seeking academic careers, for they continue to deal with cultural barriers, receive negative messages about their abilities and academic prospects during their graduate training, and face limits in acquiring select positions and serving as full members of the academic community.[8] Although women have gained access to faculty positions, their career progress can be stifled. Linda K. Johnsrud noted that although there was an increase in the number of women in administration during the period 1975–79, they continued to be employed in lower-level positions such as staff positions and received lower salaries than males. Using a number of individual and structural variables such as education, experience, race, and sponsorship, she found that the type of previous position within the institution was the most important variable associated with female administrative promotions at one university during the period 1982–85. In terms of both responsibility and earnings, males did better than women, and white women did slightly better than black and Asian women. Although Johnsrud did not directly examine the issue of discrimination, she considers this one of the possible reasons to explain male/female differences in administrative positions, along with such difficult factors to measure as ability, desire, and performance.[9] The issue of gender in obtaining positions and then receiving promotions remains a critical factor in understanding opportunities in the workplace.

Although women still face a number of obstacles, the literature on women in the public sector has shown progress within specific job categories. Amy S. Wharton found for the period 1950–81 that public sector positions became less segregated by sex than those in the private sector. In the public sector, the largest decreases in sex segregation occurred in operative and professional positions, while increases occurred in office and service positions. Wharton notes arguments made by some economists that political pressure leads public sector managers to employ individuals who were not employed in the private sector due to discrimination. She cites Martin Carnoy, Derek Shearer, and Russell Rumberger's argument that the perception of government as a "guarantor of equal opportunity for disaffected (and potentially disruptive) social groups forces it to pursue more egalitarian hiring practices than private employers."[10] The public sector may be more open to employing women and minorities than the private sector; nevertheless, positions of power still tend to be in the hands of white males. As Rita Mae Kelly notes, although women have made great strides within the public sector, few have obtained top-level administrative or staff positions but, rather, hold middle-level positions or are in clerical and maintenance positions.[11] Given past research on women's employment, we expect that white women will more likely find faculty and administrative positions in public higher education institutions rather than private institutions, for public universities are part of state governments, which we expect will attempt to move toward greater bureaucratic representativeness.

WHITE FEMALE FACULTY

In order to examine our hypothesis, we first look at white female participation rates, which increased slightly from 1979 to 1983 (from 24.03 percent to 24.8 percent) and by 1991 had reached 28.5 percent (table 8). In 1991, white females had a representation ratio of 0.73 based on their proportion of the total U.S. population in 1990 (38.8 percent). As for our hypothesis that white females were more likely to find employment in public institutions rather than private colleges and universities, we discover instead that private institutions have a slight edge over public institutions when we examine the participation rates for both 1983 and 1991. However, an examination of the representation ratios for 1983 shows no difference between public and private institutions, but the ratios for 1991 do show that private institutions have a very small lead over public ones. Why even a slight edge to private institutions? The dynamics of individual institutions and their recruitment procedures may produce these small variations. These dynamics, however, are beyond the scope of our intentions and the research data available from the EEOC.

As white males have dominated faculty positions for generations, an examination of the data for newly hired tenure-track faculty members will assist us in learning if white females are making headway. The data for 1983 and 1991 show that, overall, white females increased their share of new positions from 30.4 percent in 1983 to 34.9 percent in 1990 (table 9). During the same time period, white males suffered a decline from 57.6 percent to 47.1 percent. Thus, white males are being recruited for less than half of the available positions. White males have also fallen behind in full professorships, for there was a decline from 83.2 percent in 1983 to 64.3 percent in 1991 (table 10). White females, on the other hand, have seen a dramatic increase in their share of full professors, which rose from 9.9 percent to 24.3 percent during the same time period.

White females in private institutions have a very slight edge over those in public institutions in terms of newly hired tenure-track faculty and full professors.

Examining the individual state data, we find for 1979 (which is a combination of both public and private institutions) a range from 16.7 percent to 27.6 percent for white women's participation rates (appendix 5). The states of Delaware, Kansas, Kentucky, Maryland, Mississippi, and Missouri have the highest participation rates, all above 26.0 percent. Finding a regional pattern with regard to women is somewhat more difficult than with blacks, who have large percentages residing in the South. Nevertheless, it does appear that the border states of Delaware, Kentucky, Maryland, and Missouri along with a southern state, Mississippi, may be producing a pattern. Lee Sigelman argues that women were more likely to be hired for state and local government positions in the South and in more traditional states as efforts were made not to hire minorities.[12] To explore this aspect, we examine the representation ratios for blacks in these states, for such ratios show the relationship between the number of blacks in faculty positions and the black percentage of the state's population by sex (appendix 21 and 22). The ratios for these six states for 1979 show that Delaware has the highest ratios for black males (0.52) and black females (0.51) and Kansas the lowest (0.19 for black males, 0.23 for black females). In addition, Kentucky (0.49 for black males, 0.33 for black females) and Maryland (0.43 for black males, 0.31 for black females) show ratios above 0.40 for black males. Mississippi, the state with the largest black population, has ratios of 0.30 for black males and 0.22 for black females. For Missouri, the ratios are .41 for black males and .45 for black females. The ratios for white females in these six states range from a low of 0.57 for Kansas to a high of 0.81 for Mississippi (appendix 25). Thus, it does appear that white females rather than blacks are better represented on faculties in these states. In contrast to white females, we find that white male participation rates range from a low of 58.0 percent in Alabama to a high of 78.7 percent in Montana (appendix 6). The southern states have the lowest rates for white males, while the states with the lowest black populations have the highest rates. Representation ratios for white males are all above 1.0, ranging from a low of 1.46 in West Virginia to a high of 1.99 in Mississippi (appendix 26). Thus, while the southern states have lower participation rates for white males, when one considers their share of faculty positions as a percentage of the population, we find that white males do extremely well in such southern states as Louisiana, Mississippi, and South Carolina.

Moving to the data for 1983 for public institutions, we find that participation rates range from a low of 18.8 to a high of 32.4 percent for white females (appendix 5). The states with the highest rates include Kentucky, Maryland, Mississippi, New Jersey, and Rhode Island. In 1979 the combined data for public and private institutions show that Kentucky, Maryland, and Mississippi were among the top states employing white females as faculty members in higher education. The states with the lowest rates in 1983 in public higher education include Colorado, Idaho, New Mexico, and Utah. Looking at the southern states that have the largest black populations – Alabama, Georgia, Louisiana, Mississippi, and South Carolina – we find that the representation ratios for black males (appendix 21) and black females (appendix 22) are about half of the ratios for white females. It also appears that this trend occurs in Maryland, a border state. Where there are large numbers of blacks in the population, both black and white women benefit, but white females have the edge, which adds support to Sigelman's thesis. White women do least well in such states as Idaho and Utah, where there are also low numbers of blacks within the population.

Turning to private higher education, we find participation rates for white females ranging from a low of 13.7 percent to a high of 49.3 percent (appendix 5). The highest rates are found in the border states of Delaware, Kentucky, and West Virginia, and the southern states of Alabama and Mississippi, as well as states such as North Dakota and South Dakota with extremely low percentages of blacks. At the lower end we find the southern states of Florida and Louisiana as well as such states as Utah and Vermont that have low percentages of blacks. Representation ratios for private institutions show that the states of Alabama, Delaware, and Mississippi exceed 1.0 for white females (appendix 25). The lowest ratios are to be found in Utah and Vermont. On the other hand, for white males the representation ratios of all the states are above 1.0, with the highest ratios found in California, New Mexico, and South Carolina, and the lowest in Delaware and North Dakota (appendix 26). This is an unusual mixture of states. We would have expected that in California, with its large percentages of Asian Americans and Hispanics, and in New Mexico, with its large Hispanic population, these ratios would have been lower. In addition, we would have expected that North Dakota, with its very small percentage of blacks, would have had a larger ratio. An examination of the states of Alabama, Delaware, and Mississippi, where the representation ratios for white females are above 1.0, shows that for Alabama the ratios are 0.34 for black males (appendix 21) and 0.44 for black females (appendix 22), and for Delaware the ratios are zero for black males and black females, but in Mississippi we find 0.50 for black males and 0.41 for black females. Thus, at least in Mississippi blacks do relatively well, although white females do much better. Kentucky and Maryland are other border states, in addition to Delaware, where white females do well in public higher education. We find that white females also do well in private colleges and universities, but that black males and females do poorly, with the representation ratios below 1.0 with only a few exceptions. An examination of the white female representation ratios for the states with the largest black populations – Alabama, Georgia, Louisiana, Mississippi, and South Carolina – shows mixed results for private higher education. In the states of Alabama and Mississippi, where white female faculty have ratios above 1.0, the ratios for black males and black females are 0.5 or less (appendixes 21 and 22). In Georgia, on the other hand, we find that the ratio for black females is slightly above that for white females. In Louisiana, the ratios for black males and females exceed that for white females. In South Carolina, however, the ratios for black males and females are less than half the ratio for white females. Thus, although white women and blacks do well in private higher education in the southern states, white women do better, just as they did in public higher education. Blacks in the border states do not do as well in private higher education.

Examining the data for white female faculty in public higher education in 1991, we find the highest participation rates (32.5 percent or higher) in the states of Arkansas, Delaware, Indiana, Mississippi, Oregon, Rhode Island, and West Virginia (appendix 5). The states with the lowest rates for white females include Montana, which has an extremely low percentage of blacks, but also California and Michigan. For California, the representation ratio for white females is 0.88 (appendix 25). Black males, with a ratio of 0.68 (appendix 21), do better than black females, with a ratio of 0.45 (appendix 22), but white males, at 2.00 (appendix 26), have the highest representation ratio for 1991. Thus, white females do relatively well in California in relationship to their share of the population, but white males do the best. Examining the southern states, we find, for instance, that in the case of Mississippi, white females have a representation ratio of 1.09, while black males, at 0.44, and black females, at 0.38, have much lower ratios. For our data, white females continue to do well in the southern states and the border states. What about Rhode Island, the state with the highest participation rate for white female faculty? A look at the representation ratios in the state for 1991 shows that white females, at 0.77, do better than black males, at 0.62, and that black females, at 0.31, do poorly in relationship to the other two. Overall, the data support the conclusion that white females are the major beneficiary of affirmative action in public higher education.

A look at the representation ratios for white males shows that they continue to dominate faculty positions, although there has been some drop in their overall employment (appendix 26). White males do their best in Arizona, California, New York, South Carolina, and Texas, a mixture of states that includes the Northeast, the South, and the West. On the other hand, their ratios are the lowest in the states of Indiana, Iowa, Oregon, Rhode Island, Vermont, and West Virginia, another mixture of states that is different in that the South is not represented. All of these states have high if not the highest participation rates for white females. Thus, white males are losing their hold on faculty positions due primarily to the increase in white females.

In private higher education for 1991, we find that the participation rates for white female faculty range from 15.5 percent to 57.1 percent (appendix 5). The states with the highest rates (above 40 percent) are Delaware, Kentucky, North Dakota, South Dakota, Texas, and Vermont. This, too, is quite a mixture of states: there are three states with very low percentages of blacks – North Dakota, South Dakota, and Vermont; one border state – Delaware; and two southern states – Kentucky and Texas. North Dakota, South Dakota, and Vermont have participation rates of zero for blacks, while Texas has a rate of zero for black males (appendix 1) and 2.3 percent for black females (appendix 2). Delaware and Kentucky have participation rates for blacks that are at or below 1.5 percent, except for black females (2.2 percent) in Delaware. It would appear that Sigelman's thesis about white females and blacks is applicable in this case. His thesis seems to transcend regional boundaries.

The states with the lowest participation rates for white females in private higher education include Florida, Idaho, Indiana, Louisiana, and Wisconsin. In the case of Louisiana, white females have low rates because black males and black females have the highest participation rates for private higher education in 1991. This is not true for Florida. However, in Idaho, blacks have participation rates of zero, while in Indiana the rates are below 1.0 percent, and in Wisconsin, black males have a rate of 1.9 percent and black females have a rate of zero. On the other hand, the representation ratios for white males are among the highest in the states of Florida and Idaho, and relatively strong in the states of Indiana and Wisconsin. Blacks do less well in finding positions in relationship to white females and especially white males. It is possible that when institutions are unable to find blacks, they instead seek out white females, but this then raises concerns about the fate of other minority groups. While white females do well across regions in private higher education, they do well in public higher education in states where there are large numbers of blacks. In both cases, blacks do less well where white females do well.

To see if white women continue to have a slight edge in faculty positions in private universities rather than public institutions, we examined the data from the Department of Education's NCES survey for 1995, which shows instead the reverse. As the difference is quite close, it may be due to data collection methods. The NCES survey also shows a significant decline in white women's share of full professorships. Although we do need to consider the data with some caution, such a finding suggests that white females may find it increasingly more difficult to reach the top rank due to competition from minorities or budgetary constraints that lead colleges and universities to limit access to this higher-paying rank. There is a noticeable decline for white males in newly hired tenure-track positions and a rather small decline for white females, which is likely the result of increased competition from minorities.[13] Nevertheless, white males continue to dominate both the full professorships and the total faculty positions, although their share is declining as more minorities and white women are employed.

WHITE FEMALE ADMINISTRATORS

How well have white females done in finding positions in higher education administration? As noted above, earlier studies showed that it is quite difficult for women to move to the upper ranks of academic administration. While the data available from the EEOC do not break down positions within the administrative category so that we can learn which positions white females hold, we can discover the extent to which white females have made progress in acquiring administrative employment. The data in table 11 show that white female administrators held 24.5 percent of all positions in 1979, which increased to 28.3 percent in 1983 and to 33.8 percent in 1991. White females were more likely to find employment in private higher education institutions in both 1983 and 1991. It is also clear from the data that in 1979 white males and females together held 90.3 percent of the administrative positions in higher education. This percentage declined to 86.9 percent in 1991, as the white male hold over this job category declined from 65.8 percent in 1979 to 53.1 percent in 1991. An examination of the representation ratios shows that white males continue to have ratios above 1.0. Although steps have been taken to increase minority participation and the percentage of whites in the population has declined, whites' share of administrative positions has gone up slightly as white females replace white males. In 1991, as in 1983, white males were more likely to find employment in public higher education. On the other hand, for the private higher education data for 1991, the representation ratio for white female administrators is nearly 1.0. We had expected that white females would do better in public institutions rather than private institutions of higher education, but this is not the case; rather, white males did much better in terms of both faculty and administrative positions in public colleges and universities.

Moving to the state data for white female administrators for 1979, which is a combination of both public and private higher education, we do not find a pattern in which white females do well in the South and the border states. White females have participation rates above 30.0 percent in Massachusetts, New York, Washington, and West Virginia, the only border state (appendix 7). In these states black females (appendix 4) have participation rates of 0.1 percent or zero for administrative positions and black males have rates that range from 2.2 percent to 3.1 percent (appendix 3). Thus, in the states where white females have their best opportunities for finding administrative positions, blacks, especially black females, do rather poorly. The lowest rates for white female administrators were found in Arizona, Delaware (a border state), Idaho, Mississippi, and Wyoming. Of these states, we find that black males do relatively well in Delaware and Mississippi, but that black females have participation rates of 0.8 percent or less in all of them. White males, on the other hand, have representation ratios that range from 1.31 in Washington to 2.18 in Mississippi (appendix 28). The southern states of Mississippi, at 2.18, and South Carolina, at 2.05, are the only states with ratios above 2.0. Thus, in the case of administrative positions for 1979, white females do better outside the South, where white males do extremely well.

Data for public institutions in 1983 show that the states of Minnesota, Washington, and West Virginia have participation rates above 30.0 percent for white females (appendix 7). In these three states, participation rates for black male administrators (appendix 3) range from 1.3 percent to 2.9 percent and for black females (appendix 4) are either 1.2 or 1.3 percent. Other states where white females have strong opportunities for administrative employment include Indiana, Kansas, Louisiana, Massachusetts, Utah, Vermont, Virginia, and Wisconsin, where the participation rates are above 25. The majority of these states have low percentages of blacks, except for the states of Louisiana and Virginia. Of these states, and excluding the southern states, the participation rates for black females range from zero in Utah and Vermont to 2.8 percent in Massachusetts and for black males range from 0.6 percent in Utah to 5.7 percent in Massachusetts. The southern states with the largest black populations are at the lower end in terms of white female administrators, with the exception of Louisiana. Although some other states such as Montana, New Hampshire, North Dakota, and South Dakota are also at this lower end for white female administrators, Delaware is the lowest for female administrators in public higher education. Unlike the case for faculty positions, white females do not do as well in the southern and border states. This conclusion is supported by the representation ratios for white female administrators, which range from 0.29 to 0.78, while for white males all ratios are above 1.0 and exceed 2.0 in the southern states of Alabama, Mississippi, and South Carolina (appendix 28).

Looking at the data for private higher education for 1983, we find that the participation rates for white female administrators exceed 40.0 percent in the states of Massachusetts, New York, and Pennsylvania (appendix 7). Given that our national participation rates showed that white females do better in private institutions than public higher education, these high rates are to be expected. There are also a greater number of states in which the participation rate exceeds 30.0 percent. For the states with the largest black populations, only Louisiana (38.9 percent) is near the top, while Alabama, Georgia, Mississippi, and South Carolina are at the lower end. Utah is the lowest, at 2.2 percent, which is extreme given that all other states have rates above 10.0 percent. Looking at the three states with the highest percentages (all over 40.0 percent) for white female administrators, we find that the rates for black males (appendix 3) are above 2.0 percent in Massachusetts and Pennsylvania and above 3.0 percent in New York; the rates for black females (appendix 4) are above 4.0 percent in New York and Pennsylvania. Thus, in private higher education in 1983, white females and black females did better than black males.

Moving to the data for public higher education institutions in 1991, we find that the participation rates for white female administrators range from 15.9 percent to 48.6 percent in contrast to the range for 1983 of 12.1 percent to 34.8 percent (appendix 7). This new range reinforces the national figures, which have shown that white females have made progress in obtaining administrative positions. But unlike for faculty positions, white females have the highest participation rates in areas of the country where the percentage of blacks is relatively low, such as Minnesota, New Hampshire, Vermont, and Washington. Participation rates for white males have declined in all of these four states (appendix 8), while for blacks the rates remain relatively low (all at or below 2.1 percent) and in Vermont show a decline for black males from 1.2 to 0.7 percent (appendix 3). White females, on the other hand, have seen dramatic increases in their participation rates, moving, for example, from 16.9 percent to 41.0 percent in New Hampshire (appendix 7). Thus, white females find their best opportunities in states with low percentages of blacks, although there are such exceptions as Indiana, North Dakota, and South Dakota. Unlike for faculty positions, white females do not necessarily benefit in those states where there are large numbers of blacks; instead, blacks, especially black males, do well in these states, which may be due to better employment opportunities in historically black colleges and universities. We find that the representation ratios in the states of California, Minnesota, and Texas are above 1.0 for white females (appendix 27), and in one state, Minnesota, the ratio is below 1.0 for white males (appendix 28). Only in the state of South Carolina do we find that the ratio is above 2.0 for white males. White males are losing their dominance over this employment category as white females move into these positions.

In private higher education, where white females have found better opportunities than in public higher education, we find that the states outside the South again provide the best opportunities. Delaware, a border state, has the highest participation rate followed by Connecticut, New Hampshire, New Jersey, and Wisconsin (appendix 7). Of these states, the largest black population is in Delaware (16.9 percent), followed by New Jersey (13.4 percent); the other three states have percentages below 10.0 percent, with New Hampshire below 1.0 percent. On the other hand, the five states with the largest percentages of blacks are at the lower end for white female administrative positions, except for Louisiana. Thus in administrative positions in private higher education, blacks do not necessarily lose out to white females in the South and the border states. Nevertheless, white females are making great strides in administrative positions, for the representation ratios are at or above 1.0 in the states of Alaska, Arizona, California, Connecticut, Delaware, Louisiana, Missouri, New Jersey, New York, and Virginia (appendix 27). However, except in the state of Montana, white males continue to have ratios above 1.0. Even though white males have lost positions to white females, they continue to dominate administrative positions.

To determine if the general trend of greater administrative employment for white females in private universities rather than public higher education has continued into 1995, we examine the data from the NCES survey, which confirms this finding.[14] White males continue to lose positions as white females and minorities move into administrative employment.

WHITE WOMEN IN OTHER OCCUPATIONS

We next examined the progress of white females in the other occupations in higher education, which is also important for understanding the influence of affirmative action programs in the American states. Our expectation based on the concept of representative bureaucracy was that white females should do better in public institutions rather than in private schools. In addition, we expected that white females are more likely to find employment in secretarial/clerical positions rather than in the skilled crafts. The data in table 12 indicating the participation rates and the representation ratios for all institutions showed that, as expected, white females in 1979 dominated the traditional area reserved for women – secretarial/clerical. Their lowest participation rates were in the skilled crafts and the service/maintenance categories. In the professional category, white females and white males were relatively close in both participation rates and representation ratios. For the technical/para-professional category, white females had an edge over white males. While white males had a representation ratio above 2.0 for the skilled crafts, white females had ratios equal to or above 1.0 in the professional, secretarial/clerical, and technical/para-professional categories.

In 1983, there was a drop in the white female participation rate in the secretarial/clerical category, and a very slight decline in the technical/para-professional and service/maintenance categories. White females did increase their participation in the professional category, and there was a minor change from 4.0 percent to 4.3 percent in the skilled crafts, which returned to 4.0 percent in 1991. By 1991, there was a negligible change in the technical/para-professional category. In the secretarial/clerical category, there was a slight decline in the representation ratio between 1983 and 1991, but white females continued to dominate this category. A negligible decline also occurred in the service/maintenance category in the participation rates but not the representation ratios. White females, however, continued to increase their participation in the professional category, with the ratio climbing to 1.25 by 1991. As expected, white males continued to dominate the skilled crafts; although their participation rate declined, their representation ratio, which reflects their share of the U.S. population, remained the same, 2.09, for 1979 and 1991. During this time interval, however, white males lost positions in all categories except in the secretarial/clerical category, although the decline in service/maintenance positions was negligible. This is to be expected, as affirmative action aids minorities and women attain these positions.

For 1983 data, white females were more likely to be employed in professional positions in private higher education than in public institutions (table 13). White females, however, were more likely to hold positions in all the other categories in public higher education than in private schools. This trend continued into 1991. An examination of the representation ratios shows that white females do have some low ratios in certain categories; nevertheless, there are a number of categories for the years 1983 and 1991 in which they, like white males, have ratios above 1.0. For white females, the highest ratio remained in the secretarial/clerical category, and for white males, it was in the skilled crafts.

How did white female professionals in higher education fare in the individual American states?[15] Examining the participation rates for all higher education institutions in 1979, we found that white females did not do as well in the most populous black states as in the other states. For 1991, the participation rates for white female professionals in public higher education were scattered throughout the most populous black states, with South Carolina near the top and Louisiana and Mississippi near the bottom. For these professional positions, white males seemed to have lost to white females. In private higher education in 1991, white females found their best opportunities in Wisconsin and Vermont, where there were low numbers of blacks, while the lowest participation rates were to be found in Alabama, California, Idaho, and South Carolina. White females in private higher education, just as in public institutions, tended to have a more favorable advantage in obtaining professional positions where there were lower numbers of blacks.

For the secretarial/clerical category, white females did their best in states with low percentages of blacks; for example, in 1991, Idaho, Maine, Montana, North Dakota, and Vermont were among the states with the highest participation rates for public higher education. On the other hand, the most populous black states were near the lower end of the range of participation rates, but such states as California, New Jersey, and Texas (all states with large Hispanic populations) had the lowest rates. For private higher education, we found that white females held 100 percent of the positions in Wisconsin and had rates above 95 percent in Maine, West Virginia, and Vermont.

For 1979, there was no clear pattern for technical/para-professional positions in the most populous black states, but white females did their best in states with low percentages of blacks in public higher education. By 1991, white females were most successful in the states of Idaho, Montana, Utah, West Virginia, and Vermont and were least successful in the states of Arizona, California, and Mississippi. Arizona and California are states with relatively significant numbers of Hispanics, and Mississippi is one of the most populous black states. (The white female participation rates for the other most populous black states were also clustered near the lower end of the range.) Thus it would appear that white females in this category were losing to blacks in the South and to Hispanics in Arizona and California. For private higher education in 1991, we found that white females held 100 percent of the technical/para-professional positions in Montana, North Dakota, and Wisconsin, while in Vermont 100 percent of these positions were held by white males. The most populous black states tended to be at the lower end of the range of the rates, although they were not the lowest. White females did well where there were relatively few blacks; where white females did the least well, blacks, especially in the most populous black states, did well.

White males dominated the skilled craft positions in 1979 and continued to do so in 1991. In 1991, the participation rates for white females in public institutions ranged from a low of 1.2 percent in West Virginia to a high of 10.6 percent in Oregon. The states with the highest rates (at or above 7.0 percent) were Michigan, Nebraska, Ohio, Oregon, and Vermont. As for the most populous black states, the participation rates ranged from 3.1 percent in Alabama to 4.5 percent in Louisiana. In those states where white females did well in skilled craft positions, black males tended not to do as well, and where black males tended to have their highest participation rates, white females had their lowest rates. In private higher education institutions, white females had some very high rates, including 31.2 percent in Virginia, 20.0 percent in West Virginia, and 18.7 percent in Nebraska. However, the following states had participation rates of zero not only for white females but also for black males and black females: Delaware, Montana, Nevada, North Dakota, South Dakota, Texas, Vermont, and Wisconsin. In the most populous black states, blacks were more likely to hold these positions, with the exception of South Carolina, where the rates were higher for white females than for black males (it was zero for black females). It is in the skilled crafts that we found the least progress for minorities and females in comparison with the other categories.

Examining service/maintenance positions in 1979, we found a clear pattern in which white females had the lowest participation percentages in states with the largest numbers of blacks, while they did quite well in the states of Iowa, North Dakota, and South Dakota, which have extremely low percentages of blacks. In 1991 for public higher education, white females continued to do well in states with low percentages of blacks, with the exception of California, where there are large numbers of Hispanics; white females had their lowest rates in the southern states.

As expected, we found that white females did better in public rather than private higher education institutions, with the exception of the professional positions. We also found that white females are more likely to hold positions in the secretarial/clerical category than in the skilled crafts. It does appear that public universities rather than private institutions were more responsive to the call for affirmative action. Nevertheless, females of all races continued to dominate secretarial and clerical positions; in turn, males, especially white males, remained in control of the skilled crafts. Thus, there is some evidence to support our argument that minorities and women are more likely to be employed in lower-status and lower-paying positions such as secretarial and maintenance jobs than in higher-paying categories that include the skilled crafts.[16] Despite efforts to change this situation, past attitudes about sex roles in the workplace appear to maintain the division in employment patterns. Overall for the other categories, white females did the best in states with fewer blacks and did poorly where blacks were in their greatest numbers. Thus, in these positions white females and black males and females do compete for positions, a result that we believe was unanticipated by those who envisioned affirmative action. Nevertheless, during periods of decreasing numbers of jobs, such competition can only become even more intense. Such intensity can trigger greater resentment toward affirmative action programs and could also heighten hostility toward minorities and women in the workplace.

In our examination of white females employed in higher education, we found that by 1991, private institutions had a slight edge over public institutions for faculty and administrative positions, although the NCES data for 1995 show a reversal of this trend for faculty but not for administrative positions. Within the American states, white females tend to be most successful in public higher education institutions in the South and some border states. On the other hand, for private institutions, white women do well in states spread across the nation; it is also clear that white females do better where blacks do less well. Thus, Lee Sigelman's argument about states hiring females at the expense of minorities seems to be true across the states for private institutions and in the South and some border states for public institutions. For administrative positions, white females do extremely well in private institutions, while white males have their best opportunities in public colleges and universities. White females tend to do their best in both public and private institutions in states where there are low percentages of blacks, while white males do their best in the South, where there are large numbers of blacks. For the other positions, public higher education institutions do better than private institutions in providing positions for white females, with the exception of professional positions. We also found that white females dominate the secretarial/clerical category while white males maintain dominance over the skilled crafts. Overall, it is clear white females do better in the other job categories where there are lower numbers of blacks. Thus, competition between white females and blacks does exist.

5

Hispanics in Higher Education Employment

Unlike blacks, Hispanics (as well as Native Americans) did not found their own colleges; nor did they experience "Reconstruction during which – ever so fleetingly – they [blacks] exercised genuine political power."[1] The lack of political power and of any colleges of their own, combined with the prevailing attitudes toward race, kept Hispanics out of higher education during the nineteenth century and a good part of the twentieth century. The unavailability of college and graduate education restricted employment opportunities for them in higher education, particularly in the higher-paying and higher-status categories.

Although Mexican-Americans, the largest of the Hispanic groups in the United States, started enrolling in colleges by the end of World War I, their numbers remained modest, and such schooling was restricted to those with higher socioeconomic status.[2] Congressional laws regarding GI benefits for the veterans of World War II and, later on, financial aid for those unable to afford college education opened up opportunities for Hispanics as well as for others. Immigration of large numbers of educated Cubans to the United States after Fidel Castro came to power in Cuba in 1959 further increased the Hispanic students' population in American colleges. The immigration reforms of 1965 and later years brought large numbers of Hispanics from Mexico, Central America, and South America to the United States, which also added to the ranks of Hispanic students in American higher education. The civil rights movement of the 1950s and 1960s had primarily targeted blacks, but other minorities and women also benefited. Before long, Hispanic advocacy groups emerged and demanded better opportunities for Hispanics in higher education and employment.

As a result, Hispanic enrollment in higher education and the number of degrees earned have risen in the past three decades.[3] Despite this increase in the absolute numbers of Hispanic students in higher education, they remained underrepresented in both undergraduate and graduate programs when compared to the Hispanic population in the country. Furthermore, a majority of the Hispanic undergraduates attended two-year colleges.[4]

HISPANIC FACULTY

The underrepresentation of Hispanics in higher education is reflected in their low participation rates and representation ratios in full-time faculty employment (table 14). They made hardly any progress in obtaining faculty positions between 1979 and 1983. By 1991, however, there were more Hispanic faculty members on campuses, and the percentage increase for females was greater than that for males. Nevertheless, Hispanic female faculty still remained less than 1.0 percent in both public and private institutions. Both Hispanic males and females found public institutions more hospitable than the private ones for securing employment. Based on our view that state governments will be responsive to the goals of maintaining a representative bureaucracy, we expected that Hispanics, like other minorities and women, were more likely to be employed in public universities rather than private institutes of higher education. Overall, despite some gains, in 1991 Hispanics constituted only 2.5 percent of the faculty at public institutions and 1.6 percent at private institutions. While the Hispanic population in the country increased by over 40 percent from 1980 to 1990, this was not reflected in the combined male/female faculty representation ratios.[5] The gap between Hispanic male and female ratios narrowed by 1991, indicating progress for females but not for males. A comparison of representation ratios in public and private institutions demonstrates the availability of better opportunities for both Hispanic males and females at public schools rather than private institutions.

As the data in table 15 reveal, Hispanic men and women are also more likely to land tenure-track faculty positions at public universities rather than private institutions. In 1983, the record for private institutions in this area was somewhat better than that for the public schools. By 1991, the pattern was reversed, as public institutions hired a greater proportion of their faculty from among the Hispanic candidates than did private institutions. By that year, Hispanics were also more likely to be full professors at public institutions (table 16). However, even at such institutions, Hispanics were only 2.3 percent of the full professors. Yet, the impact of affirmative action was clear, because in 1983 only 1.1 percent of the full professors at public institutions were Hispanic. The percentage of full professors at private colleges and universities also increased, although to a lesser degree, from 1.0 percent in 1983 to 1.6 percent in 1991. At both public and private institutions, Hispanic women made greater gains in statistical terms than Hispanic men from 1983 to 1991.

Based on the late 1980s data, a study on Hispanic faculty observed: "In terms of Hispanic ethnicity, Mexican-Americans comprise the largest proportion of Hispanic faculty at all institutional types, reflecting their proportion of the

U.S. Hispanic population (about 62 percent). However, the proportion of Mexican-Americans in two-year colleges is particularly great; Mexican-Americans comprise 70 percent of Hispanic faculty in two-year colleges." This finding reflects the lower socioeconomic backgrounds of Mexican-Americans in comparison to Cubans and other Latin Americans.[6] Mexican-Americans as well as other Hispanic faculty tend to be concentrated in the humanities, social sciences, and education. More important, most of these faculty do research on "Hispanic-related topics." Some scholars suggest that Hispanic faculty participate in campus committees that are less important and that "committees concerned with larger campus, instructional, research, and related policy issues are rarely among the list of choices available to Hispanic faculty." Keeping in view the role of the Hispanic faculty in such areas, Hisauro Garza raises questions about the implementation of affirmative action, stating: "Colleges and universities have created a dumping ground for Hispanic scholars, separate from and with little interconnection to the rest of the scholarly life of the university. It is this phenomenon which has at times been referred to as the 'ghettoization' or as in this case, the 'barrioization' of the university."[7]

Other scholars have also written about the discrimination faced by Hispanics in seeking jobs and promotion in academia. A study on affirmative action concluded that "a combination of individual, institutional, and societal racism explains the absence of African-American and Hispanic faculty in predominantly white colleges and universities."[8] Another study suggests that "a significant decline in the already low number of minority professors, particularly as a percentage of total faculty, is the most probable scenario for at least the remainder of the 1990s."[9] Our data discussed above, however, show that faculty representation in colleges and universities is improving for Hispanics, albeit slowly. The most probable scenario for the remainder of the 1990s is not a decline but rather an increase in the percentage of the minority faculty.

Hispanic progress in gaining faculty positions in the 1980s was evident in some states but not in others. In New Mexico, where the Hispanic population in 1980 was 36.6 percent, the highest of any state, Hispanic males and females combined comprised 14.3 percent of the faculty in public institutions and 5.8 percent in private institutions in 1983 (appendixes 9 and 10). As the national figures suggested, public institutions were more willing to hire Hispanic faculty than were private institutions. There were a few exceptions to this trend, notably in Florida and Vermont, where Hispanic faculty were twice as numerous in private institutions as in public institutions. In most states, in both public and private institutions, Hispanics remained less than 1.0 percent of the total faculty (appendixes 9 and 10). Even in public institutions, besides New

Mexico, only in three states (California, Colorado, and Texas) did Hispanics make up 3.0 percent or higher of the faculty. In 1980, the Hispanic population in California, Colorado, and Texas was 19.2, 11.8, and 21.0 percent, respectively. In private institutions, only Florida (besides New Mexico), also a state with a large Hispanic population (8.8 percent in 1980), was in this category. Of the numerous states in which only a few Hispanics taught in colleges and universities, North Dakota stands out as an example of little opportunity. Of the faculty members reported by eleven public institutions in that state, only 0.1 percent were Hispanic males and less than 0.05 were Hispanic females. Surprisingly, in the same state, 0.8 percent of the faculty reported by five private institutions were Hispanic males. Hispanic females did not do any better in holding faculty positions in private institutions than in public institutions in North Dakota. In private institutions elsewhere, Hispanics were least likely to find teaching positions in Alabama, Arkansas, Delaware, and Montana.

Preference for male Hispanic faculty in 1983 is evident from appendixes 9 and 10. In public institutions, in only three states (California, New Mexico, and Texas) were Hispanic women over 1.0 percent of the total faculty. In private institutions, only one state (New Mexico) had a Hispanic female participation rate over 1.0 percent. In public as well as private institutions in most states, Hispanic male faculty far outnumbered Hispanic female faculty. Only in two states (Iowa and Kansas), in private institutions in both cases, were there more Hispanic female faculty than Hispanic male faculty (appendixes 9 and 10). If considered together, Hispanic males and females were only 0.5 percent of the total faculty in Iowa and 1.0 percent in Kansas in private institutions. In a handful of states, the number of Hispanic male and female faculty was equal, or nearly so, in public institutions in the states of Delaware, Idaho, Maine, and Maryland and in private institutions in the states of Kentucky, Michigan, Mississippi, North Carolina, South Dakota, and Utah. In all the four states in the public institution category, combined Hispanic males and females were less than 1.0 percent of the total faculty; in the six states in the private institution category, Hispanics remained below 1.0 percent, except in Utah, where they totaled 1.1 percent (appendixes 9 and 10).

Representation ratios for public and private institutions in 1983 clearly indicate underrepresentation of this group. In public institutions, three New England states (Maine, New Hampshire, and Vermont) and one Midwestern state (Iowa), all four with Hispanic populations below 1.0 percent in 1980, had representation ratios of 1.0 or above (appendix 29). In private institutions, in addition to the same three New England states, Maryland, Minnesota, North Dakota, and West Virginia also had representation ratios of 1.0 or above for

Hispanics in faculty positions (appendix 29). Three of these four states had Hispanic populations of less than 1.0 percent in 1980; only one, Maryland, had a Hispanic population above 1.0 percent (1.5). In states with the largest Hispanic populations in 1980 (California, New Mexico, and Texas), Hispanics in public institutions had higher representation ratios than those in private institutions. However, as anticipated from the national data, representation ratios for the Hispanic faculty remained relatively low in these states in both public and private institutions. In private institutions, the Hispanic faculty ratios were 0.20 in California, 0.39 in New Mexico, and 0.22 in Texas. The corresponding ratios for these states in private institutions were 0.12, 0.16, and 0.10, respectively. Of the other states with a large Hispanic population, in Colorado, Florida, and New York, such ratios were 0.25, 0.20, and 0.21, respectively, in public institutions and 0.21, 0.43, and 0.23, respectively, in private institutions. For Arizona, the state with the fourth largest Hispanic population in 1980 (16.2 percent), the EEOC combined its data for public and private institutions, yielding a ratio of 0.19 in 1983. (The same was done for the 1983 data for Alaska and Wyoming.) Florida is the only large Hispanic population state where Hispanics had a substantial edge in holding faculty positions in 1983 in private universities over public institutions. Overall, of the forty-six states for which separate data for public and private institutions were available, the Hispanic faculty representation ratio was 0.5 or higher in nineteen states for public institutions and in twenty-one states for private institutions. On the other hand, none of the states for public institutions but four of the states for private institutions (Alabama, Arkansas, Delaware, and Montana) had Hispanic representation ratios of 0 or nearly so.

Hispanics were more numerous in faculty positions in both public and private institutions in 1991 compared to 1983. For both types of institutions, the number of states with less than 1.0 percent of Hispanic faculty decreased to fewer than twenty. In three states (Arizona, California, and Texas), Hispanics were over 5.0 percent of the faculty in public institutions in 1991 (appendixes 9 and 10). (For New Mexico, the state with the largest proportion of Hispanics in the population in the country, separate EEOC data for public and private institutions were not available for 1991.) In private institutions, only in Arizona were Hispanics over 5.0 percent of the faculty; in Colorado, Hispanics were exactly 5.0 percent of the faculty, and in two states, Florida and Texas, Hispanics were 4.8 and 4.7 percent, respectively. In private institutions, California was the only other state with Hispanic faculty over 3.0 percent (3.4) of the total. In public institutions, only Colorado, with 4.1 percent, exceeded 3.0 percent of the total faculty, in addition to the three states listed above. A comparison of the data in appendixes 9 and 10 shows improvement in the participation rates for Hispanic faculty in most states in both public and private institutions. Public institutions continued to offer better opportunities to Hispanics than did private institutions. In four states (Delaware, Montana, North Dakota, and West Virginia), Hispanic faculty were virtually nonexistent in private institutions, with participation rates of less than 0.05 for both males and females. Of the public institutions, only in Maine for Hispanic male faculty and in South Dakota for Hispanic female faculty was there such a poor representation.

Overall, Hispanic male faculty continued to outnumber Hispanic female faculty. Hispanic females, however, made significant gains, sometimes more so than Hispanic males, particularly in private institutions. Despite the unavailability of separate data, we can assume the 1991 participation rate of Hispanic female faculty in New Mexico to be over 1.0 in both types of institutions. In addition, in public institutions in eight other states (Arizona, for which separate EEOC data for public and private institutions for 1983 were not available, California, Colorado, Delaware, Florida, New Jersey, New York, and Texas), Hispanic female faculty participation was over 1.0 percent, compared to just California, New Mexico, and Texas in 1983 (appendix 10). In Arizona, California, and Texas, the participation rate was over 2.0 percent of the faculty. In one state (Missouri), Hispanic male and Hispanic female participation rates were equal (0.5 in both cases), and in two states (Delaware and Maine), there were more Hispanic women faculty than Hispanic men faculty.

In private institutions, although in 1983 only New Mexico had a Hispanic female participation rate of over 1.0, five other states (Alaska, California, Colorado, Florida, and Texas) were over 1.0 in 1991, and Louisiana's rate was exactly 1.0 (appendix 10). Arizona had a female participation rate of 4.8, the highest of any state for public or private institutions. In five states (Arizona, Idaho, Iowa, Kentucky, and Oklahoma), Hispanic males and females had equal representation in the faculty in private institutions, and in six states (Alaska, Arkansas, Kansas, Louisiana, South Dakota, and Texas), the faculty percentage for Hispanic females exceeded that of their male counterparts (appendixes 9 and 10).

Hispanic progress in gaining faculty positions is reinforced by the representation ratios in 1991. In the 1990 census, the U.S. Bureau of the Census had compiled separate as well as combined data for males and females for each of the major race/ethnic groups. That enables us to compare male and female representation ratios, which we could not do for the 1983 data. In 1991, Hispanic males had representation ratios of 1.0 or higher in fourteen states in public institutions and in ten states in private institutions (appendix 30). For

Hispanic females, such a high ratio prevailed in only one state (Vermont) for public institutions but in six states (Alaska, Arkansas, Maine, Minnesota, New Hampshire, and South Dakota) for private institutions. In two states (South Dakota and Vermont), Hispanic males had a ratio above 2.0 in public institutions. In one state (Maine), the ratio for Hispanic males in private institutions was above 2.0, and in one other state (Tennessee), it was almost 4.0. Hispanic female faculty did not have such high overrepresentation in public or private institutions in any of the states.

In general, states with relatively small Hispanic populations had higher representation ratios for Hispanic faculty than states with relatively large Hispanic populations. In New Mexico, which continued to have the largest Hispanic population of any state (38 percent in 1990) and in which separate data for public and private institutions were not available, combined public and private institutions had a representation ratio of 0.41 for Hispanic males and 0.19 for Hispanic females (appendix 30). In California and Texas, the states with the next largest Hispanic populations (over 25 percent in both states in 1990), the ratio for Hispanic males was about 0.26 in public institutions and 0.14 in private institutions. Hispanic females had ratios below 0.25 in both states in the two types of institutions. In public institutions, their ratio in the two states was similar (0.17); in private institutions, however, they were better represented in Texas (0.23) than California (0.12). In Arizona, which remained the fourth largest Hispanic-population state in 1990 (over 18 percent), Hispanic males as well as females were better represented in private than public institutions. That was also true of Colorado, which had a Hispanic population of almost 13 percent in 1990. In Florida (with a Hispanic population of 12 percent), Hispanic males had a higher representation ratio in private institutions, but Hispanic females did somewhat better in public institutions. In New York (with a Hispanic population above 12 percent), both Hispanic males and females had higher representation ratios in public institutions than in private institutions. Overall, opportunities for Hispanics had increased; however, they continued to be underrepresented in faculty positions in a majority of the states, and their prospects of finding faculty employment were better in public schools than in private institutions. In terms of bureaucratic representativeness, we had expected such differences between public and private higher education.

HISPANIC ADMINISTRATORS

There were more Hispanic administrators, both males and females, on American campuses in 1983 compared to 1979, and more in 1991 compared to 1983 or

1979. The participation rate for Hispanics went up in every case in 1983 and 1991, indicating an increase in the country's Hispanic population and the Hispanic applicant pool for academic administrators, and possibly the application of affirmative action (table 17). Hispanic men clearly did better at public schools than in private institutions. The representation ratios of the Hispanic administrators, on the other hand, declined for men and improved for women between 1983 and 1991 in both types of institutions (table 17). Over the 1979-91 period for all institutions, such ratios for the Hispanic males first increased and then decreased, but for Hispanic females a steady increasing trend continued throughout these years.

Underrepresentation of Hispanics in administration in colleges and universities is evident from the data in table 17. Some progress did take place in their representation, with women benefiting more than men. However, Hispanic women's progress is only impressive in terms of the rate of increase. For example, their gains in public institutions from 1983 to 1991 were more than 100 percent, yet in 1991 they were merely 1.1 percent of the administrators in such institutions. Many Hispanic scholars decry such underrepresentation and consider racism or other forms of bias against members of their group responsible for so few Hispanic administrators in academia.[10] Yolanda Moses indicates that the stereotyping of Latinos (and Asians) as foreigners who lack leadership skills is responsible for their not being hired as administrators in predominantly white colleges and universities.[11] On the basis of findings from an empirical study of hiring of presidents and academic vice presidents in twenty-five public and private institutions in ten states with large Hispanic populations, Robert Haro opines: "The data paint a disturbing picture for Latino candidates. They are held to a much higher level of preparation and achievement than are either white males or white females." In his research, Haro found not only white men but also white women and non-Latino minorities who held such opinions of Latino candidates. He further states: "While the appointment of Latinos to executive and leadership positions in higher education is improving gradually, it is painfully slow and filled with examples of subtle, and in some cases overt, biases that work against them . . . the results of this study add to the body of evidence that suggests that a glass ceiling for Latinos does exist in higher education." Haro also distances his own experiences from his research: "I was a candidate for an academic vice presidency and a presidency. . . . None of the information from the searches in which I was a finalist was factored into this study."[12] Regardless of Haro's personal experience in seeking the position of an academic vice president or president, severe underrepresentation of Hispanics in campus administration is indisputable, and it is likely that a major cause of this is, indeed, bias against them.

In most states, in both public and private institutions, Hispanics were less than 1.0 percent of administrators (appendixes 11 and 12). In public institutions in 1983, only in California, Colorado, Connecticut, New Jersey, New Mexico, Texas, Utah, and Washington did male Hispanic administrators exceed 1.0 percent. (In two states, Alaska and Arizona, for which combined public and private institutions data were available, Hispanic male administrators were above 2.0 percent.) In four states (California, Colorado, New Mexico, and Texas) in public institutions that year, the participation rates of Hispanic female administrators were above 1.0. The highest participation rate for Hispanic administrators in such institutions was in New Mexico, where males and females comprised 30.2 percent and 6.5 percent, respectively, of the administrators. New Mexico was one of only four states (the other states were Montana, South Dakota, and Vermont) with a representation ratio of 1.0 or higher for Hispanic administrators. In public institutions in all the other states, Hispanics were underrepresented in administrative positions (appendix 31).

In private institutions in 1983, the underrepresentation of Hispanic administrators was even more pronounced. For Hispanic male administrators, the highest participation rate was only 5.2, in New Mexico (appendix 11). Hispanic females had the highest rate (also 5.2) in Florida (appendix 12). In addition, in California, Colorado, Florida, New York, Texas, Utah, and Washington, Hispanic male administrators in private institutions had participation rates of higher than 1.0; in New Mexico, New York, and Texas, Hispanic female administrators had such rates. As in public institutions, representation ratios reflected severe underrepresentation of Hispanic administrators – the only exceptions were Florida, New Hampshire, Vermont, and Washington (appendix 31).

By 1991, Hispanics, especially females, did make progress in gaining administrative positions in several states in both public and private institutions, though they remained underrepresented in most states (appendix 32). Although the overall participation rate of Hispanic male administrators in public institutions increased, such an increase was relatively small in most cases. In California, a state with one of the largest Hispanic populations in the country, the participation rate of Hispanic male administrators in public institutions decreased from 5.6 to 4.5 (appendix 11). In New Mexico, the decline in the participation rate of Hispanic male administrators was much greater. Data for combined public and private institutions in that state in 1991 (separate data were not available) reflected approximately a 50 percent decrease in their rate from 1983 (appendix 11). While a few states had participation rates of higher than 1.0, only one state, Arizona, exceeded the rate of 5.0, with a rate of 5.2; next came Colorado with 4.9. As a result, representation ratios for Hispanics seldom exceeded 1.0 and generally highlighted their underrepresentation. Hispanic women remained even more underrepresented in that their ratio did not equal or exceed 1.0 in any state in public institutions (appendix 32). However, they made greater gains than Hispanic men in obtaining administrative positions. Although the proportion of female administrators remained low in most states, in some of the states, notably Arizona, California, Florida, New Jersey, and New York, their gains in public institutions were impressive.

In private institutions, Hispanic women also made greater gains than Hispanic men in landing administrative positions. Even their representation ratios were higher than those of Hispanic men in some states and exceeded 1.0 in as many as four states (Alaska, Arkansas, Florida, and Maine), showing their overrepresentation. Hispanic male administrators, on the other hand, were overrepresented in only one state, Iowa, and had a ratio of 1.01 in Louisiana. A comparison of Hispanic male and female participation rates in 1983 and 1991 reinforces greater progress for females than for males in private and public institutions (appendixes 11 and 12). In both types of institutions, it seems that those in charge of hiring recruited Hispanic female administrators more aggressively than their male counterparts. In Texas in 1983, Hispanic male and female administrators were nearly equal in participation rates (1.7 and 1.8, respectively) in private institutions, but in 1991 the proportion of Hispanic females was almost five times that of Hispanic males (7.9 for females versus 1.7 for males). In Florida, another state with a large Hispanic population, while Hispanic male administrators increased from 4.4 percent to only 4.7 percent in private institutions, Hispanic female administrators increased from 5.2 percent to 8.3 percent. In public institutions also, Hispanic female administrators became more numerous than Hispanic male administrators in some states, notably in Massachusetts, New Jersey, and New York. In Florida, the participation rates for both Hispanic men and women administrators more than doubled from 1983 to 1991; however, women became even more predominant than men in these administrative positions in 1991 than they were in 1983 (appendixes 11 and 12).

Some scholars, particularly Hispanic ones, are unimpressed by such gains. Robert Haro wrote in 1990: "In such states such as Arizona, California, Colorado, Texas, and Washington, Latinos, the largest minority population in these areas, continue to be the most underrepresented group in key administrative positions."[13] Writing on the status of Hispanic administrators in the systems of the University of California, the California State University, and the University of Texas, Leonard A. Valverde comments: "The two states and their systems, in total, provide 108 executive positions, filled from relatively deep talent pools. Against the backdrop, the status of Hispanic appointments – just two people [one at the California State University system and one at the University of Texas system] – is pitiful."[14]

HISPANICS IN OTHER OCCUPATIONS

In the other five occupational categories, we expect that Hispanics are more likely to be employed in lower-paying and lower-status positions than in the better positions. That indeed is the case. Of these categories, more Hispanics were hired in the service/maintenance jobs in all institutions than in any other area. As a result, Hispanic male and female combined participation rates remained close to their proportion of the country's population in the three years of our study, which was reflected in their representation ratio of about 1.0 (table 18). Hispanics were least represented in the professional non-faculty positions, which are on the opposite end of service/maintenance positions in status and pay and require the most education among the five categories. Hispanics did gain jobs as non-faculty professionals, particularly from 1983 to 1991, with Hispanic women doing better than Hispanic men in increasing their presence in this category. Although in 1979 there were more Hispanic males than Hispanic females as non-faculty college professionals, by 1983 Hispanic females had caught up with Hispanic males and by 1991 had surpassed them (table 18). In the female-dominated secretarial/clerical jobs, Hispanic women were represented roughly in equal proportion to their population in the country. Hispanic men, on the other hand, maintained a similar record in the male-dominated skilled craft area. In the technical/para-professional category, both Hispanic women and Hispanic men remained underrepresented, but the females showed a trend similar to the professional non-faculty category. In 1979, there were more Hispanic male technicians and para-professionals than Hispanic females in this category; in 1983, their percentages were exactly the same; and in 1991, Hispanic women had a higher participation rate than Hispanic men (table 18).

Trends of all institutions were reflected in public and private institutions, with noticeable differences between them, however. In both types of institutions, Hispanics were most predominant in service/maintenance positions and least predominant in non-faculty professional jobs (table 19). Overall, public institutions rather than private institutions were more willing to hire Hispanics, particularly in 1991. In 1983, the Hispanic advantage in professional non-faculty and technical/para-professional categories in public institutions was balanced by their higher participation rates in skilled craft and service/maintenance categories in private institutions (table 19). In secretarial/clerical jobs in 1983, Hispanic participation rates were the same in both types of institutions. Although this may be considered as equal treatment of Hispanics in employment in public and private institutions, we consider public institutions more open to Hispanics than private colleges since they hired larger numbers of Hispanics in jobs that require a higher level of education and generally provide better pay and status. By 1991, private institutions had a higher percentage of Hispanic technicians and para-professionals than the public institutions. However, in every other category for that year, Hispanic participation rates and representation ratios were higher in public universities than in private institutions (table 19).

Another striking difference between public and private institutions is their hiring of Hispanic women. In 1983, both public and private universities employed Hispanic women in approximately the same percentages in the categories under consideration (table 19). By 1991, Hispanic women were visibly more numerous in these positions in public institutions than private schools. Hispanic men, on the other hand, did not consistently gain more of these positions in public institutions in comparison with the private schools.

Hispanics were underrepresented in most states in the professional non-faculty category in 1983 as well as 1991, despite some gains in the 1980s. In public institutions in 1983, the combined male and female Hispanic representation ratio (separate male and female population figures were not available in the 1980 census data) was equal to 1.0 or higher in only two states, Tennessee and West Virginia; in private institutions, the ratio was that high in Maine, Montana, and South Dakota.[15] In a majority of the states, including California, Texas, and New Mexico – the states with the largest Hispanic populations – Hispanics had higher participation rates and were better represented in public universities than in private institutions. In 1991, Hispanic professionals also remained underrepresented in most states in both public and private institutions. However, in several states, Hispanic males and, more so, females made considerable progress. In California and Texas, for example, Hispanic professional female participation rates increased in public institutions from 2.5 and 3.2 in 1983 to 3.8 and 4.5, respectively, in 1991; in private institutions, the rates increased from 2.5 and 2.4 to 3.7 and 5.4, respectively. (We cannot compare New Mexico's data since only combined data for public and private institutions were available for 1991.) In a majority of states, public institutions hired a higher percentage of Hispanic professionals, males as well as females, than did private institutions. By 1991, Hispanic professionals were less than 0.05 percent in only one state, New Hampshire, in public institutions but in nine states in private institutions (Alaska, Idaho, Montana, Nevada, North Dakota, Oregon, South Dakota, Vermont, and Wisconsin).

On the lower end, Hispanic service/maintenance workers were in demand, and the males were overrepresented, in the two years of study in many states in both types of institutions. In New Mexico in 1983, for example, Hispanic males were more than half of service/maintenance employees in public institutions and almost two-thirds in private institutions. In other states with large Hispanic populations, Hispanics, particularly males, were predominant in this job category. In no other job category were Hispanic employees as predominant as in the service/maintenance area. They did, however, make progress in most states in all other categories in both types of institutions, even though they generally remained underrepresented. Despite affirmative action efforts, Hispanic gains in higher-status and higher-paying positions remained limited.

Despite occupational progress for Hispanics in the 1980s, their preponderance in service/maintenance (males more than females), skilled craft (primarily males), and secretarial/clerical (primarily females) jobs and their relatively low numbers in faculty, administrative, and professional non-faculty positions project an image of a minority that is in demand for employment in positions with lower status and pay but that is not educated and trained sufficiently for employment in the higher echelons of academia. Progress did occur in the 1980s, at a greater rate for Hispanic females than males. Such progress was certainly due, at least in part, to the implementation of affirmative action. Even in the jobs with higher status and pay, Hispanics did make gains overall, especially in certain states; however, they remained severely underrepresented in a majority of the states. Surprisingly, their median salaries according to EEOC data were generally above those of Native American and black employees, and in the faculty ranks Hispanic women often received higher pay than white women.

The mid-1990s data, prepared by the U.S. Department of Education's National Center for Education Statistics, reveal the impact of opposition to affirmative action on the status of Hispanics in faculty and administrative ranks, despite the limitations considered in the introduction to this book.[16] In all institutions, the Hispanic share of faculty positions increased by only one-tenth of 1 percent since 1991. Surprisingly, some gains for both Hispanic men and Hispanic women occurred at private institutions. At public institutions, a minuscule increase for Hispanic female faculty was canceled by a similar decrease for Hispanic males. A somewhat similar trend prevailed in the hiring of Hispanic administrators, with the result that their gains from 1991 to 1995 were minimal. Public institutions, however, did appear more inclined toward hiring Hispanics for these positions than did private institutions.

A backlash against affirmative action may have occurred, for the proportion of Hispanics in newly hired tenure-track faculty positions and the full professor rank declined in comparison with 1991. The decrease was more marked in the full professor rank than in new hires, which may in part be due to the difficulty of comparing the EEOC and NCES data. Competition with other minorities and white women may also be responsible for such a decline.

6

Asians and Native Americans in Higher Education Employment

The presence and achievements of Asians in higher education are a major characteristic distinguishing this group from other minorities. Summarizing demographic and enrollment changes for the period 1980–90, the authors of an American Council on Education report wrote, "In most states, the percentage of Asian Americans enrolled in higher education is proportionate to or slightly larger than their representation in the state population." In many states, Asian higher education enrollment is far above their percentage of the population. In California, the state with the largest Asian population in 1990, "Asian Americans represented 9.6 percent of [the state's] population, compared with 16.5 percent of four year enrollments."[1] Asian enrollment in graduate and professional programs is also impressive; indeed, "Asian Americans are the best educated Americans."[2] Asians' performance in terms of test scores and grades is much superior to that of the other three minorities and is similar to and in some cases superior to that of whites. Asians differ from all other groups, including whites, in the selection of major fields of study, as they show greater interest in the sciences, engineering, and business programs than in education, the social sciences, and the humanities.

Asian students come from relatively stable home environments. Most analysts attribute their success to "cultural factors that stress education, discipline, and achievement."[3] One scholar, Bill Ong Hing, questions such "straightforward" explanations and argues: "The problem we can see after a review of the immigration history and a brief look at demographic factors is that because there are so many distinctive Asian American experiences, a single theory cannot address them all without simplifying their answers and negating the uniqueness of each community. . . . We must begin to appreciate the multifaceted, perhaps even contradictory, significance of achievement in Asian America."[4] Hing's argument has merit, since Asians in America include over twenty subgroups with different historical, political, and cultural experiences, and since educational and economic achievements of certain Asian subgroups are far above those of some other subgroups. Yet, the cultural theory, however straightforward it may seem, offers the best available explanation of the Asian success in education.

Overrepresentation of the Asian students in colleges and universities has led to discriminatory policies by some of the most prestigious and selective institutions of higher education. L. Ling-Chi Wang argues that these institutions, in particular the University of California–Berkeley, moved away from merit consideration in the 1980s and instead admitted students on the basis of "nonacademic and subjective criteria" and "student body diversity." Wang further notes that such criteria redefined "the concept of diversity used in *Bakke* to justify the use of affirmative action programs to admit underrepresented minorities through the noncompetitive channel." Limiting Asian students in higher education is "another manifestation of a very old anti-Asian racism deeply woven into the fabric of our society and embedded in our culture and national consciousness." Wang claims that such racism is similar to the discrimination faced by the Jewish students in elite universities in the pre–World War II period, often referred to as the "Jewish problem."[5]

Most Asian-American scholars agree with Wang. According to Jayjia Hsia, who presents a somewhat different perspective, "There is very little evidence for supporting the existence of widespread, collusive, or systematic exclusionary admissions policies. . . . Asian Americans being denied admission to the most prestigious colleges and medical schools each year are a mere handful compared to their total enrollment in higher education." Hsia, however, cautions that "other pernicious problems may surface in these institutions if current admissions policies are continued over time by perpetuating the super Asian myth, . . . exacerbating divisiveness among ethnic groups, . . . discouraging qualified and motivated Asian Americans denied access to first-choice institutions."[6]

Historically, employment discrimination against Asians was rooted in laws passed by Congress. Although Congress ended statutory discrimination against minorities by passing civil rights and immigration laws in the 1960s, prejudice against these groups did not disappear overnight. Bias against Asians in employment in higher education and other areas continued, despite immigration laws, civil rights legislation, and affirmative action programs. On the other hand, since Asians excelled in higher education and since their numbers in the country and, consequently, their political clout grew due to the removal of discriminatory immigration restrictions, we posit that their ranks in higher education employment also rose and that they increasingly faced less difficulty in finding jobs. We also hypothesize that they are more likely to be employed in public rather than private institutions because state governments are expected to move toward a more representative bureaucracy.

Asian Faculty

Asian faculty have a noticeable presence on many of the campuses in the country. Their participation rates show that they made steady gains in landing faculty positions in the 1980s, though their combined male and female representation ratios actually fell from 1983 to 1991 (table 20). Asians found public institutions more hospitable for employment than private institutions. In both types of institutions, however, the proportion of the Asian faculty increased, with Asian women experiencing a greater percentage increase than Asian men. In all institutions, Asian male faculty increased from 2.1 percent in 1979 to 2.6 percent in 1983 and to 3.6 in 1991; Asian women first experienced an increase from 0.4 percent in 1979 to 0.5 percent in 1983 and then obtained 1.0 percent of the faculty positions by 1991.

The representation ratios reflect overrepresentation of Asian male faculty and underrepresentation of Asian female faculty (table 20). Despite a decline in the Asian male representation ratios that was due to the increase in the Asian population in the United States, male ratios remained at 2.2 or higher. Asian female ratios, on the other hand, were fairly consistent, mostly in the range of 0.6 to 0.7. Both the Asian male and female populations in the United States doubled in the 1980–90 period. Apparently, a substantial increase in the Asian female faculty numbers offset any potential decline in the representation ratios.

Asian success in gaining new tenure-track positions also appears impressive. In all institutions, new Asian tenure-track hires increased from 5.2 percent in 1983 to 6.8 percent in 1991 (table 21). In public institutions their gain was markedly greater than in private institutions. Another striking aspect of the data is the difference between male and female rates of increase – Asian females increased at a much higher rate among new hires than did Asian males. There was a similar difference in rates of increase for Asians in reaching the full professor rank. Asian women tripled their presence among the full professors in public institutions from 1983 to 1991 and more than quadrupled it in private as well as all institutions (table 22). Asian men, on the other hand, also increased at the top rank, but their rate of increase was far below the Asian female rate.

Some Asian-American scholars dispute the image of Asians as the successful minority in higher education. Writing on the Asians' representation in faculty and administrative ranks and their experience in obtaining tenure at colleges and universities, Don T. Nakanishi, who received tenure at the University of California–Los Angeles after a three-year battle, notes: "The widely prevalent image of Asian Pacific Americans as a successful model minority serves to disguise their lack of representation and influence in major social institutions, including higher education." He points out three misconceptions about Asian Pacific American faculty and administrators: they "are well represented in college faculties and key administrative positions"; they "do not face discriminatory or unfair employment practices in higher educational institutions"; and those "who encounter problems in their employment or promotion are more inclined than other minority-group faculty to walk away and not contest any unfair denial of tenure or promotion."[7]

Nakanishi argues that the presence of the Asian faculty on campuses in fields such as the sciences, engineering, medicine, and Asian languages, where they are generally concentrated, "may be misleading because often the professors in these fields are Asian foreign nationals, who received a substantial portion of their higher education training in Asian countries, rather than Asian Pacific Americans."[8] In a study of Asian Americans, Jayjia Hsia makes a similar point. Using "a 1983 survey of Northeast Coast Chinese-American faculty," Hsia says that "the majority of Chinese American faculty were foreign born, received their bachelor's degrees overseas and their doctorates from highly ranked United States universities." Hsia also brings up the issue of discrimination. Citing data on the scholarly productivity of the Chinese-American faculty, he states that such professors "reported that they were burdened by heavy teaching loads and did not receive academic rewards commensurate with their training and job performance."[9]

It is generally agreed that discrimination against minorities, including Asians, and against women exists in colleges and universities as well as in other places of employment. In our view, however, just because a large number of the members of a group received substantial portions of their education in their native countries, came to the United States as foreign students, and upon completion of their education became faculty members at U.S. colleges and universities, their representation in faculty ranks cannot be discounted. A vast majority of such foreign students acquire green cards and eventually American citizenship. Instead, we argue that in considering the presence or absence of a group in faculty employment, the supply of doctorates in that group should also be kept in view. (We discuss that issue in chapter 7.)

National participation rates of the Asian faculty were reflected in the state data. Public institutions hired more Asian faculty than did private institutions.

In both types of institutions, however, Asian faculty employment, particularly of the males, remained rather high. In public institutions in 1983, over two-thirds of the forty-five states for which separate data were available for public and private institutions had a participation rate of 2.0 or higher for Asian male faculty; of these, nine states showed a rate of 3.0 or higher (appendix 13). California and Indiana, both with 3.6, had the highest Asian faculty participation rate for males. Only one state, Vermont, with a rate of 0.9, had less than 1.0 percent Asian male faculty in its public institutions. By contrast, in private institutions in the same year, one-third of the states had participation rates of 2.0 or higher, and six had rates of 3.0 or higher for the Asian male faculty; seven states (Alabama, Arkansas, Idaho, Maine, Minnesota, Montana, and Vermont) had rates below 1.0 (appendix 13). Mississippi had the highest participation rate (4.6) for Asian male faculty in its fifteen private institutions that reported data to the EEOC in 1983.

Asian females were a much smaller proportion of the faculty in 1983 in both public and private institutions than their male counterparts (appendix 14). Only in one state, California, did they make up more than 1.0 percent of the faculty in public or private institutions (1.3 in both cases). As a general rule, they were 0.5 percent or less of the faculty. In a few states (North Dakota and Vermont for public institutions; Arkansas, Idaho, Kansas, Montana, North Dakota, South Dakota, and West Virginia for private institutions), they were below 0.05 percent of the faculty.

By 1991, Asian faculty had become even more numerous on campuses in most states, and Asian females had experienced a greater rate of increase than Asian males (appendixes 13 and 14). As many as fifteen states now had participation rates of 4.0 or higher for Asian male faculty in public institutions, in contrast with eight states in private institutions. Of these states, California, Indiana, Louisiana, Michigan, and Nevada employed 5.0 percent or higher of their faculty from the Asian male group in public institutions, and Delaware, Louisiana, Mississippi, and New Jersey did so in private institutions (California's percentage was 4.2). Asian women's increase on campus faculties was evident from their being 1.0 percent or higher in the faculty in ten states in public institutions and thirteen states in private institutions (appendix 14). Arizona and California were the only states with more than 2.0 percent Asian female faculty in either private or public institutions.

Considering their population in different states, Asians, as expected from the national data, were overrepresented in faculty positions in public and private institutions, males more so than females (appendixes 33 and 34). Their overrepresentation was generally greater in states with relatively small Asian populations than in states with relatively large Asian populations. Thus, California, which has the largest Asian population of any state, had the lowest representation ratio (1.39) for the male (but not female) faculty in public institutions in 1983. For private institutions in the same year, the lowest ratio (1.11) was in Washington, also a state with a large Asian population. On the other hand, the highest Asian male ratio was in West Virginia (25.69) for public institutions and in Mississippi (35.52) for private institutions. Both West Virginia and Mississippi are among the states with the lowest Asian populations.

In public as well as private institutions in 1983, Asian females were also overrepresented in many of the states. The size of their ratio followed the same pattern as for males, that is, larger in states with small Asian populations and smaller in states with large Asian populations. Since there are fewer Asian females than their male counterparts in faculty positions and their population is somewhat greater, their ratios are smaller than those for Asian males.

By 1991, Asian overrepresentation in faculty ranks was tempered by their increase in population. In public institutions, Asian male faculty still remained overrepresented in every state, with their lowest representation ratio, 1.07, in California. In private institutions, two states, California (0.90) and Texas (0.64), had ratios below 1.0. Although Asian females had gained faculty positions at a rate greater than Asian males, it was less apparent from the representation ratios, again because of their increase in population. In both 1983 and 1991, Asian female faculty remained overrepresented in about half the states in public institutions and in about two-fifths of the states in private institutions. If one has the perspective of the half-empty glass, Asian women, despite their gains, remained underrepresented in a majority of the states in private institutions and in about half the states in public institutions.

Asian Administrators

As with other targeted groups, we expect that state governments are more inclined to support a representative bureaucracy; thus Asians will find better employment opportunities as administrators in public institutions rather than private universities. However, despite the increase in Asian population in the United States in the 1980s, Asians' stellar record in Ph.D. programs (see chapter 7), and the overrepresentation of Asian males in faculty positions, they hold relatively few positions in administration in both types of institutions, and most of those positions are in the lower echelons.[10] Asians did make some progress in gaining administrative positions, and their combined male and female participation rate rose from 1.0 in all institutions in 1979 to 1.5 in 1991 (table 23). The gains were more for women than men, reflecting perhaps the concerns of universities and colleges to hire women in a previously male-dominated job category. However, Asian women were only 0.6 percent of the administrators in all institutions in 1991, representing an impressive improvement in statistical but not substantive terms. They had the same proportion of positions in public and private institutions in 1983 (0.4 percent) and did somewhat better in private universities than public institutions in 1991 (0.7 in private institutions, 0.6 in public). Asian men, on the other hand, made gains at a slower rate than Asian women and constituted 0.9 percent of the administrators in all institutions in 1991 (table 23). Somewhat surprisingly, the gains made by Asian males in obtaining administrative jobs were greater at private schools than public institutions from 1983 to 1991, as a result of which their participation rate at both types of institutions became nearly equal in 1991 (1.0 in public institutions, 0.9 in private universities).

The representation ratio for Asian male administrators moved downward in all institutions between 1979 and 1991 but remained virtually unchanged for Asian female administrators (table 23). Asian women's representation in administrative positions did improve from 1979 to 1983 but then fell by 1991. The decline in their ratio from 1983 to 1991 was greater at public schools than private institutions, reflecting their more impressive gains at the private institutions. Asian male representation also experienced a similar trend at public and private institutions from 1983 to 1991. The combined Asian male and female representation ratio in 1991 ranged from 0.52 to 0.55 in public, private, and all institutions, higher for men than for women in every category.

In 1983, Asians were less than 1.0 percent of the administrators in most states, in public as well as private institutions. Asian male administrators had a participation rate of 1.0 or higher in seven states (California, Maryland, Michigan, New Jersey, North Dakota, Virginia, and Washington) in public institutions but in only three states (California, Delaware, and Illinois) in private institutions (appendix 15). Asian female administrators had a similar rate of 1.0 or higher in California and Washington in public institutions and in California in private institutions (appendix 16). Conversely, in private institutions in 1983, in as many as fourteen states for Asian men and twenty-one states for Asian women, the participation rate in administration was less than 0.05 percent; in public institutions, there were three states for Asian men with a rate less than 0.05 percent and fourteen states for Asian women. Both Asian men and women seemed to have experienced difficulties in obtaining administrative jobs in private institutions in several states, including Idaho, Kansas, Kentucky, Maine, Montana, Mew Mexico, North Carolina, North Dakota, South Carolina, Utah, Vermont, and West Virginia (appendixes 15 and 16). Public institutions in most states were more willing to hire Asian male administrators than were private institutions. Asian women were treated rather similarly by both types of institutions in that they were not likely to be hired by either.

Surprisingly, representation ratios in 1983 show overrepresentation of Asian male administrators in public institutions in most states and in private institutions in twenty states (appendix 35). Asian female administrators had ratios above 1.0 in only twelve states in public institutions and eight states in private institutions. In the early 1980s, Asian males and females were concentrated in certain states, notably California and Washington, and to a lesser extent in Alaska, Illinois, Maryland, New Jersey, New York, Oregon, and Nevada. In many states, they were well below 0.5 percent of the population. As a result, even a small number of administrators in a state with a low Asian population made them look overrepresented, sometimes by a wide margin. Even when they were overrepresented, most remained in the lower echelons of the administrative hierarchy.[11]

By 1991, Asian administrators had increased on campuses, although they appeared less represented in comparison to their population in the country as a whole or in different states than in 1983. Asian female administrators made greater gains than Asian male administrators. Consider the examples of public institutions in California, Massachusetts, and New Jersey. In 1983, male administrators' participation rates were 1.7, 0.4, and 1.2, respectively (appendix 15). Asian female administrators' rates in these three states were 1.0, 0.4, and 0.5, respectively (appendix 16). By 1991, Asian females were equal with men in number in administrative positions (2.5 percent) in California; in Massachusetts and New Jersey, Asian male administrators had participation rates of 0.5 and 1.7 percent, respectively, and Asian female administrators had rates of 0.6 and 1.0 percent, respectively. Similar differences between the numbers of Asian male and female administrators were noticeable in some other states in public institutions.

The increase in the Asian population decreased their representation ratios. In 1991, Asian male administrators became underrepresented rather than overrepresented in nearly half the states (appendix 35). Asian female administrators also had ratios of 1.0 or higher in fewer states than in 1983. In other words, despite the gains made by Asian females in administrative positions, they appeared underrepresented to a greater degree than in 1983. In private institutions, Asian females were better represented, yet their ratios indicated underrepresentation in most states. In private institutions, even more so than in public institutions, they achieved parity with Asian men in the number of administrative positions and in some cases held more positions than did Asian men (appendixes 15 and 16). For example, in New York and Oregon in 1991, participation rates of Asian male and female administrators were equal – 1.1 and 1.6, respectively, and in New Jersey, there were almost twice as many Asian female administrators as Asian male administrators (1.1 versus 0.6). In California, Asian female and male administrators were nearly equal in private institutions – 1.4 percent and 1.5 percent, respectively.

Asians in Other Occupations

Given the educational background of Asians, unlike that of other targeted groups, we do not expect them to be concentrated in low-paying and low-status positions. In all institutions in each of the three years of study, Asians held the largest number of jobs in the professional non-faculty category, followed by the technical/para-professional category (table 24). This finding reinforces the image of Asians as being the most educated minority. In 1979, Asian male and female non-faculty professionals were equal in their participation rates. By 1983, Asian female professionals had gone ahead of the Asian male professionals, and by 1991, that trend had become somewhat more pronounced. Asian female technicians and para-professionals remained more numerous than the Asian male technicians and para-professionals throughout the time period, and their percentage of the total exceeded the corresponding Asian male percentage by 0.5 in all three years (table 24). Overrepresentation of Asians in these two occupations is apparent from their representation ratios (table 24). The decline in their ratios from 1983 to 1991 in both of these occupational categories was due to the enormous increase in the Asian population in the country from 1980 to 1990.

In the 1980–90 decade, many of the Asians who migrated to the United States came on the basis of the family reunification provisions of the Immigration Act of 1965 rather than its qualification-based requirements. In addition, Asians immigrated on the basis of the Refugee Act of 1980 and the Immigration Reform and Control Act of 1986 (which granted legal status to the qualified illegal aliens in the country). As a result, Asians settling in the United States in the 1980s were less educated than the Asians who came earlier, especially in the middle and late 1960s and early 1970s. The change in the composition of Asian immigrants explains the fluctuations in the representation ratios and their growing number in occupations that require less education. Such change was responsible for doubling the participation rates of the Asian males in the skilled craft and service/maintenance categories from 1979 to 1991 and for more than doubling the rate of Asian females in the latter category in that period (table 24).

Combined Asian male and female participation rates in the professional non-faculty category were nearly equal in public and private institutions in 1983 (table 25). By 1991, however, public institutions had hired more Asians, both males and females, as non-faculty professionals than had private institutions. A similar trend occurred for Asians seeking positions as secretaries and clerks. Asians also found better employment opportunities in the service/maintenance area in public institutions than private institutions. On the other hand, private colleges and universities offered more jobs to the Asian technicians and para-professionals than did public colleges and universities. In the skilled craft area, private and public institutions had similar records in hiring Asians. In general, these data once again demonstrate a more vigilant implementation of affirmative action in public institutions than private universities. This finding is even more true of Asian women than men (table 25).

California has been the largest employer of Asians in both public and private institutions. In public and private institutions in 1983, combined male and female participation rates for Asians in the professional non-faculty category were 9.6 and 7.5, respectively.[12] In this category, Asians were overrepresented in most states in public institutions (females more so than males) and in a majority of states in private institutions. Asian professionals were also more evenly distributed in public universities than private institutions. Although combined Asian male and female participation rates for the professionals were similar in 1983 for both types of institutions in the national data, Asians of either gender were rarely less than 0.05 percent of the total in public institutions in any state. In private institutions, on the other hand, Asian males and females made up such an insignificant portion of the total number of professionals in several states (Alabama, Arkansas, Delaware, Idaho, Mississippi, Montana, North Dakota, and West Virginia).

By 1991, Asian males and, even more so, females had increased in both types of institutions, though their representation ratios had decreased. In California's public institutions, the participation rate for Asian professionals had risen to 13.6; in private institutions, to 10.0. Although Asian professionals, as expected, remained more numerous in states with relatively large Asian populations than in states with relatively small Asian populations, they became more evenly distributed throughout the country. However, both Asian male and female professionals were still less than 0.05 percent of the total in private institutions in eight states (Arkansas, Delaware, Montana, Nevada, North Dakota, South Dakota, Virginia, and Wisconsin) – the same number as in 1983. In public institutions, there was not a single state in this category. The overrepresentation of

Asian professionals occurred in a larger number of states in public colleges and universities than private institutions in 1991, as was the case in 1983.

A similar trend prevailed in other jobs as well, including the technical/paraprofessional category – the only category in which private institutions hired more Asians than did public institutions in 1983 as well as 1991. In ten states in 1983 (Alabama, Arkansas, Delaware, Idaho, Kansas, Maine, Mississippi, Montana, North Dakota, and Vermont) and in eleven states in 1991 (Arkansas, Delaware, Idaho, Kentucky, Mississippi, Montana, Nevada, North Dakota, South Carolina, Vermont, and West Virginia), Asian male and female technicians/para-professionals had participation rates of less than 0.05 percent in private institutions. By contrast, only in five states in 1983 (Arkansas, Maine, Nevada, New Hampshire, and South Dakota) and in just one state in 1991 (Maryland) were the Asian participation rates less than 0.05 percent in this category in public institutions. These data leave little doubt that public institutions more consistently considered affirmative action in their hiring practices than did private institutions.

Overrepresentation of Asians in several categories, especially those requiring higher levels of education, reinforces their image as the best educated group in the country. Despite some progress, not many Asians obtain administrative positions, particularly those positions with greater supervisory authority and higher pay. However, in this category the gains of Asian females, especially in private institutions, are impressive. In non-administrative occupational categories that require higher educational attainment and training, Asians clearly are the most successful minority group. Even in categories for which lower levels of education and training are needed, Asians' proportion of the total work force increased substantially in the 1980s, reflecting the change in immigration patterns. The employment record of Asians in most categories appears similar to that of whites, rather than other minorities, in that they are more often overrepresented than underrepresented. The aggregate data show that in median income also, Asians resemble whites rather than other minorities, who generally earn less than these two groups.

A recent study found that Asian federal employees, particularly the more educated males, were successful. It notes: "In the federal service, Asian Americans resemble white non-Hispanics in education, salary, grade, and supervisory authority more than they resemble other minority groups. Nonetheless, they continue to earn lower salaries, attain lower grades, and wield less supervisory authority than comparably educated and experienced whites." The study further points out: "grade gaps between comparable Asians and whites have shrunk over the past decade and have essentially disappeared among the college educated. Sizeable gaps remain, however, between Asian and white men who have not completed college. . . . Being Asian has become a disadvantage for women more so than in the recent past."[13]

Our findings, on the other hand, show Asian women making greater progress than Asian men in higher education employment. Whereas Kim and Lewis, the authors of this study on federal employees, found "the least- and best-educated" Asian women in particular faced "the disadvantage" in employment, we instead noticed Asian women making progress at a higher rate than Asian men in both high-status and low-status positions.

As a general rule, Asians were more likely to be hired by public universities than private institutions. There were, however, noticeable exceptions to this rule; for example, many more Asian female technicians and para-professionals worked in private schools than in public institutions in both 1983 and 1991. That affirmative action had an impact on Asian employment in higher education is beyond any doubt. Clearly, public institutions paid greater attention to this program than did private institutions. The rate of progress demonstrates that Asian women benefited more from this program than did Asian men.

The latest available data, at the time of this writing, from NCES provide evidence of an increasing Asian share in faculty ranks, although at a lower rate than in the 1980s.[14] (For problems in comparing the 1995 data with the 1991 statistics, see the introduction to this book.) Asian gains at private institutions during 1991–95 were greater than at public institutions, and women continued to make progress at a higher rate than men. A similar pattern occurred in the administrative positions in that women made greater progress than men, and private institutions offered more positions to Asians than did public institutions. However, Asians continued to be underrepresented in administrative positions.

The data on the hiring of tenure-track faculty present a different picture. The proportion of Asians in this category declined from 1991 to 1995, despite their gains in obtaining doctorates (see chapter 7). Asian women did make gains in this area, though not enough to compensate for Asian men's losses. In the full professor rank, Asian men advanced, but Asian women suffered a setback. Public reaction against affirmative action and competition from other minority groups and from white women perhaps influenced the decrease in the proportion of Asians among the new hires and possibly full professors.

NATIVE AMERICANS

Native Americans have been the least successful minority in gaining access to higher education. Early in the twentieth century President Theodore Roosevelt expressed the widely prevalent prejudice against Native Americans when he wrote in his presidential report of 1901: "In the Indian schools the education should be elementary and largely industrial" since "the need of higher education among the Indians is very, very limited."[15] Some progress toward higher education for Native Americans started in the 1930s with the Congressional appropriation of funds for loans and grants for college attendance. Limited Congressional support for Native American higher education continued through the next three decades and then substantially improved with the passage of the Higher Education Act in 1965. In the meantime, the Native American movement had emerged, encouraging Native Americans to attend colleges and become more aware and proud of their heritage.[16] Native American tribes wanted to preserve their cultural heritage through education in colleges controlled by them rather than by the dominant white group. The first tribally controlled college, the Navajo Community College, was founded in Tsaile, Arizona, in 1969.[17] Encouraged by congressional support and President Richard Nixon's 1968 statement that "the right of self-determination of the Indian people will be respected and their participation in planning their own destiny will actively be encouraged," some two dozen tribal colleges were established, mostly in the 1970s.[18]

Tribal colleges have helped facilitate the promotion of Native Americans' heritage and pride, a point underscored by the 1989 Carnegie Foundation report on tribal colleges; however, they are not regarded as institutions of great learning. A study of these colleges comments: "most tribal colleges are small with enrollments of fewer than 2,000 students. Geographically, two-thirds are located in North and South Dakota and Montana. Almost all are funded at levels below that of other institutions. Furthermore, 22 of 25 of these tribal schools are two-year with a large percentage of faculty with no terminal degrees."[19] Overall, Native American progress in higher education has not been impressive. Although the number of Native American students, especially females, has indeed increased in higher education, including doctoral and other graduate programs, they still remain the most underrepresented and least educated minority in higher education. Furthermore, their dropout rate in colleges is the highest of any race or ethnic group.[20]

Native American Faculty

We also expect Native Americans, like other targeted groups, to be more likely to be employed in public rather than private institutions. In an article on

American Indian faculty published in 1994, Wayne J. Stein, a Native American academic, comments: "More American Indian faculty teach in four-year institutions in the United States today than at any time in the past. Yet a recent survey of these faculty indicates that many are so frustrated by their experiences in higher education that they intend to move on to other careers."[21] The EEOC data, analyzed in our study, suggest lack of any progress in the participation rates of the Native American faculty except for Native American women at public institutions from 1983 to 1991 (table 26). At private institutions, on the other hand, while Native American women remained a mere 0.1 percent of the faculty in 1983 and 1991, the proportion of the Native American male faculty actually decreased from 0.2 percent to 0.1 percent from 1983 to 1991. "More American Indian faculty" teaching in four-year institutions really means more Indian females, rather than males, in these positions.

In 1979, in all institutions (2,882) that reported data on race/ethnicity and gender of their employees to the EEOC, 638 Native American males out of a total faculty of 326,295 had nine- to ten-month contracts. In 1991, that number had gone up to 777 out of a total faculty of 366,995 in 3,285 institutions. Native American female faculty at these institutions increased from 221 in 1979 to 463 in 1991. (The increase in the Native American female participation rate is not evident because of rounding to one place after the decimal in table 26.) Even though we do not have separate data for public and private institutions for 1979, based on the data for 1983 and 1991 we can assume that the increase in Native American female faculty numbers in the period 1979 to 1991 occurred at public, not private, institutions. The decline in the participation rate of Native American men in private institutions from 1983 to 1991 does raise the possibility of frustration, as suggested by Stein, as a factor for their leaving academia. It appears that Native American male faculty were better treated at public institutions than at the private ones, for their participation rate in the former remained stable in the 1983–91 period.

That Native Americans, females more so than males, are underrepresented in faculty positions is evident from the representation ratios in table 26. These ratios reinforce the availability of better employment opportunities for Native Americans at public universities rather than private institutions. Some of these numbers may seem puzzling to the reader, since despite the stability of the participation rates, the representation ratios went down. Note, for example, the participation rates and representation ratios for all institutions in 1979 or 1983 and in 1991. The explanation lies in the U.S. Bureau of the Census data, which indicate that the Native American population (American Indian, Eskimo, and Aleut) increased from 0.63 percent in 1980 to 0.79 percent in 1990, with males increasing from 0.31 percent to 0.39 percent and females from 0.32 percent to 0.40 percent.[22] The increase in the Native American population, which we believe was more a result of better counting than due to a natural population increase in this group, affected representation ratios. In other words, there possibly was no real decline in the Native American representation ratios from 1979 or 1983 to 1991.

Data on new hires and full professors also show that public institutions, but not private institutions, improved their record in recruiting and promoting Native Americans, especially women, from 1983 to 1991 (tables 27 and 28). Native American women did particularly well in getting hired in tenure-track positions at public institutions in 1991. In a survey of Indian faculty members conducted by Wayne Stein in 1992, one female reportedly felt "the widespread idea that a non-white and especially a non-white female can pick and choose her desired position in higher education to be a myth."[23] This idea probably is a myth. Our data give ample evidence, however, that Native American women's prospects of being hired as tenure-track faculty members at public institutions have improved. The 1983 data on tenure also suggest better treatment of Native American women at public schools than at private institutions. EEOC data on tenure for 1991 are incomplete.

In very few of the states in 1983, Native Americans made up 1.0 percent or higher of the faculty (see appendixes 17 and 18). This was the case only in the states of Idaho, Oklahoma, and South Dakota for public institutions and Kansas, North Dakota, Oklahoma, and Vermont for private institutions. Alaska was also in the same category if we consider all institutions combined (separate 1983 data for public and private institutions in Alaska were not available). Native American males were clearly more predominant in faculty ranks than their female counterparts. In both public and private institutions, Native American women were 0.1 percent or less of the total faculty in approximately two-thirds of the states. Although the corresponding proportion for Native American males was generally higher, about half of the states for public institutions and three-fifths of the states for private institutions had 0.1 percent or less Native American male faculty.

As a general rule, states with relatively large Native American populations had smaller representation ratios for the faculty from this group than states with relatively small populations (see appendixes 37 and 38). In the entire 1983 data, North Dakota was the only state with a Native American male and female population over 1.0 percent and representation ratios also over 1.0 for both; this occurred in private, but not public, institutions. In a majority of the states,

Native Americans were underrepresented, females more so than males, in both public and private institutions.

There indeed was some progress in the hiring of Native American faculty by the year 1991. Alaska, Arizona, Montana, North Dakota, and Oklahoma had combined participation rates of 1.0 or higher for males and females in public institutions (appendixes 17 and 18). For private institutions, Alaska, Montana, Oklahoma, Texas, and Wisconsin had such participation rates. In addition, New Mexico, for which separate 1991 data for public and private institutions were not available, had a combined rate of 1.8 percent Native American faculty in all institutions reporting. Overall, by 1991, Native Americans were more likely to be hired by public schools than private institutions. The number of states with participation rates of 0.1 or less declined for both Native American males and females in public institutions, but it increased for the males and stayed about the same for the females in private institutions (appendixes 17 and 18).

The trend for states with larger Native American populations having smaller representation ratios continued (appendixes 37 and 38). Female Native American faculty ratios were generally higher in public institutions than in private schools. This was even more true for the Native American males, who lost ground in landing faculty positions in private institutions.

Native American Administrators

As we expected with other targeted groups, Native Americans should find better opportunities for administrative positions in public institutions rather than private schools. The participation rate of Native Americans in administration is as low as in the faculty. In all institutions, possibly in public universities rather than private ones, Native American male administrators made some gains from 1979 to 1983 but then in 1991 went back to their 1979 level of 0.2 percent (table 29). While their proportion of the total number of administrators in public institutions remained the same in 1983 and 1991, they lost ground in private institutions. In 1,541 private institutions reporting in 1983, there were only 101 Native American males out of 51,617 administrators. In 1991, in a somewhat higher number of private institutions reporting (1,586), the number of Native American male administrators had dropped to 71 out of a total 55,544. Native American female administrators also decreased in these institutions from 51 to 45 in the 1983–91 period. Since the female decline was small, it did not show up in the participation rate. In public institutions, on the other hand, the number as well as the proportion of the Native American females, but not males, increased. In 1,470 public institutions reporting in 1983, there were 210 Native American males and 68 Native American females among their 65,869 administrators. In 1,699 such institutions in 1991, there were 214 Native American males and 173 Native American females out of a total 81,364 administrators.

Representation ratios, although somewhat distorted in 1979 and 1983 due to the possible undercounting of the Native American population in 1980, reinforce the differences between public and private institutions. While the participation rate of the Native American male administrators in public institutions was unchanged in 1991 from 1983, their representation ratio declined. The decline was much greater in private schools than public institutions (table 29). The representation ratio of Native American female administrators increased considerably in public institutions in this period but decreased in private institutions.

There are very few studies on Native American administrators in higher education. Our findings reveal some progress for Native American females but not for males. In a study of the "circumstances in which American Indian female administrators [in higher education] perceive dissonance in their work environment," Linda Sue Warner, a Comanche academic as well as an administrator, interviewed "six American Indian supervisors . . . at one institution." She found that "certain aspects of the American Indian culture were characteristically in conflict with the role of the supervisor." Warner also noted, "Although each [interviewee] appeared aware of the historical context of affirmative action programs, there was no agreement on whether this was 'good' for Indian people or whether it 'harmed' them by allowing unqualified individuals to be hired, particularly in the past."[24]

Except in a few states, mainly where Native Americans have a relatively large population, their presence among the administrators was negligible in 1983 and improved little by 1991. In South Dakota's public institutions in 1983, there were 11 Native American male administrators and 7 Native American female administrators out of a total 165 in seven institutions reporting, which gave them the highest participation rate (6.7 and 4.2, respectively) of any state (appendixes 19 and 20). For Native American males, the states following South Dakota in participation rate were Delaware, Idaho, New Mexico, Oklahoma, Missouri, and North Dakota (appendix 19). In the combined public and private institutions data for Alaska, there were 4.1 percent Native American male administrators and 0.5 percent Native American female administrators (appendixes 19 and 20). Alaska's Native American female participation rate was higher than in most other states. In fact, in a majority of the states in public institutions, Native American female administrators were less than 0.05 percent. In addition to South Dakota, Montana was the only state where they were over

1.0 percent (1.4). By contrast, Native American males were over 1.0 percent of the administrators in public institutions in seven states, listed above, and in only nine states were they less than 0.05 percent in such institutions.

In private institutions in 1983, Native American administrators were even fewer. Seven states (Kansas, Montana, New Mexico, North Dakota, Oklahoma, South Dakota, and Utah) had more than 1.0 percent Native American male administrators – in all cases but one (New Mexico) the participation rate was above 2.0 percent (appendix 19). Montana, with two Native American male administrators and two Native American female administrators out of a total of forty-four in four institutions reporting, attained the highest participation rate for males (4.5) and second highest for females, also 4.5. (The highest rate for Native American female administrators, 7.1, was in North Dakota.) In addition to Montana and North Dakota, Native American females were over 1.0 percent of the administrators in only two states – Oklahoma (1.6) and South Dakota (1.4). The general trend for Native American females, and to a lesser extent for males, was a participation rate below 0.05 (appendixes 19 and 20).

Since Native American males or females constitute much less than 1 percent of the population in most states, even a modest participation rate made them, particularly males, look well represented or even overrepresented in several states. Thus, in 1983 in as many as twenty states for public institutions and ten states for private institutions, Native American males were statistically either overrepresented or at par with their proportion of the population (appendix 39). In the rest of the states, they were underrepresented. Underrepresentation rather than overrepresentation was the norm for the Native American female administrators. In only five states in public institutions and six states in private institutions were they overrepresented or at par with their proportion of the population.

By 1991 in public institutions, there appeared to be little change in the representation of Native American male administrators, although there was progress for the females. North Dakota had the highest participation rate (5.6) of the Native American male administrators, followed by Alaska (4.1), Oklahoma (1.9), South Dakota (1.2), and Arizona (1.1) (appendix 19). New Mexico had a rate of 1.2 for both males and females for all institutions (separate data for public and private institutions were not available). The general rule for the Native American male administrators was a rate well below 1.0; in fact, it was 0.1 or less in a majority of the states. Native American females, on the other hand, made up 3.7 percent of the administrators in North Dakota, followed by 1.5 percent in Montana and Oklahoma and 1.4 percent in Alaska (appendix 20). While Native American females remained a very small part of the administrative hierarchy in most other states, the number of states with negligible rates of below 0.05 did decline. As a result, their underrepresentation, as measured by representation ratios, decreased in many of the states.

In private institutions in 1991, both Native American males and females remained less than 0.05 percent of the administrators in a majority of the states. Except Montana, where Native American males were an impressive 16.7 percent of the total administrators, North Dakota (2.5 percent), South Dakota (2.3 percent), and Oklahoma (1.7 percent), they were barely noticeable in the administrative ranks (appendix 19). Native American females also were 16.7 percent of the administrators in Montana. However, in only two other states, Oklahoma and South Dakota, did their participation rates equal or exceed 1.0. Yet it appears that private institutions in some of the states with a low Native American population, notably Arkansas and Texas, had made efforts to recruit females rather than males from this group, perhaps to satisfy the requirements of affirmative action as well as to respond to women's demands. As a result, these states had higher participation rates for Native American female administrators than for Native American male administrators (appendixes 19 and 20). Representation ratios for both Native American males and females showed their continued underrepresentation in public as well as private institutions.

Native Americans in Other Occupations
We expect to find Native Americans, similar to all other targeted groups except Asians, more likely to hold lower-paying and lower-status positions than higher-paying and higher-status positions. In all institutions, Native Americans made no progress at all in the highest of the five employment categories. Both Native American men and women remained at a participation rate of 0.2 in the professional non-faculty category in 1979, 1983, and 1991 (table 30). Of the technical/para-professional and service/maintenance jobs, Native Americans improved their share from 1979 to 1983, but not from 1983 to 1991. In secretarial/clerical positions, Native American women made steady gains from 1979 to 1991, and in the skilled craft category, Native American men had a similar experience. In general, the representation ratios of Native Americans improved somewhat from 1979 to 1983 and then declined from 1983 to 1991. This occurred due to possible undercounting by the U.S. Bureau of the Census in 1980.

As in the case of other minorities, public universities rather than private institutions showed a greater willingness to hire Native Americans. In public institutions, in four of the five categories (the exception being the technical/para-professional category), participation rates and representation ratios of

Native Americans improved from 1983 to 1991 (table 31). In private institutions in this period, on the other hand, Native Americans lost ground in every job category except the technical/para-professional category. The drop from a participation rate of 0.6 to 0.2 in the top category of professional non-faculty was precipitous, indeed, and rather inexplicable. In 1,541 private colleges and universities reporting in 1983, there were 458 Native American non-faculty professionals out of a total 88,705. By 1991, in 1,586 private institutions reporting, that number had fallen to 265 out of a total 109,266. Native American men in this category suffered a greater decline than Native American women (table 31). In three of the other four categories, the Native American female participation rate remained the same, and in one (service/maintenance) it declined. The Native American male participation rate in such institutions declined in three of the four categories, and in one (technical/para-professional) it increased. In contrast, Native American women in public institutions improved their proportion of the workforce in every category except skilled crafts, where they remained below 0.05 percent in both 1983 and 1991. The Native American male participation rate in public institutions improved in three categories, declined in one, and remained the same in another.

Although Native American males as well as females remained underrepresented in professional non-faculty positions in public institutions in most states in 1983 and 1991, they made progress in several states.[25] These states included not only the ones with relatively large Native American populations but also some with relatively small numbers of Native American inhabitants. In private institutions, on the other hand, a reverse trend prevailed. While in a few states, notably Montana and South Dakota, Native American non-faculty professionals increased, for females more than males, their participation rates, particularly of men, declined in other states. The number of states in which their representation ratios equaled or exceeded 1.0 declined, from eight to six for men, and from eleven to nine for women.

Of the other four categories, Native American men were overrepresented in skilled crafts and service/maintenance in 1983 and 1991 in public institutions in a majority of the states. In private institutions, despite the national overrepresentation of Native Americans in these two categories in 1983, they were underrepresented in a majority of the states. In such institutions, the greatest concentration of the Native American male skilled craftsmen was in Kansas and Montana and of the service/maintenance men was in Connecticut, Delaware, and Kansas. By 1991, private institutions were recruiting fewer Native American men and women in the service/maintenance category. The result was the continued underrepresentation of men in a majority of the states and of women in most states. For skilled craft jobs also, private institutions had become less receptive to Native American men by 1991. (This category remains male-dominated in most states in both public and private institutions.)

We discerned a somewhat similar trend in the secretarial/clerical category, which remains female-dominated in public and private institutions. Native American female secretaries and clerks were overrepresented in public institutions in a majority of the states but were underrepresented in private institutions in a majority of the states. While states with large Native American populations had concentrations of Native American secretaries and clerks, some states with relatively small Native American populations also aggressively recruited them. Notable among such states were Massachusetts, Rhode Island, and Vermont for public institutions and Pennsylvania for private institutions.

Although public institutions recruited more Native American technicians/ para-professionals than did private institutions, men and women of this race remained underrepresented in a majority of states in public institutions in both 1983 and 1991. Of course, their underrepresentation was in an even larger number of states in private institutions. Occasionally, public or private institutions in a state seemed to have made special efforts to recruit Native Americans for this job category. This was true of Indiana in 1983 for public institutions in the hiring of men and true of Kansas in 1983 for private institutions in the hiring of both men and women. In 1991, Pennsylvania's public institutions in the hiring of men and Kansas's private institutions in the hiring of both men and women displayed similar recruiting efforts.

Native Americans, more so than other minorities, tended to seek jobs in states with relatively large populations of their own group. Like other minorities, they found public institutions more hospitable for employment than private institutions. Their presence on campuses was far greater in occupations requiring lower levels of education and training than in occupations requiring higher levels of education and training. Native American women made greater gains than Native American men, particularly in jobs with higher status and pay. By 1991, both Native American men and women were underrepresented in a majority of the seven categories considered. In skilled craft and service/ maintenance positions, Native American men were either overrepresented or had representation ratios of 1.0 in both public and private institutions; Native American women were overrepresented in secretarial/clerical jobs in public universities but not in private institutions. The data on median salaries indicated Native Americans were generally paid less than other groups in the higher-status positions. They were clearly less experienced in these positions than members of other groups and had not built up credentials for advancement.

The 1995 data reveal modest progress for Native Americans in obtaining faculty positions and a somewhat better record in gaining administrative jobs.[26] Public institutions continued to be more responsive to their aspirations for employment. Native Americans remained almost negligible in the full professor rank. However, their entrance into tenure-track faculty positions again showed improvement, which bodes well for their future in academia. Of course, in considering these findings, the difficulties of comparing the 1995 and 1991 data must be kept in view, as discussed in the introduction.

7

Minority and Female Doctorates

As the student body in colleges and universities became diverse and white male students became a minority, pressures for hiring female and minority faculty and administrators increased. It was argued that white male administrators did not fully understand the perspectives of females and minorities and that white male faculty were less-than-satisfactory role models for students other than white males. Women faculty were needed to serve as role models for female students and to understand their concerns. Similarly, the needs of black and Hispanic students were many, and hiring of these minorities in faculty ranks was advocated. Since Asians were a much smaller minority and their representation in faculty was greater than their proportion in the general population, voices to hire Asian faculty to serve as role models for Asian students were seldom heard. A few campuses, notably in California, have had large numbers of Asian students to generate a demand for more Asian faculty and administrators. Besides, Asians as a group have little in common except region, hence they are far less organized than other minority groups. Native Americans have been so few on campuses that any demand for their hiring in the faculty or administration seldom emerged.

Pressure for hiring female and minority faculty and administrators came not only from students but also, and more forcefully, from interest groups representing women and minorities, state and federal government agencies, boards of trustees of the colleges, and, for faculty hiring, from the top college administrators. Since a doctorate is generally considered an essential qualification for faculty positions as well as for many of the top administrative positions, an analysis of the supply of female and minority doctorates is necessary. It is also important that we understand changes in the availability of white male doctorates and white male representation in faculty and administrative ranks.

WOMEN

White as well as minority women increasingly earned more doctorates in the period considered in this study, a trend that continued in the 1990s.[1] White female doctorates increased from 7,022 in 1979 to 8,525 in 1983, 10,518 in 1991, and 11,724 in 1995 (table 32). Although their share of the total doctorates awarded by American universities jumped from 22.5 percent in 1979 to 27.3 percent in 1983, it increased by only 0.9 percent from 1983 to 1995 (table 32). Their proportion of all female doctorates also increased from 1979 to 1983, from 78.6 percent to 80.9 percent, but then it declined to 75.8 percent in 1991 and to 71.8 percent in 1995, indicating the entry of large members of minority women in doctoral programs.

Asian women surpassed women of all other groups by a wide margin in their increase among doctorate recipients (table 32). In the period 1979–91, the supply of Asian women doctorates accelerated by 271 percent, more than twice the rate of any other female group and more than five times the rate of white women. Minority women of all groups except blacks surpassed white women in their rates of increase in obtaining doctorates in this period; however, if the next four years (1991–95) are considered, black women had joined other minority women in this trend. By 1995, 28.2 percent of the total doctorates were awarded to white women, an increase of less than 6 percentage points since 1979. However, Asian women in this period raised their share of the total doctorates from 1.4 percent to 6.2 percent, increasing from 444 doctorates in 1979 to 2,588 in 1995. In comparison with Asian women, the gains of all other minority women in this respect were modest. Overall, minority women clearly increased their share of the total doctorates at a faster pace than did white women. The male-female doctorate ratio narrowed considerably by the mid-1990s, and black women emerged as the only female group to have earned more of such degrees than men in their race category.

Of the women doctorates, more degrees for every group except Asians are awarded in education. Asian women prefer the life sciences over other fields. In engineering, women continue to be a small minority. This field is clearly the least preferred by women for their doctorates. Asian women, however, prefer engineering to professional/other fields such as business and management, communications, and library science. On the whole, white and minority women are more apt to pursue doctorates in education and the social sciences, particularly psychology, than in other fields, including the humanities.

It is apparent that women are heading toward parity with men in the number of doctorates granted annually. In 1967, the first year in which the National Research Council (NRC) compiled data on doctorate recipients, females earned 11.9 percent of such degrees. By 1979, the first year of focus in our study, that number had more than doubled to 28.6 percent. As table 32 reveals, the female share of all doctorates was 33.7 percent in 1983, 37.0 percent in 1991, and 39.3

percent in 1995. NCES estimates, in its "middle alternative projections," that women will earn 18,700 doctorates (43.4 percent) out of a total of 43,100 in the year 2000 and 20,700 (48.0 percent) out of the same projected total in 2005.[2]

Earlier data gathered by NCES and the American Council on Education reveal that the percentage of female doctorates was slightly above 1 in 1890, shot up to 6 in just twenty years, surpassed 15 by 1920, but then declined in the 1930s and 1940s.[3] Comparing such information to the data on women faculty in the period 1890–1989, Harold Orlans noted that "historically, the proportion of faculty who were women has greatly exceeded the proportion of women among Ph.D. recipients" and that "only in the early 1980s did the flood of women into graduate and professional schools change that situation."[4] Such conclusions are disputed by some other scholars who interpret the same data differently. Martha West wrote in an article in *Academe*: "In 1920, when women won the right to vote, 26 percent of full-time faculty in American higher education were women. In 1995, 31 percent of full-time faculty in American higher education are women – an increase of 5 percent over seventy-five years! . . . Women's exceedingly slow integration of the faculty ranks, particularly during more recent times, is most distressing given the rapid increase in the percentage of American Ph.D.s obtained by women in the 1970s and 1980s."[5]

Our own data show that women held 26.1 percent of the full-time faculty positions in 1979, 27.9 percent in 1983, and 32.8 percent in 1991 (table 33).[6] Comparing these numbers to the female shares of doctorates, it is clear that women are no longer able to obtain faculty positions in the same proportion as the supply of their doctorates. Orlans, however, is accurate in interpreting the data from a historical perspective. It is true that in the late nineteenth century and much of the twentieth century, the percentage of women faculty was higher than their percentage of the Ph.D.s awarded.[7] Such data do not signify any discrimination against men who controlled academia, were better paid, and held higher positions than women. There is no doubt that women continue to face discrimination in obtaining faculty as well as administrative positions in higher education. There are fewer of them in such jobs in Ph.D.-granting institutions than in comprehensive universities, undergraduate colleges, and community colleges. They also hold a much smaller percentage of tenured professorships and higher-level administrative jobs than men, particularly in prestigious research universities, and on average, they earn less than men at the same ranks. Other studies also reveal systematic gender discrimination in American academia.[8]

A close look at the data also reveals that minority women are more likely to face discrimination in the academic market than white women. As is apparent from the data in tables 32 and 33, in 1979, white women held a slightly higher proportion of the faculty ranks than their share of doctorates. In 1983, fewer white women held faculty positions than could be expected by doctorates awarded to them that year. This discrepancy, however, was corrected by 1991.[9] On the other hand, Hispanic women, Asian women, and to a lesser extent Native American women clearly faced a greater degree of discrimination than did white women. (Black women are the only female group that held a higher proportion of faculty positions than the proportion of their doctorates in all three years in the data.) Asian women possibly faced the greatest discrimination. In 1991, for example, they received 4.4 percent of the doctorates but held only 1.0 percent of the faculty positions. Of course, some of the Asian female foreign students returned home after obtaining doctorates in the United States, yet the discrepancy between the two percentages (4.4 and 1.0) is much too large to ignore the possibility of a systematic discrimination against Asian women. Like Asian women, Hispanic women also faced discrimination during the period in the study, although to a lesser extent.

Although anecdotes on campuses abound to show that white males are facing great difficulties in being hired as faculty members due to the onslaught of affirmative action and, in particular, the preference for minority and white women, we find no evidence in our data to support such opinions.[10] Even white women, who faced less discrimination than minority women, held faculty positions in 1979 and 1991 exceeding their share of doctorates by only 0.5 percent, and in 1983, in fact, they held 2.5 percent fewer positions than their share of doctorates. Black women, who exceeded their proportion of doctorates in obtaining faculty ranks, did so by small margins except in 1991 (see tables 32 and 33). Black women did better than other minority women in gaining faculty positions, but "doing better" is relative. In 1991, black women held only 2.3 percent of the total faculty positions in American higher education. Asian, Hispanic, and Native American women combined represented only 1.9 percent of the total faculty that year. In 1991, white males still controlled 59.4 percent of all faculty positions, and they continue to be the dominant group in better-paying and more prestigious positions.

A similar pattern is evident in employment in administration in higher education. With more women earning higher degrees and with pressure by women's groups and affirmative action agencies, the male-female ratio in the administrative hierarchy has been changing. Women's overall share of administrative positions increased from 28.1 percent in 1979 to 40.1 percent in 1991. The increase in women administrators has occurred more at the lower ranks than at the higher ranks. Of the female groups, once again, it is white and black women who have gained the most. White women's share of the administrative jobs expanded from 24.5 percent in 1979 to 28.3 percent in 1983 and then to 33.8 percent in 1991 (table 33). Conversely, minority women, except blacks, made little advancement in this area. Black female administrators increased from 0.1 percent in 1979 to 3.1 percent in 1983 and to 4.5 percent in 1991. Hispanic, Asian, and Native American women administrators combined remained at 1.9 percent in 1991, despite a statistically impressive gain of over 100 percent in the 1979–91 period (table 33).

Despite the difficulty of comparing the 1995 NCES data with the earlier EEOC data (see the introduction), it is apparent that the campus anecdotes reflecting concerns of discrimination against white males remained unsubstantiated.[11] In 1995, white males still held nearly 56 percent of the faculty positions and 49 percent of the administrative positions. According to these data, all minority women combined occupied less than 5 percent of the faculty positions, half of which were held by black women, and 7 percent of the administrative positions, about two-thirds of which were in black women's hands; white women controlled 29 percent of the faculty positions and 36 percent of the administrative jobs. We found no evidence to believe that white male domination over the jobs with higher status and higher pay in either of these two categories had decreased by any substantial degree.

We analyzed data on newly hired tenure-track faculty in order to understand the relationship between the supply of doctorates for different groups and the positions obtained by them. EEOC data for new hires were available for 1983 and 1991, but not 1979. We excluded administrators from this discussion since a doctorate is seldom required for the lower ranks, and since several years of experience along with a doctorate are usually necessary for higher positions. Women clearly are gaining more faculty positions at the expense of men (table 34). In 1983, women earned 33.7 percent of doctorates and gained 34.0 percent of the new positions; in 1991, however, their share of such positions was 5 percent greater than their share of doctorates, 42.0 versus 37.0 (tables 32 and 34). Men, on the other hand, landed 5 percent fewer new faculty positions in 1991 than their share of doctorates that year, although in 1983 these two percentages were nearly equal for men as well as women (tables 32 and 34). Much of the gain for females went to white women, who obtained 34.9 percent of the new positions in 1991, 4.5 percent more than in 1983, even though the increase in their doctorates was less than 1 percent, from 27.3 to 28.0. Of the minority women, every group's hiring record improved in 1991 over 1983. If we compare job offers and doctorates, black women did the best, Asian women the worst (tables 32 and 34). White men's dominance in doctorates earned and new tenure-track positions decreased; however, they continued to be hired at a rate much higher than their proportion of doctorates (tables 32 and 34).

We also compared the 1995 doctorate data with the 1995 newly hired tenure-track faculty data prepared by NCES and found the continuation of a similar trend.[12] White and black women had the most success in gaining such positions in comparisons to their doctorates; Asian women had the least success. Many more white men were hired than the supply of their doctorates would suggest; however, the gap between their proportion of new tenure-track faculty positions and that of their doctorates did decline.

As the presence of women in faculty and administrative categories continues to increase, we expect gender discrimination to further decrease. We share the views expressed by scholars such as Helen Astin and M. B. Snyder and by Howard Bowen and Jack Schuster that progress has occurred in gender equality in academe and that before long (we hope sooner rather than later) discrimination against women will be eliminated.[13] We believe, however, that such an optimistic forecast is more applicable to white and black women than to Asian, Hispanic, or Native American women.

BLACKS

Commenting on the scarcity of doctorates earned by blacks, Horace Mann Bond noted in a study published in 1972, "The scarcity of Negro scholars in the American intellectual community throws into sharp relief not the deficiencies of the Negro intellect, but the imperfections of a system that now produces perhaps one percent of its greatest human asset from one-tenth of its population."[14] In an earlier study, Harry Washington Greene, after studying doctorates awarded to blacks during the period 1876–1943, also pointed out an equally discouraging scenario for blacks. Edward S. Bouchet, a physicist who received a doctorate from Yale in 1876, was the first black to earn a Ph.D. from an American university.[15] By the end of the nineteenth century, only six more blacks were granted doctorates in the United States. It was not until the 1930s and 1940s before blacks started earning doctorates in noticeable numbers. Yet, from 1940 to 1943, only 128 blacks received such degrees.[16] According to estimates prepared by Bond, a steady increase in the number of black doctorates occurred in the 1940s, 1950s, and early 1960s. In the period 1960–62, the estimated number of black doctorates was 480, that is, 160 a year; however, the ratio of white to black doctorates stood at 68:1 for those three years.[17] In the 1960s and 1970s, there was an improvement in the number of doctorates awarded to blacks, partly in response to the civil rights movement and partly due to increased demand for employees with Ph.D.'s in higher education, industry, and government. In 1979, the first year in our study, 1,443 blacks received doctorates, 4.6 percent of such degrees awarded that year (table 32). That brought down the white-black ratio for doctorates to 16:1. The number of black doctorates decreased to 1,384 in 1983 (4.4 percent of the total number of doctorates granted that year) but bounced back to 1,458 in 1991 (3.9 percent) and 1,798 in 1995 (4.3 percent). The white-black ratio for the first two of these years was 17:1; then it dropped to 15:1.

Within the black group, women have made greater gains than men in obtaining doctorates. While the number of black women graduating with doctorates was similar in 1979 and 1983, there was an increase in 1991 and even more so in 1995 (table 32). However, the number of doctorates earned by black men and their share of the total number of doctorates awarded declined from 1979 to 1983 and again in 1991; in 1995, black male doctorates increased (table 32).

When considering fields of doctorates, the NRC separates U.S. citizens and those with U.S. permanent visas from the foreign students studying on temporary visas in the United States. A racial/ethnic breakdown is available for the former group. Although the number and proportion of foreigners earning doctorates in the United States, particularly in the sciences and engineering, has been increasing, the citizen/permanent resident group remains predominant and was awarded three-fourths of the doctorates in 1995. Blacks in this group received 4.2 percent of the doctorates in 1979; this figure declined to 3.9 percent in 1983 and then moved up to 4.1 percent in 1991 and 4.6 percent in 1995 (table 35). As the data in table 35 reveal, the largest number of black graduate students have been in education and the social sciences. Although a majority of the black doctorates were in education in 1979 and 1983, this proportion did drop to about four-tenths in 1991 and 1995, signaling a trend among black students toward higher enrollment in other fields, including the sciences and engineering.

Other studies have also noted black students' preference for education and the social sciences and have lamented their lack of interest in the sciences and engineering.[18] Harry Greene's study of 368 black doctorates in the period 1876–1943 included 71 in education and 77 in the social sciences.[19] According to Greene, 58 blacks earned doctorates in the physical sciences and 35 in the biological sciences. These numbers reflect a greater interest of blacks in the sciences, if one considers the proportion of the total number of black degrees represented by these science degrees. Analyzing the NRC data for 1975, 1981, and 1983, Alan Fechter wrote: "Although the number of black Ph.D.'s increased dramatically in the life sciences and in the broad field that includes mathematics, computer sciences, and engineering, little or no change occurred in the black shares of the populations in these fields. Both the number and proportion of blacks in physical science fields fell."[20]

Our data also reveal that the number of blacks and their share of doctorates in the physical sciences fell from 1979 to 1983 but then rose in 1991 and 1995.[21] In engineering and the life sciences, blacks also increased their numbers and shares of doctorates. We also discerned steady black gains in professional fields. In a study published in 1989, a sociologist, however, wrote: "The black scientist is both rare and relatively unknown: rare because of an educational philosophy that produced laborers not scholars, and unknown because white society has often refused to recognize the contributions of those able to overcome the obstacles placed before them."[22]

Our analysis of the recent data reveals a more optimistic trend. It is true, of course, that despite gains in receiving doctorates in the sciences, engineering, and other fields, blacks remain severely underrepresented among the holders of such degrees. Several explanations have been advanced for black underrepresentation in doctorates.[23] There is little doubt that discrimination, poor academic preparation, low economic status, and lack of role models have kept many blacks from pursuing doctoral programs.[24] To these must be added poor job prospects and low pay in academia, where a majority of doctoral recipients want to work. In their study based on over five hundred interviews conducted in 1983 and 1984 at thirty-eight campuses across the country, Howard Bowen and Jack Schuster point out that "poor compensation [in academia] is the most frequently cited explanation" for good students from both historically black schools and white-dominated campuses not pursuing a doctorate. They also noted that "the extended 'pledgeship' at a subsistence level of income during graduate school, as well as the problematic prospects of attaining tenure after an arduous probationary period, make academic careers even less attractive to talented, mobile minorities."[25]

Poor compensation, the hardship of graduate student life, and the difficulties of attaining tenure are reasons why many among the best and the brightest of any race or ethnicity do not chose a career in academia. However, these reasons do not account for the low numbers of blacks in the sciences and engineering, which traditionally have provided better prospects for employment in higher education and also in industry. Alan Fechter provides empirical evidence to show that "blacks are more likely [than whites] to report that they are being underutilized – that is, they are either unemployed, employed part-time but seeking full-time work, or employed in a nonscience or nonengineering job because science or engineering jobs were not available."[26] As a result, black students may be discouraged from enrolling in doctoral programs, even in the sciences or engineering. Donald Deskins gives another explanation for relatively few black science doctorates and many more education doctorates:

> Blacks' awareness of job ceilings and the lack of role models cause many who have the ability to succeed in academia to reject what they perceive as dead-end fields and channel their efforts to fields in which their greatest chances for success lie. The fact that blacks have traditionally selected doctoral training in education is an example of blacks adjusting their expectations and pursuing careers in a field in which possibilities for success are high. Conversely, they also steer away from those fields that have little or no black participation or that hold little promise of opening up to them, especially the scientific specialities.[27]

Although black women held a larger proportion of faculty positions than their share of doctorates in all three years in our study, this was the case for black men only in 1991 (tables 32 and 33). A similar pattern also existed among new hires (tables 32 and 34). Combined male and female black new hires exceeded the black share of doctorates, particularly in 1991 (tables 32 and 34). In the administrative ranks, black progress, or rather the progress of black females, was impressive. Combined male and female black share of administrative positions jumped from 4.4 percent in 1979 to 7.1 percent in 1983 and to 8.7 percent in 1991 (table 33). Black men remained at 4.0 to 4.2 percent of administrators in all three years; black women, on the other hand, continued gaining such positions, moving from 0.1 percent in 1979 to 3.1 percent in 1983 to 4.5 percent in 1991 (table 33).

The above data clearly show that, by 1991, black males and females were well-represented in faculty positions and the administrative ranks, in view of their shares of doctorates. Of course, they were underrepresented in light of their proportion of the country's population. A study on black academics, published in 1991, argued that "significant numbers of highly qualified African American candidates are overlooked or deemed unqualified, in part because of the contested assumption in academia that 'quality rises to the top.' According to this assumption, if black candidates are not found in the graduate programs of the universities considered to be the best in a field, then it is often incorrectly concluded that no other black candidates are available."[28] There is some truth to this argument, since other studies have documented the preponderance of black faculty in historically black colleges.[29] It is also true that the percentage of blacks in top positions in the faculty or administration remains relatively low. At the same time, even though blacks are not advancing in their share of doctorates, their share of administrative ranks and, to a lesser extent, faculty ranks has increased.[30]

HISPANICS

Mexican-Americans and Puerto Ricans, the largest of Hispanic groups in the United States, were virtually excluded from higher education for a long time. "The collegiate history of Mexican-Americans," writes Meyer Weinberg, "had barely begun by World War I." Puerto Ricans in the United States did worse: "before the 1960's, Puerto Ricans rarely attended mainland colleges."[31] Very few Mexican-Americans or Puerto-Ricans were able to pursue doctoral programs. With Fidel Castro's assumption of power in Cuba in 1959, large numbers of Cubans fled to the United States. Other Hispanics also came to the United States with the passage of the Immigration Act of 1965 that abolished the quota system, which had been designed to favor Europeans, and later legislation, in particular the Immigration Reform and Control Act of 1986, which provided amnesty to large numbers of illegal aliens living in the United States. Immigration reform has dramatically increased the Hispanic population in the United States, resulting in the enrollment of more Hispanics in the doctoral programs than in the past. Hispanics, however, still receive a very small proportion of the total number of doctorates granted in the United States.

In 1979 and 1983, Hispanics earned only about 3 percent of the total doctorates. Even though their numbers went up appreciably in 1991 and then again in 1995, they remained below 4.0 percent (table 32).[32] From 1979 to 1991 and from 1991 to 1995, the Hispanic share of doctorates did increase, but it did not reflect their population increase in the United States since the 1980 census. The number of doctorates earned by Hispanic males decreased in number as well as proportion from 1979 to 1983 and then increased in 1991 and 1995, more in number than proportion. Hispanic females made gains in both respects. The number of doctorates earned by Hispanic females more than doubled from 1979 to 1991 and nearly tripled from 1979 to 1995 (table 32). Their share of total doctorates doubled from 1979 to 1991 and again increased in 1995.

Like blacks, Hispanics stay away from the sciences and engineering and specialize in education, the social sciences, and the humanities (table 36). Although doctorates for Hispanics in the physical and life sciences and in engineering have shown a rising trend over the years in this study, in 1991 and 1995 such degrees in education, humanities, and the social sciences still amounted to about 60 percent of the doctorates earned by Hispanics. Doctorates earned by Hispanics in professional studies followed the pattern of degrees in the sciences and engineering.

The underrepresentation of Hispanics in doctorates, particularly in the sciences and engineering, is due to the same handicaps that blacks experience in pursuing this degree – the effects of historic discrimination, inadequate financial resources, poor preparation for college, and the diminishing returns in pay and status in employment for Ph.D.'s. There are more blacks with doctorates than Hispanics. This gap, however, has narrowed considerably since 1979. Since the Hispanic population is growing much faster than the black population, Hispanics are likely to surpass blacks in the number and proportion of doctorates earned in the near future.[33]

In faculty and administrative positions in higher education, there are far fewer Hispanics than blacks. Both groups made gains in securing such jobs in the 1979–91 period; black gains, however, were substantially greater than those of Hispanics. In 1991, when Hispanics earned 3.5 percent of doctorates compared to 3.9 percent for blacks, they held only 2.2 percent of faculty positions and 2.6 percent of administrative positions (tables 32 and 33). By comparison, in that same year, blacks held more than twice as many faculty positions and more than three times as many administrative positions as those held by Hispanics (table 33). If we compare black and Hispanic doctorates and new faculty hires, it is apparent that blacks made far more impressive gains from 1983 to 1991 than Hispanics (tables 32 and 34). One advantage enjoyed by blacks over Hispanics and other minorities is the existence of historically black colleges. Furthermore, the civil rights movement, which helped uplift blacks and bring more of them into higher education, was primarily a black movement. Also, affirmative action was first targeted at blacks rather than any other group. It clearly has benefited blacks more than other minorities. Another explanation for the relative success of blacks in securing employment in higher education is simply their numbers and white guilt dating back to the slavery era. Blacks are the largest minority so far, and they were treated more shabbily than other minorities. It makes sense to many in power positions in government and academia to give a greater consideration to blacks in employment than to other minorities.

ASIANS

Although Asians faced discrimination in the past and even today have to contend with an unwritten enrollment quota system in some of the major universities in the country and a glass ceiling in the corporate world and several other areas, they have overcome many of these difficulties and have excelled in higher education, including doctoral programs. Indeed, in a pattern strikingly different from any other group, Asians increased their share of total doctorates from 8.3 percent in 1979 to 20.1 percent in 1991 and to 23.3 percent in 1995, thanks in part to the doubling of the Asian population in the United States in the 1980–90 period and the influx of Asian foreign students into American universities. Another different feature of Asians who earned doctorates that distinguishes them from other minorities as well as whites is the impressive increase in both female and male doctorates. The number of Asian females who earned doctorates, however, did increase by a higher margin than for Asian males. While Asian males earned 6.9 percent of the total number of doctorates awarded in 1979 and 17.1 percent in 1995, corresponding percentages for Asian females were 1.4 percent in 1979 and 6.2 percent in 1995 (table 32). A unique feature of doctorates awarded to Asians is their concentration in the sciences and engineering (table 37). Of the doctorates awarded to Asian citizens and permanent residents, over two-thirds were in the physical sciences, engineering, and life sciences in 1979, 1983, and 1991, and over three-fourths were in those fields in 1995. These proportions are much higher than the corresponding proportions for other groups, including whites (tables 35, 36, 37, 38, 40). Contrary to the educational and career interests of other minorities, Asians showed little interest in the field of education, receiving less than 2.0 percent of doctorates in 1979 and 1983 and 3.0 percent or less in 1991 and 1995 (table 37). Their interest in the social sciences and humanities, despite an increase over the years, also remained low. Of the nonscientific fields, the Asian share of doctorates remained most visible in professional/other fields.

The surge in Asian doctorates, particularly in the sciences and engineering, is due more to the influx of foreign students from Asia, especially China, Taiwan, Korea, and India, than to the increase in the Asian population in the United States. Asian foreign students earned 57.8 percent of the doctorates awarded to all Asian students in the American universities in 1979 (table 39). This percentage rose to 66.7 in 1983, accelerated to 80.2 in 1991, and then dropped to 55.7 in 1995. From 1991 to 1995, doctorates awarded to Asians who were U.S. citizens or permanent residents increased from 1,491 to 4,300, while the degrees for Asian foreign students decreased from 6,031 to 5,396. The job market of the early 1990s had perhaps convinced many American-born and permanent resident Asians to pursue graduate studies in the sciences or engineering. It is also likely that the children of the Asian immigrants of the 1960s, many of whom were scientists or engineers, were encouraged by their home environments to pursue fields chosen by their parents.

The United States continues to absorb a large number of scientists and engineers emigrating from Asia. A National Science Foundation (NSF) report pointed out that in the United States, "Asian scientists and engineers are over-whelmingly foreign-born. Foreign-born scientists and engineers constitute 81 percent of the Asian S & E [science and engineering] labor force in 1990 and 91 percent of the U.S.-educated Asian doctoral S & E labor force in 1991."[34]

Another NSF study found that "immigrants from the Far East constitute a large and growing proportion of all S & E immigration. In 1991, 44.7 percent of all scientists and engineers admitted were from the Far East, and this percentage rose to 55.3 percent in 1992." Asians are very visible and indeed overrepresented in the U.S. science and engineering labor force. The NSF reported their percentage of such labor force at 6.2 in 1990. Equally telling is the statistic that "in 1991, Asians constituted 10.2 percent of the doctoral S & E labor force."[35]

The share of doctorates earned by Hispanic foreign students, in contrast to Asian students, steadily fell from 41.1 percent in 1979 to 31.1 percent in 1995 (table 39). Although Hispanic citizens and permanent residents increased their number as well as proportion of doctorates, including those in science and engineering, they remained far behind Asians (tables 36, 37, and 39). The same is true of blacks and Native Americans.

In educational opportunities and home environment, Asians have been fortunate and are at a level equal to or higher than that for whites. The other three minorities have a long way to go before they catch up with Asians and whites. Commenting on the Asian-black contrast in "the academic record, credentials [including doctorate], and employment," Harold Orlans writes: "Many Asians received their early education in nations where schools provide academic preparation, not detention, entertainment, or a battlefield where teachers and students fight for attention and control. . . . Both foreign and American-born Asians come from intact families, study earnestly, and are not mocked or harassed for doing so. . . . Many black students suffer the ills of distressed neighborhoods, turbulent schools, and broken homes."[36]

Different home and societal environments for the race/ethnic groups have shaped their attitudes toward education in general and particular fields of education. Such differences explain higher numbers of blacks and Hispanics in the fields of education, the humanities, and the social sciences than in the sciences and engineering. These two groups view the sciences and engineering differently from the way Asians and whites do. Blacks and Hispanics do not consider the benefits of scientific research as favorably, for example, as do Asians and whites. This is true not only of less educated blacks and Hispanics but also of those with college educations.[37]

Doctorates have provided Asians access to faculty positions. As a result, by 1991, there were almost as many Asian faculty members on American campuses as blacks. However, although more Asians than blacks were hired in 1983, the reverse was the pattern in 1991 (table 34). NCES 1995 data place blacks and Asians at nearly the same percentages in both categories (total faculty and new hires).[38] Moreover, the Asian percentage of total faculty positions and of the new hires remained well below their share of doctorates, so discrimination against them cannot be ruled out.[39] Since a large proportion of the Asian Ph.D.'s were in the sciences and engineering, many of these students were perhaps able to get employment in industry. In addition, although a majority of the Asian foreign students with U.S. doctorates stay on in the United States, many do go back to their native countries. While discrimination against Asians in faculty hiring may be debatable, that does not seem to be the case with administrative positions. Despite their singular record in earning doctorates, Asians remain severely underrepresented in academic administration (table 33). Asians possibly continue to face discrimination and a glass ceiling in academic administration.

NATIVE AMERICANS

Native Americas are the least visible minority in doctoral programs. They were the last minority to enter higher education. "During the nineteenth century," writes Meyer Weinberg, "Indians only rarely enrolled in colleges." Even when colleges claimed to be interested in educating Native Americans, the results were disappointing. Dartmouth College's charter, for example, included "among its purposes the education and Christianizing of Indians, Utes and others"; however, "during the college's first century, a single Indian was graduated."[40] Later, attention to the education of Native Americans, particularly in the 1960s and 1970s, brought this group into higher education, including graduate programs. Over the years, the number of doctorates earned by Native Americans has increased but still remains a minuscule portion of total American doctorates. Despite progress in the number of Native American doctorates in the periods 1979–91 and 1991–95, they remained a mere 0.4 percent of total doctorates, barely a rise of 0.1 percent since 1979 (table 32). Women's gains were more impressive, even spectacular in terms of percentage increase, but the total number of doctorates earned by them was only 58 in 1991 and 67 in 1995. Since gains by Native American men were substantially less, the gap between doctorates earned by Native males and females narrowed considerably by 1995.

The field of education was the first choice for doctoral programs with Native Americans, as was the case with blacks and Hispanics (tables 35, 36, 40). While very few Native Americans enrolled in doctoral programs in the physical sciences and engineering, their doctorates in the life sciences surpassed those in the humanities, particularly in 1991, and came close to the number of such degrees in the social sciences in 1991 and 1995 (table 40). Native Americans also increasingly earned doctorates in professional/other fields, such as business, communications, and social work. In general, Native Americans suffered many of the same handicaps in pursuing higher education – in particular, doctoral education – that Hispanics and blacks did. In other words, discrimination, economic conditions, and poor preparation for college have made higher education rather inaccessible to them. A declining job market for doctorates and promising employment prospects without earning such a degree perhaps also dissuaded some baccalaureate degree holders from pursuing doctoral education.

Despite an increase in the number of doctorates they earned, Native Americans remained almost rare in academia in faculty and administrative ranks (table 33). Their share of faculty positions was 0.3 percent in all three years of our study, 0.2 percent for men and 0.1 percent for women. The same pattern was evident in 1983 among the new faculty hires; however, by 1991 Native American women surpassed men in landing positions (table 34). The number of Native American women administrators did increase in 1991, but that of men first increased in 1983 and then in 1991 returned to their 1979 level. Overall, in 1991 as well as in 1983, Native Americans held only 0.4 percent of administrative positions, an increase from 0.3 percent in 1979.

SUPPLY AND DEMAND

When Theodore Caplow and Reece McGee published their now classic study of the academic marketplace in 1958, academia was almost exclusively controlled by white men.[41] Not only did white males receive most of the doctorates (female doctorates accounted for approximately 10 percent of the total in the 1950s), but they also kept a tight rein over hiring. Personal contacts were the primary credentials for getting academic jobs, particularly in research universities. Professors in research universities have not forsaken the practice of hiring Ph.D. students or graduates largely on the basis of recommendations by their friends, and the white male grip over faculty and administrative positions, especially in the higher echelons, remains very firm. However, affirmative action, pressure by women and minorities, and the growing number of female and minority students on campuses have compelled white male administrators and professors to broaden the pools of applicants for positions, which now must be advertised, and to consider women and minorities for faculty and administrative ranks.

By the time the study by Neil Smelser and Robin Content appeared in 1980, bureaucratic rules of affirmative action were in place and those responsible for hiring had no choice but to consider, or at any rate give the appearance of considering, minorities and women for the advertised positions. However, Smelser and Content were much more concerned with the overall dynamics of the academic market, including bureaucratic procedures imposed by changing conditions in academia in general and by affirmative action in particular, budgetary constraints, and the growth of political constituencies on campuses than with the hiring of women and minorities.[42] A study of the academic profession by Howard R. Bowen and Jack H. Schuster, published six years later, provided a comprehensive and empirical analysis of supply and demand, based on the assumption that academia was in serious difficulties, in part because fewer of the best and the brightest were opting for teaching careers. This study analyzed 532 interviews with administrators, department chairs, and faculty members from thirty-eight campuses and considered such variables as the number of Ph.D. degrees awarded, faculty workload, salaries, work environment, and faculty attrition. Bowen and Schuster gave more attention to minorities and women than most previous studies of the academic market; their primary concern, however, was the health and future of the professoriate.[43] Another study, published in 1989, focused on the supply and demand of faculty positions projected to 2012 in various fields of the arts and sciences without giving special attention to women and minorities.[44] A study of the academic market, published in 1988, considered women and minorities, without making them its primary concern.[45]

Studies forecast better job prospects for women in higher education than for minorities, largely because women will, before long, achieve near parity with men in the number of doctorates awarded; minorities, however – blacks, Hispanics, and Native Americans, but not Asians – will continue to be underrepresented in the granting of such degrees in the foreseeable future.[46] A vexing issue on many campuses has been an inadequate supply of black and Hispanic doctoral students, especially in certain fields, who can be hired to meet the demands placed on academic departments by administrators, affirmative action offices, and minority students. Those responsible for hiring faculty members generally complain that notwithstanding their intentions and efforts, qualified black or Hispanic candidates are not available. A study by Valora Washington and William Harvey disputed such claims of the seemingly well-meaning professors and administrators: "The availability pool of African-Americans and Hispanics who hold [a] doctorate is definitely a problem: There are too few of these individuals and they are not evenly distributed across the range of academic fields. But, even when the availability pool was somewhat larger and faculty hiring was on the increase, African-American and Hispanic academicians did not receive faculty positions in predominantly white institutions in proportion to their representation in the total pool of Ph.D.s."[47]

Supply-Demand Projections

The most extensive projections on supply and demand of faculty in arts and sciences, but not in other fields, were prepared by William G. Bowen and Julie Ann Sosa. Bowen and Sosa considered factors such as age distributions of faculty and their exit probabilities, population trends, enrollment projections, student/faculty ratios, and the supply of new doctorates, and then constructed four models for projecting net faculty positions. They next prepared supply and demand projections by field of study for five-year periods starting in 1987 and ending in 2012. Based on such projections, they predicted shortfalls in supply in the humanities, the social sciences, mathematics, and the physical sciences, but not in the biological sciences and psychology, as the twentieth century approached its end. Even by the end of the period 2007 to 2012, the supply-demand ratio for these fields would not be in balance and would reflect more positions than doctorates.[48] Shortages of doctorates in engineering (and the physical sciences) in relation to demand have also been predicted, and even in education a shortage of doctorates is suggested.[49]

The most extensive estimates of minority doctorates by the year 2000 were prepared by Donald Deskins with the NRC data. Deskins notes:

The white share of all Ph.D.s awarded is projected to decline from 60.1 percent in 1990 to 51.8 percent in 2000. . . . Among the minority groups, only Asians and Hispanics are projected to increase their percentage of Ph.D.s, Asians increasing from 1.7 percent in 1990 to 2.2 percent by the end of the century, offsetting the black percentage decline. During the period, the black percentage is forecast to move downward, from 2.3 to 1.9 percent. Although the Native American percentage of degrees acquired during the entire period is forecast to remain below 1 percent, they will still decline over time.[50]

Blacks, according to this estimate, will experience a decline in doctorates in the physical sciences, the humanities, and education and gains in other fields. Their overall decline will be 13.8 percent. Asians and Hispanics, on the other hand, will earn more doctorates in all fields. Native Americans will also move forward in the number of such degrees in every field; however, their gains will be small enough compared to other minorities that their share of the total will decline.[51]

In order to make up for anticipated shortfalls in the number of doctorates,

Deskins suggested "significant increases in current graduate enrollment." Since whites' share of doctorates will also decline, he concluded that "perhaps much of the demand will be met by nonresidents, who are rapidly increasing their share of doctorates, expected to reach 31.7 percent by the year 2000."[52]

Most people with Ph.D.'s who were looking for employment in the early or mid-1990s perhaps felt far less optimistic about their future prospects than the above forecasts would seem to suggest. If these predictions do turn out to be true, U.S. higher education institutions, industry, and the economy in general would indeed be in serious trouble by the dawn of the twenty-first century. If the high growth rates of Asian economies return and the quality of life in the United States does not improve, many of those who come to the United States to earn Ph.D.'s may go back to their native countries. In the early 1990s, as many as two hundred thousand foreign-born people, most of them highly qualified Asians from countries like India, Taiwan, and South Korea and many of them with American Ph.D.'s, were annually leaving the United States for better and more secure employment prospects in their original countries.[53] Considering that development, combined with the historic discrimination faced by minorities in the United States, it is all the more important that serious efforts be made to attract the best and the brightest to doctoral programs.

8

The Political and Socioeconomic Determinants of Higher Education Employment

Why do the patterns that we have found in higher education employment in the American states exist? We next attempt to discover if various macrolevel political and socioeconomic factors have had an influence on the employment of minorities and women in faculty and administrative positions, as access to these higher-status and higher-paying positions reveals to a greater degree the effectiveness of affirmative action programs than access to lower-level positions. Our model is based on scholarly efforts to examine the political and socioeconomic determinants of social policies at the state level. Although patronage employment has had a long history in government employment, we are not arguing that a patronage connection exists in higher education employment. Instead, based on the theory of representative bureaucracy, we expect that specific state political factors will create a more conducive environment for the employment of minorities and women in public higher education institutions rather than private institutions. We also seek to uncover which variables are associated with greater minority and female employment in some states than others.

POLITICAL AND SOCIOECONOMIC FACTORS

Although an extensive literature exists on minority and female employment in the public sector at the municipal level, there have been few studies at the state level.[1] These studies have focused on the conditions under which minorities and women have increased their share of public employment primarily in terms of their representativeness on city councils and in mayoral positions. The results of such studies, however, have been mixed. Although some research has shown that minorities on city councils can influence black and Hispanic employment, other works have pointed out a stronger association with minority or female mayors.[2] Research has also focused on the significance of government structure, the type of electoral system, racial divisions, and unionism.[3] In addition, competition between minorities and women has been examined in a number of municipal employment studies.[4] For example, in one study a negative relationship was found between white female municipal employment and the percentage of blacks and Hispanics in the population.[5] In another study, Hispanics did poorly in municipal positions in cities with large numbers of blacks.[6] As noted in chapter 4, Lee Sigelman found that region was a significant factor: white women were more likely to be employed in state and local employment in the South and other more traditional areas in place of minorities.[7] J. Edward Kellough also found that region of the country – in this case, the Southwest, where the Hispanic population was the largest – was associated with Hispanic employment in federal positions.[8] Related to this regional effect, numerous studies at the municipal level have shown that blacks and Hispanics are more likely to be employed in municipal positions where their numbers are the greatest.[9]

Although there have been only a few studies on affirmative action at the state level, there is a vast scholarly literature on the determinants of various social policies within the American states. V. O. Key Jr. argued that party politics and policies supporting the less well-off were interrelated. Thus, he stated that "in the two-party states the anxiety over the next election pushes political leaders into serving the interests of the have-less elements of society."[10] Research by Richard E. Dawson and James A. Robinson, however, showed that interparty competition was not independent of socioeconomic factors in the adoption of various social policies.[11] Other scholars also found that socioeconomic factors rather than party competitiveness were the determining forces in shaping policies in the American states.[12] Nevertheless, some scholarly research has shown that party competitiveness is an independent factor.[13] However, Sung-Don Hwang and Virginia Gray note that the view that party competition has little independent effect on policymaking in the American states is generally accepted.[14] Given that these studies have shown that such socioeconomic variables as wealth, industrialization, and urbanization have had a major impact on state policies, we examine these factors in relationship to minority and female faculty employment in higher education in the American states. Beginning with Edward T. Jennings Jr., new attempts were made to qualify and refine this literature.[15] Jennings's argument that it was necessary to show that party distinctions did exist and that one party did indeed represent the less well-off generated new research in the area.[16] In terms of political ideology, Democrats are usually considered more liberal and, therefore, more likely to support programs that assist the poor.[17] Research on Democratic party control in the states has shown mixed results; for example, some studies showed a relationship with greater welfare spending, but there were major exceptions as well.[18]

Another way to examine such differences among the states is through state political culture. Daniel J. Elazar has developed a model of state political culture in which migration and settlement patterns have shaped three distinct political cultures (although hybrid variations may also be present).[19] In the moralistic political subculture, the emphasis is on good government and communal efforts; in the individualistic subculture, the focus is on the marketplace and the individual; and in the traditionalistic subculture, there is tension between the values of the marketplace and those of paternalism, elitism, and the status quo. Research on the application of this model to state politics and various policy issues in the American states has produced uneven results.[20] In our own research using EEOC data for black male and female faculty members in 1983, we found that a variable for states with Elazar's traditionalistic subculture was not significant; however, using Ira Sharkansky's adoption of Elazar's model, we did find that region (the southern states plus the border states) was significant along with black voting strength.[21] We concluded that while region was a better measure than state political culture, region represented a measure of the distribution of blacks in that area of the country. Political factors with this set of variables were weak, as we did not find an association between Democratic-controlled legislatures and black male and female faculty employment.

One major problem with using Democratic party control as an indicator of party liberalism is that although Democrats dominated the southern states for generations, as Jeff Stonecash notes, they tended to be politically conservative rather than liberal.[22] An alternative method is to use political ideology rather than Democratic party control. Gerald C. Wright, Robert S. Erikson, and John P. McIver have developed a measure of state political ideology based on public opinion surveys that can be used to evaluate attitudes toward various policy issues within the American states.[23] They argue that although the past literature has shown that socioeconomic factors rather than political ones are more likely to explain state public policies, little has been done to examine the issue of public opinion at the state level.[24] Using political ideology as a surrogate for public opinion, they find that liberal states are more liberal and conservative states are more conservative when making public policies. However, they also find that parties in control of state legislatures respond not just to their ideological positions but also to public opinion when making these decisions. This model is not without criticism. Thomas M. Holbrook-Provow and Steven C.

Poe, examining a number of possible measures of state political ideology, questioned their measure in terms of representative sampling.[25] Wright and his colleagues, however, did take steps to ensure that their measure was both reliable and valid.[26] Given that a number of studies have examined the role of Democratic governors and legislatures, in addition to political ideology, we also include these variables in our statistical model to discover their association with affirmative action outcomes for faculty and administrative employment. Previously we examined the association of black legislators and female legislators with black and female faculty employment.[27] Our findings indicated that the number of black legislators was significant for black faculty employment in public higher education, but neither the number of female legislators nor any of the other political and socioeconomic variables were significant for female employment. Since comparable data were not available for other minority groups, in part because of the extremely small number of other minority legislators, we were unable to examine the variable of legislators' race/ethnicity in this larger study. Instead, we developed a measure of each minority group's share of a state's population.

METHODS

First, we examine the relationship between the representation ratios and the independent variables for 1991. We expect to find a greater association between the political variables and public higher education institutions than private schools, as public colleges and universities, we believe, would be more responsive to state efforts to promote a representative bureaucracy. Second, we consider the association between the independent variables (which are lagged to account for the time factor) and the 1991 participation rates. We examine both these measures (ratios and rates), for the numbers provide two different interpretations, although often reinforcing ones, about affirmative action. As noted earlier, the representation ratios do provide higher numbers in states with lower percentages of minorities; on the other hand, to simply use participation rates does not give us a complete picture of how minorities and women are doing in relationship to white males.

Some data problems, however, reduced the number of states we were able to use in our model since complete data were not available for the states of Alaska, Hawaii, Maryland, New Mexico, Utah, Washington, and Wyoming. We also deleted Nebraska due to its unicameral legislature and Nevada for reasons mentioned below, giving us a total of forty-one states.

Our first independent variable is a measure of political ideology. We use Erikson, Wright, and McIver's measure of unweighted scores for liberal political ideology. However, the authors found problems with their measure of state ideology for the state of Nevada, so we deleted this state from our study as they had done.[28] We expect a positive association between employment opportunities for minorities and women and liberal political ideology.

In order to measure the impact of Democratic governors and legislatures, we developed two measures of Democratic party control. For governors for the year 1988, we use a dummy variable of 1 for Democratic governors and a 0 for Republican governors.[29] For Democratic-controlled legislatures, using data for those holding office as of the beginning of 1989, we combined the number of Democrats in the lower and upper houses and divided it by the total number of seats.[30] We expect a positive relationship between these two variables and minority and female employment.

Next, we consider the impact of each minority group's percentage of the population within a state. Given that the representation ratios have this percentage in the denominator for each group, we need to construct dummy variables to serve as surrogates for population percentages. Data from the 1990 census for the percentages of blacks, Hispanics, Asians, and Native Americans within each state are used; however, we assign a 1 to a state whose population of a group is equal to or exceeds the percentage of the national population for that group or a 0 if it does not.[31] In addition, we also consider the association of the percentage of whites in a state's population with white male and female employment by constructing a similar dummy variable. For consistency, we use the same measure when we examine the participation rates. We expect a positive association between this variable and faculty and administrative positions.

Finally, we include the socioeconomic variables of wealth, industrialization, and urbanization.[32] Given that one set of our dependent variables (representation ratios) is based on a proportion of each state's population and that the usual measure of wealth is per capita income by state, we use an alternative method of measuring wealth. Instead of per capita income, we use median income for each state for 1989 divided by the national median income.[33] Industrialization is measured as the number of employees in nonfarm establishments as a percentage of the total civilian labor force in 1989. Urbanization is the percentage of the population living in metropolitan areas for the year 1988 for each state. We expect a positive association between these variables and opportunities for minorities and women.

To avoid problems with multicollinearity, a regression analysis for each independent variable with the other variables was done to discover if any of the coefficients of determination were close to 1, as suggested by Michael S. Lewis-Beck.[34] None of the coefficients were found to be close to 1.

For public higher education, the results for the black representation ratios (tables 41 and 42) show that the political ideology variable is positive and statistically significant. However, the variables for Democratic governors and Democratic-controlled legislatures (the latter carries a negative sign for black males and females) are not significant, thereby raising questions about the direct influence of liberal ideology on black faculty representation. There is also an association for black male and female representation and less urbanized states. The findings for the participation rates (tables 43 and 44) demonstrate a positive association for black male and female participation and the black population variable, suggesting the southern states and the border states where blacks tend to reside in greater numbers. Further examination of the results for the participation rates shows that the variable of Democratic-controlled legislatures is statistically significant and positive for black males and females; nevertheless, although the political ideology variable is to some extent associated with black female rates, it carries a negative sign for males and females, suggesting that it is region rather than politics that is the critical factor in that the southern states and that the border states tend to be ideologically more conservative while maintaining Democratic-controlled legislatures. While these results support our earlier conclusion in chapter 3 that blacks tend to do well in the southern states and the border states, it is fair to note that the variable of Democratic-controlled legislatures is not just a measure of southern Democratic control and that some states may be pursuing active affirmative action policies motivated by liberal ideology.

For white female representation, there is an association with states that have smaller numbers of whites and states that have Democratic-controlled legislatures. The political ideology variable is not significant but carries a negative sign, suggesting a relationship with ideologically more conservative states. Such a finding is consistent with our conclusion in chapter 4 that white females do better in the southern states and the border states, in which there are greater numbers of blacks and which tend to be ideologically conservative while maintaining Democratic-controlled legislatures. This is supported by the results for the participation rates, as the political ideology variable is not statistically significant and carries a negative sign, and the variable of Democratic-controlled legislatures is statistically significant and positive. Given these results and the ones for blacks, we consider the variable of Democratic-controlled legislatures with a positive sign an indicator of region – the South along with the border states, rather than liberal Democratic legislative support – unless we also find that the political ideology variable is both statistically significant and positive.

For white males, we find an association with the representation ratios for states with fewer whites, suggesting better representation in the southern states and the border states where there are larger numbers of blacks. There is some evidence that more urbanized states also provided better representation. The findings for the participation rates show an association with states that have larger white populations, which tend to be outside the South. The negative sign of the variable of Democratic-controlled legislatures, which is statistically significant, also suggests states outside this region. It is apparent that white males maintain strong representation ratios in the southern states and the border states and high participation rates outside this region, which in great part has been due to their past control over faculty positions.

Examining the representation ratios for Hispanic males, we find that neither the Hispanic population variable nor the political variables are significant. There is some evidence showing that Hispanic females and males are better represented in less wealthy states, although Hispanic females also do well in more industrialized states. Recent global economic transformations that have led to downsizing and industrial flight may explain why the median income variable carries a negative sign and the industrialization variable is positive, as these states have become poorer.[35] Greater participation for Hispanic males and females is associated with states where Hispanics are found in larger numbers. None of the political variables are significant. As some studies have shown that Hispanics are in competition with blacks for public sector positions, we ran a second regression model for Hispanic males and Hispanic females using the black population variable in place of the Hispanic population variable.[36] The results did show a negative relationship for Hispanic males, but they were not statistically significant; the relationship for Hispanic females and the black population variable was positive but not significant. Thus for faculty positions there does not seem to be strong evidence that Hispanics do poorly due to the presence of a large black population.

Asian male representation is associated with less wealthy states, while Asian female representation to some extent is related to less urbanized states. The results for the participation rates show that Asian male participation and to a lesser extent Asian female participation are associated with more urbanized states. Although Asian female participation is associated with states with larger numbers of Asians, this variable is not relevant for males. These findings suggest that other factors such as education should be considered in assessing Asian faculty outcomes.

To some extent there is a positive relationship for Native American male and female representation and political ideology. However, for the participation rates, this variable is not significant and carries a negative sign for Native American males and females. Since neither of the other two political variables is statistically significant for the ratios or the rates, these findings suggest that greater Native American representation is to be found in a more liberal environment, while they raise questions about the direct political forces at play to produce these results. Native American male representation is also associated with states with fewer Native Americans and to some extent less wealthy states, but no other relationships are discovered for Native American females. For Native American male and female participation, the findings demonstrate a relationship with states with larger numbers of Native Americans and states that are less industrialized. Just as region is a significant indicator for blacks and white women, it also appears that this is the case for Native Americans despite the findings for political ideology.

Overall, the population variable for each group appears to be the strongest indicator associated with faculty positions in public higher education. Although it carries little significance for the representation ratios except for white males, white females, and Native American males, it is very relevant for the participation rates except for white females and Asian males. The dominance of the white population throughout the states has assisted white males, but it apparently has no relevance for white female participation, which may be related to past discriminatory practices and other individual factors. As for the participation of Asian males, education is most likely the major indicator for their employment outcomes; in addition, the weakness of the results for the representation ratios also suggests the role of other factors.

As for our political factors, we found little evidence to suggest that ideology, Democratic governorship, and Democratic-controlled legislatures had an association with faculty outcomes. These findings suggest that although public faculty employment decisions are insulated from undue political pressures, there is little opportunity to influence positive affirmative action outcomes for minorities and women.

Moving to the data for private higher education faculty (tables 45 and 46), we find that none of the variables are significant for the representation ratios for blacks. For the participation rates (tables 47 and 48), the black population variable and the Democratic-controlled legislatures variable are statistically significant and positive for black males and females. The political ideology variable, although not significant, is negative. Such findings demonstrate that region is a crucial factor for black faculty opportunities in private colleges and universities.

White female representation is to some extent associated with states where there are fewer whites, such as those in the southern states and the border states. The results for the participation rates show that less urbanized states are an important indicator, while states with greater numbers of whites are not. None of the political variables are significant for either the ratios or the rates, but since nearly all carry negative signs, there is some evidence suggesting that region should be considered. These results reinforce our conclusion in chapter 4 that white women in private higher education are to be found throughout the United States, although some border states and southern states do offer greater opportunities than other states. For white males, the only statistically significant variables that also carry positive signs are the urbanization variable for the representation ratios and the white population variable for the participation rates, which suggest that past dominance of faculty positions is the key factor for explaining their very strong employment record.

For Hispanic male representation, the strongest relationships are found with states that are less wealthy, ones that are more industrialized, and to a smaller degree states that have fewer Hispanics. Only industrialization is a factor for Hispanic female representation. There is some weak evidence suggesting an association for Hispanic male representation and participation with states with less Democratic-controlled legislatures. The results do show that Hispanic male participation rates are strongly associated with states where there are greater numbers of Hispanics and to lesser degrees with more urbanized states and less wealthy ones. Hispanic female participation is also strongly associated with states with greater numbers of Hispanics, demonstrating for Hispanics the importance of this factor for faculty employment in private higher education.

Asian male and female representation is not associated with the Asian share of a state's population. There is an association for Asian male representation with less wealthy states and to a lesser extent with more industrialized states for Asian males and females. The results for Asian males also show that the variable of Democratic-controlled legislatures is significant and positive and the political ideology variable, although not significant, is positive, suggesting that a weak relationship exists between Asian male representation and states with liberal Democratic-controlled legislatures. However, for the participation rates, while the variable of Democratic-controlled legislatures is significant and positive, the political ideology variable is not significant and has a negative sign, providing little clear support for an association between Asian male faculty outcomes and states with liberal Democratic-controlled legislatures. There is a weak relationship between the Asian male participation rates and states where there are greater numbers of Asians, but this is not the case for Asian female participation, as none of the variables are found to be significant. It is more likely for Asians that the determinants of their progress are such microlevel factors as education.

For Native American males and females, none of the variables are statistically significant for the representation ratios. For the participation rates, there is some evidence showing that Native American males have better participation in more liberal states and in states where there are greater numbers of Native Americans. However, because the variable of Democratic-controlled legislatures has a positive sign and the Democratic governorship variable has a negative sign and because neither is significant, there is some question about how such liberalism has a direct relationship with greater faculty employment opportunities. Native American female participation rates are associated with less industrialized states only. The small number of Native American doctorates is no doubt a contributing factor to such findings and demonstrates the need to consider a variety of educational and social obstacles faced by Native Americans.

Overall for faculty positions in private colleges and universities, a group's share of a state's population continues to be the most consistent indicator; however, it is less relevant for private higher education employment than was the case for employment in public higher education. For the representation ratios for private higher education, the share of a state's population was significant only for white females and Hispanic males, for whom the results were negative and marginal. For the participation rates, the share of population was significant to varying degrees for all the male groups but only for black females and Hispanic females. It appears that while the population results for black female and Hispanic female participation may be the result of greater concentrations of blacks and Hispanics in some states, other factors such as education may be related to the results for Asian female and Native American female rates. As for white females, once again we discovered that the dominance of the white population was not associated with white female participation, but there was an association with the representation ratios, suggesting that more microlevel factors need to be considered.

We also completed a statistical analysis of administrative positions, which provided similar but weak evidence. The population variable continued to be the most important of the variables for examining female and minority employment in administrative positions. Nevertheless, we did find that the population variable was not significant for any of the representation ratios. The political factors continued to be weak, leading us to again argue that of our variables, population rather than political factors plays the primary role in shaping minority and female administrative employment outcomes in higher education.

Our approach has been to examine the macrolevel factors that might show that some states have an environment more conducive to greater faculty and administrative employment for minorities and women than other states. However, such decisions as those made by deans, department chairs, and search committees in the hiring process and by individual candidates about residence, family, and salaries are all significant for explaining faculty and administrative employment outcomes. Prejudice also cannot be ruled out. Discussions with personnel directors and affirmative action officers at higher education institutions, public and private, might provide some alternative avenues for further research. However, the problem of gaining access to individual college and university records, due to privacy restrictions, limits the extent to which such data can be uncovered, and the data, if available, would not be readily applicable to studies using EEOC aggregate data at the state level.

Our statistical models provide little evidence to suggest a relationship between the political factors and greater employment of minorities and white women in faculty and administrative positions that carry higher status and pay in higher education. Instead, a group's population distribution within each state tends to indicate why progress may be occurring to a greater degree in some states rather than others. This evidence does not support the claims of those who believe that government has too much power; nor does it reassure those who look to government as a means to achieve equality. Although we have not examined the impact of the federal government on hiring, it does seem that state political factors carry little weight in shaping positive affirmative action outcomes in higher education employment.

Believing that state governments would be more likely to respond to calls for a representative bureaucracy, we hypothesized that better employment opportunities for minorities and women would be discovered in public higher education rather than private higher education. Our examination of the participation rates and representation ratios has provided considerable evidence to support this position. However, our analysis of such political factors as party of the governor, Democratic-controlled legislatures, and state political ideology found that these factors were not relevant for explaining why greater opportunities exist for minorities and women in public higher education rather than private higher education. Why do public higher education institutions have a better track record for the implementation of affirmative action? One possible explanation comes from Gregory B. Lewis's finding that minorities and women did better in federal white-collar employment under President Reagan, who opposed affirmative action efforts, than under President Carter, who supported them.[37] Lewis suggests that given the vast number of individual personnel decisions made in the federal government, any significant policy change affecting the composition of federal employment should take a considerable amount of time. He also considers bureaucratic resistance as a factor, for a number of top administrators continued to support affirmative action. James N. Baron, Brian S. Mittman, and Andrew E. Newman suggest that the integration of women into the California civil service is related to the degree to which past agency heads have institutionalized affirmative action through bureaucratic routine so that leadership changes had little effect.[38] Perhaps public higher education institutions are more bureaucratic, which in turn means that rules and guidelines set for affirmative action implementation produce better results. As noted in chapter 3, the growth of administrative positions in higher education employment for the period 1983–91 was much larger than that for faculty positions. This is especially the case for public higher education institutions, which experienced a greater growth in administrative positions than private higher education institutions. The increased focus on administration, which brings about further bureaucratization, may in turn enhance the implementation of affirmative action. This possibility opens up a new avenue for further research, as a comparative study of individual college and university rules and guidelines for affirmative action implementation might explain why public higher education is more likely to provide better employment opportunities to minorities and women than private higher education.

9
Summary and Conclusions

In this book, we have examined the problem of discrimination and its impact on higher education employment. Early racial attitudes by such notables as Thomas Jefferson demonstrate that even those who might have favored the abolition of slavery were not willing to grant full rights or intellectual status to blacks. These attitudes and the resulting practices spilled over into white relations with Hispanics, Asians, and Native Americans. Clearly throughout American history efforts were made to discourage equal employment opportunities for minorities. In a different manner, social attitudes toward women also limited their access to employment and raised questions about their intelligence and abilities to perform certain types of work. The past history of American values and attitudes toward race, ethnicity, and gender has produced a climate in which equal opportunities for minorities and women have often been severely limited. Efforts since the 1960s to combat these obstacles have led to greater public awareness and public policies such as affirmative action to expand equal employment opportunities for minorities and women within American society in both the public and private sectors. Affirmative action, a product of a tortuous set of executive orders, bureaucratic rules, and often contradictory judicial decisions, has created one of the most controversial policy issues of the times. Although affirmative action has not been an easy policy to implement, it should be understood within the context of the long history of discrimination against blacks, Hispanics, Asians, Native Americans, and women.

Our interest has been to examine the impact of affirmative action on the employment opportunities of minorities and women in higher education. Of course, the changing demographics of America, along with heightened awareness about the need to include larger numbers of minorities and women in employment, pose a major and difficult process of change. This is especially true as employment opportunities for both minorities and whites are increasing at a slow pace and decreasing in some segments of the job market. Thus, a commitment to expand employment serves as an indicator not only to minorities and women but also to white males about the need to be more inclusive of the diverse segments of American society. In turn, such diversity, especially in the area of higher education employment, serves as a means to encourage minority and female students to attend higher education institutions.

FINDINGS: A SUMMARY

Our research shows that as minorities and women have entered higher education employment, white male domination in these positions has eroded. The overall white male faculty participation rates steadily declined during the 1979-91 period, ending at below 60 percent in *all* (public and private) institutions. White male faculty experienced a similar decrease in public and private institutions from 1983 to 1991, although they remained somewhat more numerous at private institutions. Their declining participation rates are reflected in their representation ratios; nevertheless, white males still remained overrepresented in faculty positions. Data on new hires and full professors reinforce this trend. By 1991, less than 50 percent of the newly hired tenure-track faculty were white males – a drop of about 10 percentage points from 1983. White males lost ground to a greater extent in the highest academic rank during the same period, moving from over 80 percent to under 66 percent.

White females were the greatest beneficiaries of faculty employment changes that, to a considerable extent, were a result of the implementation of affirmative action. Despite a drop in the white male representation ratio, the increase in the white female ratio kept white faculty slightly more overrepresented at the beginning of the 1990s than at the end of the 1970s. The data on new hires demonstrate that white women will continue to increase their overall participation rate among the faculty and before long may reach a representation ratio of 1.0. Their gains in the full professor rank were even more impressive than among the new hires or the overall faculty. The shift in the 1980s in this rank was mostly from white males to white females. As a result, white female full professors increased from nearly 10 percent to over 24 percent in public as well as private institutions from 1983 to 1991.

Black progress in faculty positions was relatively minor except in private institutions, which essentially moved closer to public institutions in the 1983–91 period. In 1991, they made up 5 percent or less of the total faculty in public, private, and all institutions and experienced only a small improvement in their representation ratio from 1979 to 1991 and from 1983 to 1991. Data on black new hires and black full professors, however, present a different picture. Blacks constituted about 7 percent of the new hires in 1991, a gain of nearly 2 percent. Black male and female gains were approximately the same.

Black women, however, attained full professor rank at a rate much higher than black men. There were three times as many black female full professors in 1991 as in 1983. Overall, black full professors increased from 2.2 percent in 1983 to 4.3 percent or more in 1991. Although black gains in participation rates among the total faculty do not appear impressive, their record in gaining new positions and promotion to the highest rank is a harbinger of an era of more black faculty in higher education in the future.

Our data show that Hispanics remained virtually as underrepresented in faculty positions in 1991 as in 1979, and that the increase in their participation rate, greater at public than private institutions from 1983 to 1991, also was relatively small; nevertheless, the proportion of Hispanic new hires and full professors bodes well for their progress. Public institutions offered them more faculty positions than did private institutions, and Hispanic women faculty increased at a higher rate than Hispanic men at both types of institutions. By 1991, 2.1 percent of the full professors were Hispanic, more of them at public than private institutions and with women surpassing men in the rate of progress. Despite a nearly 100 percent increase, 2.1 indeed is a very modest number. Based on our findings, we anticipate a steady increase in the overall number of the Hispanic faculty, including full professors, even though they will continue to lag behind blacks in this area.

Asians made progress in their participation rate among the faculty, females at a higher rate than males, and remained more numerous at public than private institutions. They were the only minority group in our study that remained overrepresented for the time span considered. In this respect Asians resemble whites rather than any other minority group. Asian male faculty, like their white counterparts, were overrepresented. Asian female faculty, also like their white counterparts, were not overrepresented but ended up with nearly the same representation ratio as that for white women (0.7) in all institutions in 1991. In that year Asian and white women had similar ratios in public institutions, but white women had a higher ratio in private institutions.

The data on new hires and full professors show that blacks have caught up with Asians in participation rates. While more Asian male faculty were hired than black male faculty in public as well as private institutions in 1983 and 1991, the percentage of newly hired black males increased at a higher rate than that of the Asian males. Besides, black female faculty were hired in larger numbers than Asian female faculty at both types of institutions in the two years. As a result, total hiring of new black faculty in all institutions was lower than new

Asian faculty hiring in 1983 but exceeded it in 1991 by a small margin. In the full professor rank, a somewhat similar trend prevailed, with the result that although blacks did not catch up with Asians, they came close to it and appeared heading toward exceeding the Asian participation rate in the near future.

Of the groups considered in the study, only the participation rate for Native American faculty remained unchanged in all institutions during the time period under study. Native American females gained more faculty positions in public institutions in 1991 than in 1983, but Native American males' share of such positions declined in private institutions in this period, resulting in the same overall rate for all institutions. As discussed in chapter 6, their representation ratio declined in 1991 due to a possible correction in the census count for 1990 as compared to 1980.

The data on Native American new hires and the full professor rank raise little hope for this group except for females. Native American females increased their share of new hires as well as full professor positions in public, but not private, institutions from 1983 to 1991. By 1991, in public institutions, more Native American females than males were hired for tenure-track positions. Although Native American females lagged behind Native American males in the full professor rank, they made progress in public institutions. The Native American male participation rate in these two categories showed some fluctuation but remained the same for all institutions in 1983 and 1991.

In the administrative ranks, the predominance of white males decreased at a faster rate than in faculty positions. Starting with control of nearly two-thirds of the administrative positions in 1979, they declined to a little over half of the total positions in 1991. The decrease in the participation rate of white male administrators was greater at public institutions than private schools from 1983 to 1991, demonstrating once again that public institutions were more committed to implementing affirmative action than private institutions by hiring women and minorities in place of white men. However, white males still remained overrepresented, although their representation ratio did decline.

As in faculty positions, white women gained the most from the decline of white men in administrative positions. They increased their share of such jobs from nearly one-fourth to over one-third from 1979 to 1991. White female administrators were far more numerous in private institutions than public schools in 1983. While they gained even more positions in private institutions by 1991 and still exceeded public institutions in their share of the total administrative positions, the gap in their participation rates in public and private institutions narrowed considerably from 1983 to 1991. In private institutions, white female administrators had attained a representation ratio of nearly 1.0, and if the 1983–91 trend holds, it will not be long before they reach this number in public institutions as well.

Black women also made substantial gains at the cost of white men in administrative positions. In 1979, black females held a negligible proportion of such jobs in all institutions and had a representation ratio of only 0.02. By 1991, their participation rate rose to over 4.0 percent and their representation ratio surpassed 0.7 in these institutions. Black women remained more numerous in private institutions than public schools, and there is little to suggest in our data that this pattern will change.

Black male administrators, on the other hand, remained at about the same participation rate in 1991 as they were in 1979. Their gains in private institutions from 1983 to 1991 were canceled by their losses in public institutions, showing in this case the willingness of private institutions to implement affirmative action by hiring more black men as well as black women in administrative positions. Since the black male participation rate showed little change from 1979 to 1991 and their population in the country increased, their representation ratio experienced a small decline. Black male administrators, however, did retain a respectable ratio of above 0.7 in public, private, and all institutions in 1991. Due to the increase in the number of black women administrators, overall black progress in the 1980s was remarkable. The total black share of administrative positions doubled from 4.3 to 8.7, and their representation ratio also increased by the same margin, from 0.37 to 0.74.

Hispanic females, like white and black females, increased their participation rates substantially in administrative positions. Both public and private institutions hired them in increasing numbers, with the result that they did not fare better to any significant degree at one type of institution over the other. The representation ratio for Hispanic female administrators also increased, virtually doubling by 1991 from 0.13 in 1979. Compared to white and black women, Hispanic women were severely underrepresented in administration, notwithstanding their strides in statistical terms. The data, however, suggest an unmistakable trend toward a higher representation ratio for Hispanic women in administration. It is possible that they will catch up with black, if not white, women in administration in terms of the representation ratio. However, this is not likely to occur before 2010 or even 2020, assuming that their rate of growth in administration for the 1983–91 period continues to improve.

The experience of Hispanic male administrators has been different from that of the white or black administrators. While the representation ratio of white males decreased, and that of black males remained steady, for Hispanic males it increased. They gained more positions at public institutions than private schools, but their rate of growth at both types of institutions remained below that of Hispanic females. The gap between the Hispanic male and female participation rates in administration has been narrowing and is clearly proceeding toward extinction, as has happened in the case of black male and female administrators.

Asian females also moved closer to the Asian male participation rate in administration during the period considered. Their representation ratio, however, declined in both public and private institutions from 1983 to 1991, more so in the public institutions than in private schools. There was little change in this ratio for them from 1979 to 1991. Nevertheless, they were less underrepresented than Hispanic female administrators. The data, however, presage a reversal in their underrepresentation levels. In other words, before long Hispanic women will be better represented than Asian women in administration.

Although the Asian male participation rate in administration increased from 1983 to 1991, more so in private institutions than public ones, and from 1979 to 1991 in all institutions, their representation ratio decreased. The increase in the number of Asian male administrators did not keep up with their increase in the population. If this trend were to continue – and perhaps it will – the representation ratio for Asian males will continue to decline.

Among Native Americans, women made progress in administration, and men, despite some fluctuation in their participation rate, ended up with exactly the same rate in all institutions in 1991 as they had in 1979. Male representation ratios decreased, while those for females increased. Both groups held more positions in public institutions than private schools by 1991. Their representation ratio in all institutions, however, was virtually the same (0.50 and 0.51). Although the combined male and female representation ratio for Native Americans as well as Asians was similar in all institutions in 1991, that may change. Asians will perhaps slip in their representation ratio, but Native Americans may not. On the other hand, Hispanics will likely surpass these groups, though it will take time. Blacks, particularly females, are likely to stay ahead of these three minorities in administrative positions.

Despite the difficulties of comparing 1995 data from the Department of Education's National Center for Education Statistics (NCES) with the earlier data from the Equal Employment Opportunity Commission (EEOC) as discussed in the introduction, the mid-1990s data do reflect the public mood in the 1990s on the issue of affirmative action. Although white male control over faculty and administrative positions further decreased, the gains by minorities and women in these ranks also slowed down. Of course, white males remained the dominant group in both areas, and public opposition to affirmative action may have been helpful to them. White women's progress continued in administrative positions but decelerated in faculty positions, especially full professorships.

Black males and females seem to have lost some ground in the top faculty rank. However, black women, but not black men, continued to increase their share of tenure-track positions, although only to a slight degree. Public institutions remained more favorable to hiring blacks, especially women, than private institutions. It also appears that black men do better in administrative positions in public institutions rather than private schools, while the advantage for black women in private institutions has narrowed.

Hispanics only marginally increased their proportion of the faculty in the 1991–95 period, and their gains occurred primarily in private higher education. Their progress also slowed down in administration, although public universities rather than private institutions were more inclined to hire them. We also discerned a decline in the Hispanic share of newly hired tenure-track faculty positions and the full professor rank. These findings, however, must be viewed in light of the difficulties of comparing the two sets of data.

Asian advance from 1991 to 1995 in both faculty and administration was greater at private institutions rather than public schools, and Asian women made greater progress than Asian men in both employment categories. The underrepresentation of Asians in administration continued. Their gains in newly hired tenure-track faculty positions and the highest academic rank were mixed, in that Asian men lost ground in tenure-track positions, and Asian women experienced a similar trend in the full professor rank. However, Asian men advanced in the full professor rank, and Asian women did the same in the newly hired tenure-track positions.

Native Americans, it appears, made modest gains in the first half of the 1990s, more so in administration than faculty positions. Public institutions remained more hospitable to the Native American search for these jobs than private institutions. Their presence, or rather lack thereof, in the full professor rank barely changed; however, they did attain a few more tenure-track faculty positions.

Of the other occupational categories, white males' hold over skilled craft jobs was the strongest. They experienced a small decline in their participation rate from 1979 to 1991, yet they controlled over three-fourths of such positions in 1991. That gave them a representation ratio of above 2.0 in all institutions in the time period considered. The only category in which white males remained severely underrepresented was that of secretarial/clerical, but that likely was due to their own choice rather than reverse discrimination. One can make a case for reverse discrimination against white males in the professional non-faculty category (and, of course, in administration and, to a lesser extent, in faculty ranks) because they experienced a decline of 8 points in their participation rate (from 42.3 to 34.2) from 1979 to 1991. (The white male participation rate for faculty positions also fell by nearly the same number of points; in administration, however, the decline in the white male participation rate was greater.) White males, however, did have a representation ratio of 0.9 or higher in this job category in public, private, and all institutions in 1991. In the technical/para-professional category, they also lost jobs, though by a lower rate than in the professional non-faculty category, and in the service/maintenance area they encountered little fluctuation in their participation rate or representation ratio. In both these categories, white males remained represented roughly in proportion to their population in the country.

White male loss of professional non-faculty positions benefited white females more than any other group. As a result, the white female representation ratio in this category increased from 1.07 in 1979 to 1.25 in 1991. They had similar ratios in public and private institutions that year. White females remained overrepresented to a greater extent in secretarial/clerical jobs. In the technical/para-professional category, their ratio was close to 1.0 most of the time. They were underrepresented in service/maintenance jobs, possibly by choice, and they remained severely underrepresented in the skilled craft jobs, perhaps because of the male dominance over this category and a reluctance to accept women as coworkers.

In nearly all of the "other" occupations, black men and women had higher participation rates and representation ratios in private universities than public institutions. Similar to white females, black females were more numerous in the professional non-faculty category than black males. Also like white females, black females made strides in obtaining jobs in this category. Black men, unlike white men, did not experience a decline in their participation in such positions from 1979 to 1991 (in all institutions); however, they made hardly any gains. Black women remained overrepresented in secretarial/clerical positions, and black men remained overrepresented in skilled craft jobs, echoing the experience of white women and white men. Despite some decline in the participation rate and the representation ratio, black women were also overrepresented in technical/para-professional positions, surpassing white women (in their representation ratio) in this category. Black men, on the other hand, had a lower ratio than white men in these jobs in 1979 and 1983 but caught up with them in 1991. As anticipated, black men were underrepresented in the secretarial/clerical category, and black women were underrepresented in the skilled craft classification. The last category, service/maintenance, reflects the difference between the dominant majority group and an aspiring minority group. White men and women experienced little change in their representation ratios in these jobs from 1979 to 1991. Both black men and women, on the other hand, were overrepresented. However, their ratios declined, more for females than for males, pointing to their entry into higher-category jobs.

Hispanics did make progress, more so in public institutions than private colleges, in landing non-faculty professional positions, which carry the highest pay and prestige among the "other" five categories; by 1991, Hispanic women surpassed Hispanic men in public, private, and all institutions in participation rate and representation ratio. However, both Hispanic men and women remained underrepresented, with a combined male/female representation ratio far lower than their ratio in the other four categories. They also lagged far behind blacks in obtaining positions in this classification. On the other end, in the service/maintenance category, their ratio dropped from 1983 to 1991 in private and all institutions and remained below that of blacks, but the trend of their shift from lower to higher positions was not as marked as for blacks. In the middle three categories also, blacks remained more numerous than Hispanics. The pattern of Hispanic male and female employment in secretarial/clerical and skilled craft jobs was similar to that of whites and blacks. In the technical/para-professional category, the Hispanic male and female pattern was different: whereas black (as well as white) female para-professionals and technicians were consistently more numerous than their male counterparts, Hispanic male and female representation fluctuated.

Asians, the best educated group in our data, expectedly were overrepresented in the professional non-faculty and technical/para-professional categories. Their representation ratios in these positions did decline over the years, indicating their substantial increase in the country's population. Asian female and male employment in these two classifications was similar to that of whites and blacks, in that females, as a general rule, were more numerous than males. In skilled craft and secretarial/clerical jobs, Asian male and female presence reflected the experience of other groups. In the service/maintenance category, the representation ratio for Asian males and females declined from 1983 to 1991, once again reinforcing the image of a well-educated group.

The representation ratios for Native Americans were lower in professional non-faculty and technical/para-professional categories than in the other three categories. There is little evidence of a shift from lower-level to higher-category jobs in this group, except for professional non-faculty positions in public institutions. In the service/maintenance category, the combined male and female Native American representation ratio did decline from 1983 to 1991 in all institutions, but that was perhaps due to their possible undercounting in the 1980 census rather than to job mobility in this group. The male and female pattern of employment in professional non-faculty and technical/para-professional jobs, apparent among whites, blacks, and Asians, did not exist among Native Americans. Male and female patterns for skilled craft and secretarial/clerical jobs were the same as for the other four groups. The oldest, smallest, and least educated minority in the country clearly benefited less from affirmative action than did some other groups, particularly white women and black women.

Overall, women gained more from affirmative action than did men; white women, in particular, and black women made greater progress than Hispanic, Asian, or Native American women. White male dominance over employment certainly decreased but not white dominance as such, since most of the positions, especially in higher categories (faculty, administration, and professional non-faculty), that were lost by white males apparently went to white females. White women's exceptional gains leave the suspicion that racial prejudice is more deep-rooted than gender prejudice. Of the minority groups, blacks gained the most from affirmative action, and Native Americans gained the least. Hispanic progress was marred by their continued severe underrepresentation in the higher categories.

One issue we wished to examine was the validity of Thomas Sowell's argument that preferential policies tend to be concentrated on prestigious benefits that accrue only to those at the top of a targeted group.[1] We instead argued that higher education employment could be divided into higher-status and lower-status positions and that minorities and women would be more likely to make gains in lower positions. However, we found that white females did well in faculty positions and in obtaining the full professor rank. Black women also made gains in faculty positions. This was the case for administrative positions as well, where white women and black women appeared to be the biggest winners. On the other hand, in the "lower" categories, we found that blacks and to a lesser extent Hispanics continued to be predominant in service/maintenance employment, and that women remained overrepresented in secretarial/clerical positions. Thus our findings were quite mixed. The most prestigious positions – faculty and administrative – did open up for white females and black females. On the other hand, women and minorities remain overrepresented in such occupations as secretarial/clerical and service/maintenance.

A FINAL WORD

Affirmative action was established to bring equality in employment for minorities and women. White males still dominate faculty and administrative positions in higher education, but their grip over these two top employment categories has certainly loosened – a trend that our study establishes is likely to continue. A similar trend is likely to persist in the professional non-faculty employment category.

Women as a general rule, and white women in particular, have made greater gains than minority men. White women have been noticeably more successful in obtaining jobs in faculty, administrative, and professional non-faculty categories. Of the women from the four minority groups, blacks' record of employment is the most impressive. Relative to their command over doctoral degrees, white women and black women emerged as the greatest winners in obtaining faculty and administrative employment. If we consider combined male/female data for minorities, the order of success for employment, especially for the "higher" three categories, places blacks at the top and Native Americans at the bottom, with Asians and Hispanics in the middle.

The gains by women and minorities in higher education employment, though impressive in some categories, are still rather modest. To call such gains a system of preferences would be an exaggeration. The increased entry of women and minorities into higher education employment, however, has clearly been due in part to the application of affirmative action. This has given rise to hostility toward the program. Not only white males but also members of minority groups who believe that they have benefited less than others from affirmative action are opposed to it. Opposition to affirmative action also comes from some scholars and others who argue that this program has primarily helped the affluent and the privileged among minorities and women. The approval of Proposition 209 in California in the 1996 election and of Proposition 200 in Washington in the 1998 election were expressions of such opposition to affirmative action.

Our analysis of the political and socioeconomic determinants of faculty and administrative positions in higher education employment in the American states demonstrated that only demography played a significant role in shaping outcomes. These results suggest that government policies have not been as intrusive as critics charge, nor have they been as effective as advocates of affirmative action would like them to be. To understand such findings, it is necessary to consider past practices and values that continue in contemporary American society to maintain barriers to equal employment opportunity. Nevertheless, programs such as affirmative action have been developed, and although they produced unequal results, they have led to greater opportunities for minorities and women. Our finding that public institutions rather than private universities tend to be more open to employing minorities and women in higher education suggests that governments can play a role, although a limited one, in shaping employment outcomes. By setting standards and maintaining government agencies, efforts have been made to promote the ideal of a representative bureaucracy. Such steps, which are more inclusive of the diversity of the nation's population, do show that the share of minority and female employment can be increased. Furthermore, despite criticisms of the practices of affirmative action, its underlying concept of equality in employment for minorities and women continues to be supported. That would assure the continuation of affirmative action, albeit in a substantially altered form or even under a different name.

Tables

Table 1. Black Full-Time Faculty in Public, Private, and All
Institutions

	1979* All	1983 Pu.	Pr.	All	1991 Pu.	Pr.	All
Participation rates							
Male	2.4	2.4	1.9	2.2	2.6	2.5	2.6
Female	2.1	2.2	1.6	2.0	2.4	2.1	2.3
Total	4.5	4.6	3.5	4.2	5.0	4.6	4.9
Representation ratios**							
Male	0.44	0.44	0.35	0.41	0.46	0.45	0.46
Female	0.34	0.36	0.26	0.33	0.39	0.34	0.37
Total	0.39	0.40	0.30	0.37	0.42	0.39	0.42

Source: Equal Employment Opportunity Commission.
*Separate 1979 data for public and private institutions were not available.
**Representation ratios were calculated by dividing a group's participation rate by its percentage of the country's total population.
For 1979 and 1983, 1980 U.S. Bureau of the Census population figures were used; for 1991, 1990 census data were used.

Table 2. Participation Rates of Newly Hired Tenure-
Track Black Faculty

	1983 Pu.	Pr.	All	1991 Pu.	Pr.	All
Male	2.6	2.7	2.6	3.9	3.5	3.8
Female	2.1	2.1	2.1	3.3	3.2	3.2
Total	4.7	4.8	4.7	7.2	6.7	7.0

Source: Equal Employment Opportunity Commission.

Table 3. Participation Rates of Black Full Professors

	1983 Pu.	Pr.	All	1991 Pu.	Pr.	All
Male	1.5	1.7	1.6	2.4	2.3	2.4
Female	0.7	0.5	0.6	2.0	1.6	1.9
Total	2.2	2.2	2.2	4.4	3.9	4.3

Source: Equal Employment Opportunity Commission.

Table 4. Black Administrators in Public, Private, and All
Institutions

| | 1979* | | 1983 | | | 1991 | | |
	All	Pu.	Pr.	All	Pu.	Pr.	All
Participation rates							
Male	4.2	4.4	3.5	4.0	4.2	4.1	4.2
Female	0.1	2.5	3.5	3.1	3.9	5.3	4.5
Total	4.3	7.2	7.0	7.1	8.1	9.4	8.7
Representation ratios							
Male	0.78	0.81	0.65	0.74	0.75	0.73	0.75
Female	0.02	0.46	0.57	0.51	0.63	0.85	0.73
Total	0.37	0.63	0.61	0.62	0.69	0.80	0.74

Source: Equal Employment Opportunity Commission.
*Separate 1979 data for public and private institutions were not available.

Table 5. Changes in Higher Education Employment, 1979–1991 (%)

	1979–1983	1983–1991	1979–1991
Faculty (9–10 month)	3.3	8.8	12.5
Public		18.0	
Private		-10.8	
Administrators	7.4	16.5	25.2
Public		3.5	
Private		7.6	
Non-Faculty & Administrators	9.4	14.6	25.4
Public		22.0	
Private		0.7	

Source: Equal Employment Opportunity Commission.

Table 6. Blacks in "Other" Occupations in All Institutions

Occupational category	1979			1983			1991		
	Male	Female	All	Male	Female	All	Male	Female	All
Participation rates									
Prof. Non-Faculty	2.7	4.8	7.5	3.0	5.0	8.0	2.8	5.9	8.7
Secr./Clerical	1.3	11.7	13.0	1.5	12.8	14.3	1.7	14.5	16.2
Tech./Para-Prof.	4.6	11.5	16.1	4.6	11.2	15.8	5.0	10.9	15.9
Skilled Craft	9.0	1.1	10.1	9.1	0.9	10.0	10.0	1.1	11.1
Serv./Maint.	17.6	17.5	35.1	17.9	16.3	34.2	17.2	14.8	32.0
Representation ratios									
Prof. Non-Faculty	0.50	0.79	0.65	0.56	0.82	0.70	0.50	0.95	0.74
Secr./Clerical	0.24	1.92	1.13	0.28	2.10	1.24	0.30	2.34	1.37
Tech./Para-Prof.	0.85	1.89	1.40	0.85	1.84	1.37	0.89	1.76	1.35
Skilled Craft	1.67	0.18	0.88	1.69	0.15	0.87	1.79	0.18	0.94
Serv./Maint.	3.26	2.87	3.05	3.31	2.67	2.97	3.07	2.39	2.71

Source: Equal Employment Opportunity Commission.

Table 7. Blacks in "Other" Occupations in Public and Private Institutions

Occupational category	1983			1991		
	Male	Female	All	Male	Female	All
Participation rates						
Public institutions						
Prof. Non-Faculty	2.5	4.7	7.2	2.7	5.4	8.1
Secr./Clerical	1.3	11.8	13.1	1.4	13.1	14.5
Tech./Para-Prof.	4.1	10.0	14.1	4.4	10.2	14.6
Skilled Craft	8.7	1.0	9.7	9.2	0.8	10.0
Serv./Maint.	16.6	15.5	32.1	16.3	13.9	30.2
Private institutions						
Prof. Non-Faculty	4.0	5.6	9.6	3.0	7.0	10.0
Secr./Clerical	1.9	14.7	16.6	2.4	17.4	19.8
Tech./Para-Prof.	5.6	13.4	19.0	6.3	12.5	18.8
Skilled Craft	8.7	1.0	9.7	9.2	0.8	10.0
Serv./Maint.	20.5	17.8	38.3	19.3	16.6	35.9
Representation ratios						
Public institutions						
Prof. Non-Faculty	0.46	0.77	0.63	0.48	0.87	0.69
Secr./Clerical	0.24	1.93	1.14	0.25	2.11	1.23
Tech./Para-Prof.	0.76	1.64	1.23	0.79	1.65	1.24
Skilled Craft	1.61	0.16	0.84	1.64	0.13	0.85
Serv./Maint.	3.07	2.54	2.79	2.91	2.24	2.56
Private institutions						
Prof. Non-Faculty	0.71	0.92	0.81	0.54	1.13	0.85
Secr./Clerical	0.35	2.41	1.41	0.43	2.81	1.68
Tech./Para-Prof.	1.04	2.20	1.61	1.13	2.02	1.59
Skilled Craft	1.83	0.13	0.91	2.18	0.27	1.18
Serv./Maint.	3.80	2.92	3.25	3.45	2.68	3.04

Source: Equal Employment Opportunity Commission.

Table 8. White Full-Time Faculty in Public, Private, and All Institutions

| | *1979** | *1983* | | | *1991* | | |
	All	*Pu.*	*Pr.*	*All*	*Pu.*	*Pr.*	*All*
Participation rates							
Male	67.04	65.5	67.0	66.0	59.0	60.6	59.4
Female	24.03	24.8	25.0	24.8	28.4	29.0	28.5
Total	91.07	90.3	92.0	90.8	87.4	89.6	87.9
Representation ratios**							
Male	1.73	1.69	1.73	1.71	1.60	1.64	1.61
Female	0.59	0.61	0.61	0.61	0.73	0.75	0.73
Total	1.14	1.13	1.16	1.14	1.15	1.18	1.16

Source: Equal Employment Opportunity Commission.
*Separate 1979 data for public and private institutions were not available.
**Representation ratios were calculated by dividing a group's participation rate
by its percentage of the country's total population. For 1979 and 1983, 1980 U.S. Bureau of
the Census population figures were used; for 1991, 1990 census data were used.

Table 9. Participation Rates of Newly Hired Tenure-
Track White Faculty

| | *1983* | | | *1991* | | |
	Pu.	*Pr.*	*All*	*Pu.*	*Pr.*	*All*
Male	57.8	57.3	57.6	46.4	48.4	47.1
Female	30.1	30.8	30.4	34.5	35.7	34.9
Total	87.9	88.1	88.0	80.9	84.1	82.0

Source: Equal Employment Opportunity Commission.

Table 10. Participation Rates of White Full Professors

| | *1983* | | | *1991* | | |
	Pu.	*Pr.*	*All*	*Pu.*	*Pr.*	*All*
Male	82.9	83.7	83.2	64.1	65.2	64.3
Female	09.8	10.0	09.9	24.1	24.9	24.3
Total	92.7	93.7	93.1	88.2	90.1	88.6

Source: Equal Employment Opportunity Commission.

Table 11. White Administrators in Public, Private, and All Institutions

| | *1979** | | *1983* | | | *1991* | | |
	All	*Pu.*	*Pr.*	*All*	*Pu.*	*Pr.*	*All*
Participation rates							
Male	65.8	65.8	55.8	61.4	56.0	48.8	53.1
Female	24.5	23.5	34.5	28.3	31.0	37.8	33.8
Total	90.3	89.3	90.3	89.7	87.0	86.6	86.9
Representation ratios							
Male	1.70	1.70	1.44	1.59	1.52	1.32	1.44
Female	0.60	0.57	0.84	0.69	0.80	0.97	0.87
Total	1.13	1.12	1.13	1.13	1.15	1.14	1.15

Source: Equal Employment Opportunity Commission.
*Separate 1979 data for public and private institutions were not available.

Table 12. Whites in "Other" Occupations in All Institutions

| *Occupational category* | *1979* | | | *1983* | | | *1991* | | |
	Male	*Female*	*All*	*Male*	*Female*	*All*	*Male*	*Female*	*All*
Participation rates									
Prof. Non-Faculty	42.3	43.9	86.2	39.1	46.7	85.8	34.2	48.4	82.6
Secr./Clerical	05.2	76.3	81.5	05.3	74.2	79.5	05.6	69.7	75.3
Tech./Para-Prof.	36.1	41.0	77.1	36.3	40.4	76.7	33.3	40.5	73.8
Skilled Craft	81.0	04.0	85.0	80.2	04.3	84.5	77.3	04.0	81.3
Serv./Maint.	37.0	20.4	57.4	37.0	19.8	56.8	36.9	19.3	56.2
Representation ratios									
Prof. Non-Faculty	1.09	1.07	1.08	1.01	1.14	1.08	0.93	1.25	1.09
Secr./Clerical	0.13	1.87	1.02	0.14	1.81	1.00	0.15	1.80	0.99
Tech./Para-Prof.	0.93	1.00	0.97	0.94	0.99	0.96	0.90	1.04	0.97
Skilled Craft	2.09	0.10	1.07	2.07	0.11	1.06	2.09	0.10	1.07
Serv./Maint.	0.96	0.50	0.72	0.96	0.48	0.71	1.00	0.50	0.74

Source: Equal Employment Opportunity Commission.

Table 13. Whites in "Other" Occupations in Public and Private
Institutions

Occupational category	1983 Male	Female	All	1991 Male	Female	All
Participation rates						
Public institutions						
Prof. Non-Faculty	41.7	44.8	86.5	34.6	48.0	82.6
Secr./Clerical	05.1	75.5	80.6	05.5	70.9	76.4
Tech./Para-Prof.	36.4	42.0	78.4	33.9	41.2	75.1
Skilled Craft	80.7	04.4	85.1	77.7	04.3	82.0
Serv./Maint.	38.6	20.7	59.3	37.4	19.7	57.1
Private institutions						
Prof. Non-Faculty	34.2	50.1	84.3	33.1	49.3	82.4
Secr./Clerical	05.7	71.8	77.5	06.0	67.3	73.3
Tech./Para-Prof.	36.2	37.4	73.6	31.9	38.7	70.6
Skilled Craft	79.1	04.0	83.1	76.2	03.2	79.4
Serv./Maint.	34.0	18.1	52.1	35.8	15.3	54.1
Representation ratios						
Public institutions						
Prof. Non-Faculty	1.08	1.10	1.09	0.94	1.24	1.09
Secr./Clerical	1.13	1.85	1.01	0.15	1.83	1.01
Tech./Para-Prof.	0.94	1.03	0.98	0.92	1.06	0.99
Skilled Craft	2.09	0.11	1.07	2.11	0.11	1.08
Serv./Maint.	1.00	0.51	0.74	1.01	0.51	0.75
Private institutions						
Prof. Non-Faculty	0.88	1.22	1.06	0.90	1.27	1.09
Secr./Clerical	0.15	1.76	0.97	0.16	1.73	0.97
Tech./Para-Prof.	0.94	0.91	0.92	0.86	1.00	0.93
Skilled Craft	2.04	0.10	1.04	2.07	0.08	1.05
Serv./Maint.	0.88	0.44	0.65	0.97	0.47	0.71

Source: Equal Employment Opportunity Commission.

Table 14. Hispanic Full-Time Faculty in Public, Private, and All
Institutions

	1979*	1983			1991		
	All	Pu.	Pr.	All	Pu.	Pr.	All
Participation rates							
Male	1.0	1.2	0.9	1.1	1.6	1.0	1.4
Female	0.5	0.5	0.4	0.5	0.9	0.6	0.8
Total	1.5	1.7	1.3	1.6	2.5	1.6	2.2
Representation ratios**							
Male	0.31	0.38	0.28	0.34	0.35	0.22	0.30
Female	0.16	0.16	0.13	0.16	0.20	0.14	0.18
Total	0.23	0.27	0.20	0.25	0.28	0.18	0.24

Source: Equal Employment Opportunity Commission.
*Separate 1979 data for public and private institutions were not available.
**Representation ratios were calculated by dividing a group's participation
rate
by its percentage of the country's total population. For 1979 and 1983, 1980
U.S. Bureau of the Census population figures were used; for 1991, 1990
census data were used.

Table 15. Participation Rates of Newly Hired Tenure-
Track Hispanic Faculty

	1983			1991		
	Pu.	Pr.	All	Pu.	Pr.	All
Male	1.2	1.3	1.3	2.3	1.8	2.1
Female	0.5	0.6	0.5	1.8	1.2	1.6
Total	1.7	1.9	1.8	4.1	3.0	3.7

Source: Equal Employment Opportunity Commission.

Table 16. Participation Rates of Hispanic Full
Professors

	1983			1991		
	Pu.	Pr.	All	Pu.	Pr.	All
Male	0.9	0.8	0.9	1.5	1.1	1.4
Female	0.2	0.2	0.2	0.8	0.5	0.7
Total	1.1	1.0	1.1	2.3	1.6	2.1

Source: Equal Employment Opportunity Commission.

Table 17. Hispanic Administrators in Public, Private, and All
Institutions

| | 1979* | 1983 | | | 1991 | | |
	All	Pu.	Pr.	All	Pu.	Pr.	All
Participation rates							
Male	1.0	1.4	0.9	1.2	1.6	1.2	1.5
Female	0.4	0.5	0.6	0.6	1.1	1.0	1.1
Total	1.4	1.9	1.5	1.8	2.7	2.2	2.6
Representation ratios							
Male	0.31	0.44	0.28	0.38	0.35	0.26	0.33
Female	0.13	0.16	0.19	0.19	0.25	0.23	0.25
Total	0.22	0.30	0.23	0.28	0.30	0.24	0.29

Source: Equal Employment Opportunity Commission.
*Separate 1979 data for public and private institutions were not available.

Table 18. Hispanics in "Other" Occupations in All Institutions

Occupational category	1979			1983			1991		
	Male	Female	All	Male	Female	All	Male	Female	All
Participation rates									
Prof. Non-Faculty	1.0	0.8	1.8	1.0	1.0	2.0	1.3	1.7	3.0
Secr./Clerical	0.5	3.0	3.5	0.5	3.4	3.9	0.7	4.8	5.5
Tech./Para-Prof.	1.9	1.5	3.4	1.9	1.9	3.8	2.6	2.8	5.4
Skilled Craft	3.5	0.2	3.7	3.9	0.2	4.1	5.3	0.3	5.6
Serv./Maint.	4.1	1.8	5.9	4.6	2.2	6.8	6.1	2.9	9.0
Representation ratios									
Prof. Non-Faculty	0.31	0.25	0.28	0.31	0.31	0.31	0.28	0.39	0.33
Secr./Clerical	0.16	0.94	0.55	0.16	1.06	0.61	0.15	1.09	0.61
Tech./Para-Prof.	0.59	0.47	0.53	0.59	0.59	0.59	0.56	0.64	0.60
Skilled Craft	1.09	0.06	0.58	1.22	0.06	0.64	1.15	0.07	0.62
Serv./Maint.	1.28	0.56	0.92	1.44	0.69	1.06	1.33	0.66	1.00

Source: Equal Employment Opportunity Commission.

Table 19. Hispanics in "Other" Occupations in Public and Private Institutions

Occupational category	1983			1991		
	Male	Female	All	Male	Female	All
Participation rates						
Public institutions						
Prof. Non-Faculty	1.1	1.0	2.1	1.4	1.9	3.3
Secr./Clerical	0.5	3.4	3.9	0.7	5.2	5.9
Tech./Para-Prof.	2.1	1.9	4.0	2.4	2.9	5.3
Skilled Craft	3.6	0.2	3.8	5.5	0.3	5.8
Serv./Maint.	4.1	2.2	6.3	6.2	3.2	9.4
Private institutions						
Prof. Non-Faculty	0.8	1.0	1.8	1.0	1.5	2.5
Secr./Clerical	0.6	3.3	3.9	0.8	3.8	4.6
Tech./Para-Prof.	1.7	1.9	3.6	3.0	2.5	5.5
Skilled Craft	4.6	0.1	4.7	4.7	0.2	4.9
Serv./Maint.	5.6	2.1	7.7	5.8	2.3	8.1
Representation ratios						
Public institutions						
Prof. Non-Faculty	0.34	0.31	0.33	0.30	0.43	0.37
Secr./Clerical	0.16	1.06	0.61	0.15	1.18	0.66
Tech./Para-Prof.	0.66	0.60	0.63	0.52	0.66	0.59
Skilled Craft	1.13	0.06	0.59	1.20	0.07	0.65
Serv./Maint.	1.28	0.69	0.98	1.35	0.73	1.04
Private institutions						
Prof. Non-Faculty	0.25	0.31	0.28	0.22	0.34	0.28
Secr./Clerical	0.19	1.03	0.61	0.17	0.86	0.51
Tech./Para-Prof.	0.53	0.59	0.56	0.65	0.57	0.61
Skilled Craft	1.44	0.03	0.73	1.02	0.05	0.54
Serv./Maint.	1.75	0.66	1.20	1.26	0.52	0.90

Source: Equal Employment Opportunity Commission.

Table 20. Asian Full-Time Faculty in Public, Private, and All Institutions

| | *1979** | | | | *1983* | | *1991* | |
	All	*Pu.*	*Pr.*	*All*	*Pu.*	*Pr.*	*All*
Participation rates							
Male	2.1	2.7	2.4	2.6	3.7	3.1	3.6
Female	0.4	0.6	0.5	0.5	1.0	0.9	1.0
Total	2.5	3.3	2.9	3.1	4.7	4.0	4.6
Representation ratios**							
Male	3.00	3.86	3.43	3.71	2.64	2.21	2.57
Female	0.50	0.75	0.63	0.63	0.67	0.60	0.67
Total	1.67	2.20	1.93	2.06	1.62	1.38	1.59

Source: Equal Employment Opportunity Commission.
*Separate 1979 data for public and private institutions were not available.
**Representation ratios were calculated by dividing a group's participation rate by its percentage of the country's total population. For 1979 and 1983,1980 U.S. Bureau of the Census population figures were used; for 1991, 1990 census data were used.

Table 21. Participation Rates of Newly Hired Tenure-Track Asian Faculty

| | *1983* | | | *1991* | | |
	Pu.	*Pr.*	*All*	*Pu.*	*Pr.*	*All*
Male	4.5	3.9	4.3	5.1	4.2	4.8
Female	0.9	1.0	0.9	2.1	1.7	2.0
Total	5.4	4.9	5.2	7.2	5.9	6.8

Source: Equal Employment Opportunity Commission.

Table 22. Participation Rates of Asian Full Professors

| | *1983* | | | *1991* | | |
	Pu.	*Pr.*	*All*	*Pu.*	*Pr.*	*All*
Male	3.5	2.8	3.2	3.9	3.6	3.8
Female	0.3	0.2	0.2	0.9	0.9	0.9
Total	3.8	3.0	3.4	4.8	4.5	4.7

Source: Equal Employment Opportunity Commission.

Table 23. Asian Administrators in Public, Private, and All
Institutions

| | 1979* | | 1983 | | | 1991 | |
	All	Pu.	Pr.	All	Pu.	Pr.	All
Participation rates							
Male	0.7	0.8	0.5	0.7	1.0	0.9	0.9
Female	0.3	0.4	0.4	0.4	0.6	0.7	0.6
Total	1.0	1.2	0.9	1.1	1.6	1.6	1.5
Representation ratios							
Male	1.00	1.10	0.71	1.00	0.71	0.64	0.64
Female	0.38	0.50	0.50	0.50	0.40	0.47	0.40
Total	0.67	0.80	0.60	0.73	0.55	0.55	0.52

Source: Equal Employment Opportunity Commission.
*Separate 1979 data for public and private institutions were not available.

Table 24. Asians in "Other" Occupations in All Institutions

Occupational category	1979			1983			1991		
	Male	Female	All	Male	Female	All	Male	Female	All
Participation rates									
Prof. Non-Faculty	2.0	2.0	4.0	1.8	2.1	3.9	2.5	2.9	5.4
Secr./Clerical	0.2	1.3	1.5	0.3	1.5	1.8	0.5	1.9	2.4
Tech./Para-Prof.	1.2	1.7	2.9	1.3	1.8	3.1	2.0	2.5	4.5
Skilled Craft	0.6	0.1	0.7	0.7	0.1	0.8	1.2	0.1	1.3
Serv./Maint.	0.7	0.4	1.1	1.0	0.5	1.5	1.4	0.9	2.3
Representation ratios									
Prof. Non-Faculty	2.86	2.50	2.67	2.57	2.63	2.60	1.79	1.93	1.86
Secr./Clerical	0.29	1.63	1.00	0.43	1.88	1.20	0.36	1.27	0.83
Tech./Para-Prof.	1.71	2.13	1.93	1.86	2.25	2.07	1.43	1.67	1.55
Skilled Craft	0.86	0.13	0.47	1.00	0.13	0.53	0.86	0.07	0.45
Serv./Maint.	1.00	0.50	0.73	1.43	0.63	1.00	1.00	0.67	0.79

Source: Equal Employment Opportunity Commission.

Table 25. Asians in "Other" Occupations in Public and Private Institutions

Occupational	1983			1991		
category	Male	Female	All	Male	Female	All
Participation rates						
Public institutions						
Prof. Non-Faculty	1.7	2.2	3.9	2.6	3.0	5.6
Secr./Clerical	0.3	1.5	1.8	0.5	2.1	2.6
Tech./Para-Prof.	1.3	1.6	2.9	2.0	2.4	4.4
Skilled Craft	0.7	0.1	0.8	1.2	0.1	1.3
Serv./Maint.	1.1	0.6	1.7	1.5	1.0	2.5
Private institutions						
Prof. Non-Faculty	1.9	1.9	3.8	2.3	2.6	4.9
Secr./Clerical	0.3	1.4	1.7	0.5	1.6	2.1
Tech./Para-Prof.	1.3	2.1	3.4	2.1	2.8	4.9
Skilled Craft	0.8	0.1	0.9	1.3	0.1	1.4
Serv./Maint.	0.7	0.4	1.1	1.1	0.6	1.7
Representation ratios						
Public institutions						
Prof. Non-Faculty	2.43	2.75	2.60	1.86	2.00	1.93
Secr./Clerical	0.43	1.88	1.20	0.36	1.40	0.90
Tech./Para-Prof.	1.86	2.00	1.93	1.43	1.60	1.52
Skilled Craft	1.00	0.13	0.53	0.86	0.07	0.45
Serv./Maint.	1.57	0.75	1.13	1.07	0.67	0.86
Private institutions						
Prof. Non-Faculty	2.71	2.38	2.53	1.64	1.73	1.69
Secr./Clerical	0.43	1.75	1.13	0.36	1.07	0.72
Tech./Para-Prof.	1.86	2.63	2.27	1.50	1.87	1.69
Skilled Craft	1.14	0.13	0.60	0.93	0.07	0.48
Serv./Maint.	1.00	0.50	0.73	0.79	0.49	0.59

Source: Equal Employment Opportunity Commission.

Table 26. Native American Full-Time Faculty in Public, Private, and All Institutions

| | 1979* | | | 1983 | | | 1991 |
	All	Pu	Pr.	All	Pu.	Pr.	All
Participation rates							
Male	0.2	0.2	0.2	0.2	0.2	0.1	0.2
Female	0.1	0.1	0.1	0.1	0.2	0.1	0.1
Total	0.3	0.3	0.3	0.3	0.4	0.2	0.3
Representation ratios**							
Male	0.65	0.65	0.65	0.65	0.51	0.26	0.51
Female	0.31	0.31	0.31	0.31	0.50	0.25	0.25
Total	0.48	0.48	0.48	0.48	0.51	0.25	0.38

Source: Equal Employment Opportunity Commission.
*Separate 1979 data for public and private institutions were not available.
**Representation ratios were calculated by dividing a group's participation rate by its percentage of the country's total population. For 1979 and 1983, 1980 U.S. Bureau of the Census population figures were used; for 1991, 1990 census data were used.

Table 27. Participation Rates of Newly Hired Tenure-Track Native American Faculty

| | 1983 | | | 1991 | | |
	Pu.	Pr.	All	Pu.	Pr.	All
Male	0.2	0.3	0.2	0.2	0.2	0.2
Female	0.1	0.1	0.1	0.3	0.1	0.3
Total	0.3	0.4	0.3	0.5	0.3	0.5

Source: Equal Employment Opportunity Commission.

Table 28. Participation Rates of Native American Full Professors

| | 1983 | | | 1991 | | |
	Pu.	Pr.	All	Pu.	Pr.	All
Male	0.1	0.2	0.2	0.2	0.1	0.2
Female	*	*	*	0.1	*	0.1
Total	0.1	0.2	0.2	0.3	0.1	0.3

Source: Equal Employment Opportunity Commission.
*Less than 0.05 percent.

Table 29. Native American Administrators in Public, Private, and All Institutions

| | 1979* | 1983 | | | 1991 | | |
	All	Pu.	Pr.	All	Pu.	Pr.	All
Participation rates							
Male	0.2	0.3	0.2	0.3	0.3	0.1	0.2
Female	0.1	0.1	0.1	0.1	0.2	0.1	0.2
Total	0.3	0.4	0.3	0.4	0.5	0.2	0.4
Representation ratios							
Male	0.65	0.97	0.65	0.97	0.77	0.26	0.51
Female	0.31	0.31	0.31	0.31	0.50	0.25	0.50
Total	0.48	0.63	0.48	0.63	0.63	0.25	0.51

Source: Equal Employment Opportunity Commission.
*Separate 1979 data for public and private institutions were not available.

Table 30. Native Americans in "Other" Occupations in All Institutions

| Occupational category | 1979 | | | 1983 | | | 1991 | | |
	Male	Female	All	Male	Female	All	Male	Female	All
Participation rates									
Prof. Non-Faculty	0.2	0.2	0.4	0.2	0.2	0.4	0.2	0.2	0.4
Secr./Clerical	*	0.3	0.3	0.1	0.4	0.5	0.1	0.5	0.6
Tech./Para-Prof.	0.2	0.2	0.4	0.3	0.2	0.5	0.2	0.3	0.5
Skilled Craft	0.5	*	0.5	0.6	*	0.6	0.7	*	0.7
Serv./Maint.	0.3	0.2	0.5	0.4	0.2	0.6	0.4	0.2	0.6
Representation ratios									
Prof. Non-Faculty	0.65	0.63	0.63	0.65	0.63	0.63	0.51	0.50	0.51
Secr./Clerical	0.00	0.94	0.48	0.32	1.25	0.79	0.26	1.25	0.76
Tech./Para-Prof.	0.65	0.63	0.63	0.97	0.63	0.79	0.51	0.75	0.63
Skilled Craft	1.61	0.00	0.79	1.94	0.00	0.95	1.79	0.00	0.89
Serv./Maint.	0.97	0.63	0.79	1.29	0.63	0.95	1.03	0.50	0.76

Source: Equal Employment Opportunity Commission.
*Less than 0.05 percent.

Table 31. Native Americans in "Other" Occupations in Public and Private Institutions

Occupational	1983			1991		
category	Male	Female	All	Male	Female	All
Participation rates						
Public institutions						
Prof. Non-Faculty	0.1	0.2	0.3	0.2	0.3	0.5
Secr./Clerical	0.1	0.4	0.5	0.1	0.6	0.7
Tech./Para-Prof.	0.4	0.2	0.6	0.3	0.3	0.6
Skilled Craft	0.6	*	0.6	0.8	*	0.8
Serv./Maint.	0.4	0.2	0.6	0.5	0.3	0.8
Private institutions						
Prof. Non-Faculty	0.4	0.2	0.6	0.1	0.1	0.2
Secr./Clerical	0.1	0.3	0.4	*	0.3	0.3
Tech./Para-Prof.	0.1	0.2	0.3	0.2	0.2	0.4
Skilled Craft	0.7	*	0.7	0.4	*	0.4
Serv./Maint.	0.6	0.2	0.8	0.2	0.1	0.3
Representation ratios						
Public institutions						
Prof. Non-Faculty	0.32	0.63	0.48	0.51	0.75	0.63
Secr./Clerical	0.32	1.25	0.79	0.26	1.50	0.89
Tech./Para-Prof.	1.29	0.63	0.95	0.77	0.75	0.76
Skilled Craft	1.94	0.00	0.95	2.05	0.00	1.01
Serv./Maint.	1.29	0.63	0.95	1.28	0.75	1.01
Private institutions						
Prof. Non-Faculty	1.33	0.63	0.95	0.26	0.25	0.25
Secr./Clerical	0.33	0.94	0.63	0.00	0.75	0.38
Tech./Para-Prof.	0.33	0.63	0.48	0.51	0.50	0.51
Skilled Craft	2.26	0.00	1.11	1.03	0.00	0.51
Serv./Maint.	1.94	0.63	1.27	0.51	0.25	0.38

Source: Equal Employment Opportunity Commission.

*Less than 0.05 percent.

Table 32. Doctorates Earned by Minorities and Whites

		1979	1983	1991	1995
Race/Ethnicity					
Black	Total	1,443 (4.6)	1,384 (4.4)	1,458 (3.9)	1,798 (4.3)
	Men	898 (2.9)	835 (2.7)	784 (2.1)	872 (2.1)
	Women	545 (1.7)	549 (1.8)	674 (1.8)	926 (2.2)
Hispanic	Total	908 (2.9)	969 (3.1)	1,318 (3.5)	1,530 (3.7)
	Men	681 (2.2)	635 (2.0)	805 (2.2)	906 (2.2)
	Women	227 (0.7)	334 (1.1)	513 (1.4)	624 (1.5)
Asian	Total	2,602 (8.3)	3,125 (10.0)	7,522 (20.1)	9,696 (23.3)
	Men	2,158 (6.9)	2,543 (8.1)	5,875 (15.7)	7,108 (17.1)
	Women	444 (1.4)	582 (1.9)	1,647 (4.4)	2,588 (6.2)
Native Amer.	Total	84 (0.3)	82 (0.3)	132 (0.4)	148 (0.4)
	Men	59 (0.2)	51 (0.2)	74 (0.2)	81 (0.2)
	Women	25 (0.1)	31 (0.1)	58 (0.2)	67 (0.2)
White	Total	23,682 (75.8)	23,838 (76.2)	25,325 (67.5)	26,993 (64.9)
	Men	16,660 (53.3)	15,313 (49.0)	14,807 (39.5)	15,269 (36.7)
	Women	7,022 (22.5)	8,525 (27.3)	10,518 (28.0)	11,724 (28.2)
Unknown Race/Ethnicity					
	Total	2,520 (8.1)	1,884 (6.0)	1,763 (4.7)	1,445 (3.5)
	Men	1,846 (5.9)	1,372 (4.4)	1,303 (3.5)	1,041 (2.5)
	Women	674 (2.2)	512 (1.6)	460 (1.2)	404 (1.0)
Total	Men	22,302 (71.4)	20,749 (66.3)	23,648 (63.0)	25,277 (60.8)
Total	Women	8,937 (28.6)	10,533 (33.7)	13,870 (37.0)	16,333 (39.3)
Total	Both	31,239	31,282	37,518	41,610

Source: National Research Council, *Doctorate Recipients from United States Universities,* summary reports, 1993, 1994, and 1995.

Note: These statistics include foreign students. Since National Research Council keeps updating doctorate data, statistics for a particular year are not necessarily from the council's report for that year. Percentages of total (men and women) doctorates are within parentheses. Some may not equal the total percent for a group or the overall total of 100.0 due to rounding.

Table 33. Minority and White Shares of Faculty and Administrative
Positions

		1979		1983		1991	
		Fac.	*Adm.*	*Fac.*	*Adm.*	*Fac.*	*Adm.*
Race/Ethnicity							
Black	Total	4.3	4.4	4.2	7.1	4.9	8.7
	Men	2.3	4.2	2.2	4.0	2.6	4.2
	Women	2.0	0.1	2.0	3.1	2.3	4.5
Hispanic	Total	1.5	1.4	1.6	1.8	2.2	2.6
	Men	1.1	1.0	1.1	1.2	1.4	1.5
	Women	0.4	0.4	0.5	0.6	0.8	1.1
Asian	Total	2.9	1.0	3.1	1.1	4.6	1.5
	Men	2.3	0.7	2.6	0.7	3.6	0.9
	Women	0.6	0.3	0.5	0.4	1.0	0.6
Native Amer.	Total	0.3	0.3	0.3	0.4	0.3	0.4
	Men	0.2	0.2	0.2	0.3	0.2	0.2
	Women	0.1	0.1	0.1	0.1	0.1	0.2
White	Total	91.0	90.3	90.8	89.7	87.9	86.9
	Men	68.0	65.8	66.0	61.4	59.4	53.1
	Women	23.0	24.5	24.8	28.3	28.5	33.8
Total	Men	73.9	71.9	72.1	67.5	67.2	59.9
	Women	26.1	28.1	27.9	32.5	32.8	40.1

Source: Equal Employment Opportunity Commission.
Note: The numbers in this table are percentages of the total positions in *all* institutions.
They may not add to the total percent for a group or to the overall total of 100.0 due to
rounding.

Table 34. Minority and White Shares of Newly Hired Tenure-
Track Faculty

Race/Ethnicity		1983	1991
Black	Total	740 (4.8)	1,131 (7.0)
	Men	409 (2.6)	610 (3.8)
	Women	331 (2.1)	521 (3.2)
Hispanic	Total	278 (1.8)	601 (3.7)
	Men	195 (1.3)	344 (2.1)
	Women	83 (0.5)	257 (1.6)
Asian	Total	801 (5.2)	1,093 (6.8)
	Men	659 (4.3)	775 (4.8)
	Women	142 (0.9)	318 (2.0)
Native Amer.	Total	47 (0.3)	78 (0.5)
	Men	34 (0.2)	36 (0.2)
	Women	13 (0.1)	42 (0.3)
White	Total	13,621 (88.0)	13,164 (81.9)
	Men	8,917 (57.6)	7,560 (47.1)
	Women	4,704 (30.4)	5,604 (34.9)
Total	Men	10,214 (66.0)	9,325 (58.0)
Total	Women	5,273 (34.0)	6,742 (42.0)

Source: Equal Employment Opportunity Commission.
Note: These data are from *all* institutions. Percentages of the total positions are within parentheses. Some may not equal the total percent for a group or the overall total of 100.0 due to rounding.

Table 35. Doctorates Awarded to Blacks, by Field (U.S. Citizens and Non–U.S. Citizens with Permanent Visas)

Field	1979	1983	1991	1995
Physical sciences	52 (1.5)	32 (1.0)	53 (1.4)	62 (1.3)
Engineering	20 (1.2)	29 (2.0)	55 (2.3)	71 (2.1)
Life sciences	61 (1.4)	74 (1.6)	116 (2.3)	186 (3.1)
Social sciences (incl. Psychology)	220 (4.0)	199 (3.8)	231 (4.9)	278 (5.1)
Humanities	130 (3.4)	79 (2.6)	101 (3.0)	124 (2.9)
Education	570 (8.6)	516 (8.1)	438 (7.8)	610 (10.3)
Professional/Other	51 (4.3)	69 (4.9)	88 (5.2)	124 (6.0)
Unspecified	2	2	0	0
Total recipients	1,106 (4.2)	1,000 (3.9)	1,082 (4.1)	1,455 (4.6)
Total U.S. citizens & permanent visa holders	26,683	25,564	26,535	31,910

Source: National Research Council, *Doctorate Recipients from United States Universities,* summary reports, 1979, 1983, 1991, 1995.
Note: Foreign students with temporary U.S. visas are excluded from this table and tables 36, 37, 38, and 39. Percentages of the total doctorates held by blacks in a field are within parentheses.

Table 36. Doctorates Awarded to Hispanics, by Field (U.S. Citizens and Non–U.S. Citizens with Permanent Visas)

Field	1979	1983	1991	1995
Physical sciences	51 (1.4)	44 (1.3)	99 (2.6)	106 (2.2)
Engineering	24 (1.5)	29 (2.0)	59 (2.5)	77 (2.3)
Life sciences	61 (1.1)	59 (1.3)	126 (2.5)	179 (3.0)
Social sciences (incl. Psychology)	107 (1.9)	150 (2.9)	197 (4.1)	227 (4.2)
Humanities	130 (3.4)	113 (3.7)	144 (4.3)	161 (3.7)
Education	165 (2.5)	185 (2.9)	184 (3.3)	255 (4.3)
Professional/Other	12 (1.0)	24 (1.7)	34 (2.0)	50 (2.4)
Unspecified	0	0	0	0
Total	550 (2.1)	604 (2.4)	843 (3.2)	1,055 (3.3)
Total U.S. citizens & permanent visa holders	26,683	25,564	26,535	31,910

Source: National Research Council, *Doctorate Recipients from United States Universities,* summary reports, 1979, 1983, 1991, 1995.
Note: Percentages of the total doctorates held by Hispanics in a field are within parentheses.

Table 37. Doctorates Awarded to Asians, by Field (U.S. Citizens and Non–U.S. Citizens with Permanent Visas)

Field	1979	1983	1991	1995
Physical sciences	244 (6.9)	216 (6.4)	306 (8.1)	1,201 (24.9)
Engineering	305 (18.9)	247 (16.7)	401 (17.0)	1,031 (30.9)
Life sciences	227 (5.3)	239 (5.2)	324 (6.5)	1,110 (18.3)
Social sciences (incl. Psychology)	127 (2.3)	109 (2.1)	154 (3.2)	394 (7.3)
Humanities	72 (1.9)	47 (1.5)	84 (2.5)	217 (5.0)
Education	85 (1.3)	118 (1.9)	124 (2.2)	174 (3.0)
Professional/Other	36 (3.0)	64 (4.5)	98 (5.7)	173 (8.4)
Unspecified	1	0	0	0
Total	1,097 (4.1)	1,040 (4.1)	1,491 (5.6)	4,300 (13.5)
Total U.S. citizens & permanent visa holders	26,683	25,564	26,535	31,910

Source: National Research Council, *Doctorate Recipients from United States Universities*, summary reports, 1979, 1983, 1991, 1995.
Note: Percentages of the total doctorates held by Asians in a field are within parentheses.

Table 38. Doctorates Awarded to Whites, by Field (U.S. Citizens and Non–U.S. Citizens with Permanent Visas)

Field	1979	1983	1991	1995
Physical sciences	2,926 (82.6)	2,935 (87.4)	3,229 (85.6)	3,373 (70.0)
Engineering	1,154 (71.4)	1,127 (76.1)	1,788 (75.8)	2,086 (62.5)
Life sciences	3,655 (85.9)	4,132 (89.5)	4,300 (86.6)	4,494 (74.2)
Social sciences (incl. Psychology)	4,767 (85.5)	4,596 (88.2)	4,087 (86.0)	4,457 (82.1)
Humanities	3,230 (84.8)	2,769 (89.4)	2,992 (88.3)	3,735 (86.6)
Education	5,442 (81.7)	5,399 (84.8)	4,748 (84.9)	4,779 (81.1)
Professional/Other	1,033 (86.0)	1,219 (86.2)	1,460 (85.5)	1,684 (81.9)
Unspecified	15	12	0	0
Total	22,222 (83.3)	22,189 (86.8)	22,604 (85.2)	24,608 (77.1)
Total U.S. citizens & permanent visa holders	26,683	25,564	26,535	31,910

Source: National Research Council, *Doctorate Recipients from United States Universities*, summary reports, 1979, 1983, 1991, 1995.
Note: Percentages of the total doctorates held by whites in a field are within parentheses.

Table 39. Doctorates Awarded to Hispanics and Asians—A Comparison

	1979	*1983*	*1991*	*1995*
Hispanics				
Citizens & permanent residents	535 (58.9)	604 (62.3)	843 (64.0)	1,055 (69.0)
Foreign students	373 (41.1)	365 (37.7)	475 (36.0)	475 (31.1)
Total	908	969	1,318	1,530
Asians				
Citizens & permanent residents	1,097 (42.2)	1,040 (33.3)	1,491 (19.8)	4,300 (44.4)
Foreign students	1,505 (57.8)	2,085 (66.7)	6,031 (80.2)	5,396 (55.7)
Total	2,602	3,125	7,522	9,696
Total doctorates awarded	31,239	31,282	37,518	41,610

Source: National Research Council, *Doctorate Recipients from United States Universities*, summary reports, 1979, 1983, 1991, 1995.
Note: Percentages of the total doctorates awarded to Hispanics or Asians are within parentheses. Some percentages may not equal 100.0 due to rounding.

Table 40. Doctorates Awarded to Native Americans, by Field (U.S. Citizens and Non–U.S. Citizens with Permanent Visas)

Field	*1979**	*1983*	*1991*	*1995*
Physical sciences		9 (0.3)	14 (0.4)	11 (0.2)
Engineering		1 (0.1)	6 (0.3)	10 (0.3)
Life sciences		7 (0.2)	19 (0.4)	27 (0.5)
Social sciences (incl. Psychology)		12 (0.2)	21 (0.4)	29 (0.5)
Humanities		6 (0.2)	10 (0.3)	19 (0.4)
Education		44 (0.7)	53 (1.0)	40 (0.7)
Professional/Other		1 (0.1)	7 (0.4)	12 (0.6)
Total		80 (0.3)	130 (0.5)	148 (0.5)
Total U.S. citizens & permanent visa holders	26,683	25,564	26,535	31,910

Source: National Research Council, *Doctorate Recipients from United States Universities*, summary reports, 1979, 1983, 1991, 1995.
Note: Percentages of the total doctorates held by Native Americans in a field are within parentheses.
*1979 data for Native American doctorates are excluded because they appeared unreliable to us.

Table 41. Multiple Regression Analysis: Male Public Faculty Representation Ratios

Independent variables	Dependent variables				
	Black	White	Hispanic	Asian	Native American
Political ideology	.115**	-.001	.017	-.012	.056*
	(.045)	(.006)	(.031)	(.253)	(.030)
Democratic governorship	.109	.033	-.071	-1.183	-.207
	(.248)	(.036)	(.169)	(1.39)	(.171)
Democratic legislatures	-.004	-.002	-.007	.041	.004
	(.010)	(.001)	(.007)	(.055)	(.007)
% Population	-.048	-.213****	-.391	-1.040	-.504**
	(.289)	(.043)	(.279)	(2.989)	(.215)
Median income	.486	.039	-1.963*	-15.814**	-2.137*
	(1.623)	(.235)	(1.133)	(8.986)	(1.112)
Industrialization	.010	-.005	.037	.137	-.002
	(.036)	(.005)	(.024)	(.192)	(.025)
Urbanization	-.027***	.002*	-.006	-.060	.008
	(.008)	(.001)	(.007)	(.045)	(.006)
Constant	-.905	2.039****	.095	13.530	1.533
	(2.178)	(.031)	(1.447)	(11.653)	(1.649)
Adjusted R-squared	.264	.487	.171	.326	.285

Regression coefficients (b's) are presented in the table. Standard errors of estimates are in parentheses. *p<.10, **p<.05, ***p<.01, ****p<.001

Table 42. Multiple Regression Analysis: Female Public Faculty Representation Ratios

	Dependent variables				
Independent variables	Black	White	Hispanic	Asian	Native American
Political ideology	.046**	-.006	.016	.053	.058*
	(.021)	(.004)	(.015)	(.040)	(.030)
Democratic governorship	.085	.011	-.111	-.029	-.273
	(.116)	(.025)	(.081)	(.221)	(.172)
Democratic legislatures	-.002	.003***	-.004	-.004	-.009
	(.005)	(.001)	(.003)	(.009)	(.007)
% Population	-.012	-.164****	-.199	-.376	-.363
	(.135)	(.030)	(.134)	(.476)	(.216)
Median income	-.075	.164	-1.197**	-2.159	-1.355
	(.759)	(.166)	(.545)	(1.432)	(1.117)
Industrialization	.004	-.003	.037***	.022	.014
	(.017)	(.004)	(.011)	(.031)	(.025)
Urbanization	-.011***	.000	-.004	-.013*	-.002
	(.004)	(.000)	(.003)	(.007)	(.006)
Constant	.177	.836****	-1.319*	1.709	.455
	(1.018)	(.214)	(.695)	(1.857)	(1.656)
Adjusted R-squared	.216	.592	.228	.201	.043

Regression coefficients (b's) are presented in the table. Standard errors of estimates are in parentheses. *p<.10, **p<.05, ***p<.01, ****p<.001

Table 43. Multiple Regression Analysis: Male Public Faculty Participation Rates

Independent variables	Dependent variables				
	Black	White	Hispanic	Asian	Native American
Political ideology	-.058	.222	-.011	-.030	-.018
	(.053)	(.189)	(.023)	(.061)	(.013)
Democratic governorship	.287	-.049	.033	-.184	.017
	(.295)	(1.072)	(.130)	(.335)	(.076)
Democratic legislatures	.036***	-.157***	-.005	.015	.004
	(.012)	(.043)	(.006)	(.013)	(.003)
% Population	2.271****	4.256***	1.679****	.435	.342***
	(.344)	(1.273)	(.214)	(.720)	(.096)
Median income	-1.248	.516	.238	.238	.427
	(1.929)	(6.963)	(.871)	(2.165)	(.495)
Industrialization	.029	-.037	-.027	-.034	-.029**
	(.043)	(.147)	(.018)	(.046)	(.011)
Urbanization	.014	-.052	.011**	.023**	.002
	(.010)	(.037)	(.005)	(.011)	(.002)
Constant	-1.869	67.988****	2.551**	4.412	2.169***
	(2.588)	(9.001)	(1.111)	(2.807)	(.733)
Adjusted R-squared	.743	.569	.784	.075	.455

Regression coefficients (b's) are presented in the table. Standard errors of estimates are in parentheses. *p<.10, **p<.05, ***p<.01, ****p<.001

Table 44. Multiple Regression Analysis: Female Public Faculty Participation Rates

	Dependent variables				
Independent variables	*Black*	*White*	*Hispanic*	*Asian*	*Native American*
Political ideology	-.085*	-.030	-.015	.013	-.014
	(.046)	(.155)	(.017)	(.016)	(.012)
Democratic governorship	.069***	-.928	-.005	.074	.052
	(.258)	(.879)	(.095)	(.088)	(.068)
Democratic legislatures	.034***	.093**	-.003	-.002	.002
	(.011)	(.035)	(.004)	(.003)	(.003)
% Population	2.726****	.437	1.179****	.591***	.263***
	(.302)	(1.045)	(.157)	(.190)	(.084)
Median income	-2.710	4.000	.379	.189	.499
	(1.692)	(5.715)	(.638)	(.571)	(.434)
Industrialization	.025	-.004	-.008	-.010	-.020**
	(.037)	(.121)	(.013)	(.012)	(.010)
Urbanization	.019**	-.036	.006	.005*	.000
	(.008)	(.030)	(.004)	(.003)	(.002)
Constant	.084	23.342***	.853	.942	1.468**
	(2.270)	(7.393)	(.815)	(.740)	(.634)
Adjusted R-Squared	.839	.075	.757	.418	.368

Regression coefficients (b's) are presented in the table. Standard errors of estimates are in parentheses. *p<.10, **p<.05 , ***p<.01, ****p<.001

Table 45. Multiple Regression Analysis: Male Private Faculty Representation Ratios

Independent variables	Dependent variables				
	Black	White	Hispanic	Asian	Native American
Political ideology	-.017	.003	.027	.146	-.047
	(.039)	(.013)	(.039)	(.264)	(.055)
Democratic governorship	-.128	-.030	-.222	-2.421	-.237
	(.215)	(.071)	(.216)	(1.450)	(.312)
Democratic legislatures	.003	-.002	-.016*	.131**	-.007
	(.009)	(.003)	(.009)	(.057)	(.013)
% Population	-.238	-.094	-.622*	-.257	.118
	(.252)	(.084)	(.355)	(3.120)	(.392)
Median income	-.319	.262	-4.481***	-20.781**	-.787
	(1.411)	(.462)	(1.444)	(9.381)	(2.027)
Industrialization	.039	-.011	.109***	.341*	-.011
	(.031)	(.010)	(.030)	(.201)	(.049)
Urbanization	-.003	.006**	.007	-.027	.011
	(.007)	(.002)	(.008)	(.047)	(.010)
Constant	-2.010	1.914***	-4.156**	-11.574	1.185
	(1.893)	(.598)	(1.843)	(12.166)	(3.005)
Adjusted R-squared	-.117	.222	.227	.358	-.102

Regression coefficients (b's) are presented in the table. Standard errors of estimates are in parentheses. *p<.10, **p<.05, ***p<.01, ****p<.001

Table 46. Multiple Regression Analysis: Female Private Faculty Representation Ratios

	Dependent variables				
Independent variables	Black	White	Hispanic	Asian	Native American
Political ideology	-.013	-.004	-.016	-.087	-.031
	(.027)	(.011)	(.024)	(.074)	(.034)
Democratic governorship	-.041	-.012	-.077	-.349	-.134
	(.151)	(.064)	(.132)	(.407)	(.192)
Democratic legislatures	.005	-.000	-.003	.000	.006
	(.006)	(.003)	(.006)	(.016)	(.0087)
% Population	-.208	-.147*	-.119	-.058	-.189
	(.176)	(.076)	(.218)	(.876)	(.241)
Median income	-.780	-.010	-1.212	-2.583	.479
	(.988)	(.416)	(.886)	(2.633)	(1.248)
Industrialization	.025	.004	.032*	.105*	-.025
	(.022)	(.009)	(.018)	(.056)	(.028)
Urbanization	.002	-.002	-.001	-.007	.009
	(.005)	(.002)	(.005)	(.013)	(.006)
Constant	-1.135	.747	-.543	-2.849	1.722
	(1.325)	(.538)	(1.130)	(3.414)	(1.851)
Adjusted R-squared	-.077	-.026	.034	.048	-.014

Regression coefficients (b's) are presented in the table. Standard errors of estimates are in parentheses. *$p<.10$, **$p<.05$, ***$p<.01$, ****$p<.001$

Table 47. Multiple Regression Analysis: Male Private Faculty Participation Rates

	Dependent variables				
Independent variables	Black	White	Hispanic	Asian	Native American
Political ideology	-.227	.247	-.002	-.017	.087**
	(.173)	(.486)	(.037)	(.077)	(.032)
Democratic governorship	1.331	-2.006	.059	-.373	-.066
	(.962)	(2.756)	(.204)	(.426)	(.184)
Democratic legislatures	.090**	-.115	-.018*	.038**	.002
	(.0393)	(.109)	(.009)	(.017)	(.008)
% Population	2.698**	8.773**	1.438****	1.694*	.436*
	(1.124)	(3.275)	(.337)	(.915)	(.231)
Median income	-2.324	10.042	-2.414*	-2.044	-.179
	(6.303)	(17.911)	(1.367)	(2.752)	(1.194)
Industrialization	-.074	-.350	.032	.075	-.037
	(.139)	(.379)	(.028)	(.059)	(.026)
Urbanization	.043	.105	.019**	.019	-.004
	(.031)	(.096)	(.008)	(.014)	(.006)
Constant	5.504	(69.818)***	.140	-5.074	1.881
	(8.455)	(23.170)	(1.745)	(3.569)	(1.770)
Adjusted R-squared	.392	.218	.592	.334	.232

Regression coefficients (b's) are presented in the table. Standard errors of estimates are in parentheses. *p<.10, **p<.05, ***p<.01, ****p<.001

Table 48. Multiple Regression Analysis: Female Private Faculty Participation
Rates

	Dependent variables				
Independent variables	Black	White	Hispanic	Asian	Native American
Political ideology	-.260	.102	-.049	-.026	-.008
	(.154)	(.435)	(.036)	(.031)	(.016)
Democratic governorship	1.241	-1.610	.216	.042	-.045
	(.857)	(2.470)	(.198)	(.172)	(.093)
Democratic legislatures	.096**	-.046	-.006	-.000	.007
	(.035)	(.098)	(.008)	(.007)	(.004)
% Population	2.449**	.968	1.610****	.425	.163
	(1.001)	(2.934)	(.327)	(.370)	(.117)
Median income	-.344	-3.935	-.855	-.143	.667
	(5.616)	(16.049)	(1.328)	(1.113)	(.603)
Industrialization	-.114	.389	-.004	.025	-.030**
	(.124)	(.340)	(.028)	(.024)	(.013)
Urbanization	.037	-.192**	.009	.006	.002
	(.028)	(.086)	(.008)	(.006)	(.003)
Constant	7.601	15.090	2.108	-1.206	1.586*
	(7.533)	(20.761)	(1.695)	(1.443)	(.894)
Adjusted R-squared	.434	.056	.526	.065	.098

Regression coefficients (b's) are presented in the table. Standard errors of estimates are in
parentheses. *p<.10, **p<.05, ***p<.01, ****p<.001

Appendixes

Faculty is defined as those employed as professors, associate professors, assistant professors, instructors, lecturers, or the equivalent whose major activities include teaching, research, and community service. Also included are those holding such ranks as deans or department chairs whose primary activity is teaching.[1]

Administrators (defined by the EEOC as executive, administrative, and managerial) are those whose principal function is management. This category includes those involved in the business aspects of the university as well as presidents, deans, and department chairs whose primary duty is an administrative one. Those who hold supervisory positions for the various other categories such as professional non-faculty are reported with that category.[2]

The *participation rate* represents the percentage of each ethnic/racial group by sex holding these positions.

The *representation ratio* is the participation rate divided by each racial/ethnic group by sex as a percentage of the state's population.

Complete data were not available for the states of Maryland, New Mexico, Utah, Washington, and Utah.

TABLE INFORMATION

*Participation rates were not available for this year.

**Public and private participation rates are combined under public.

***Incomplete data.

****Separate population figures for Hispanic males and females were not available for 1980, thus representation ratios are calculated for total faculty and administrative positions for 1979 and 1983.

0.0 for the participation rates tables refers to zero or less than .05.

Appendix 1. Participation Rates: Black Male Faculty

State	1979 Combined	1983 Public	1983 Private	1991 Public	1991 Private
Alabama	7.7	3.7	4.0	4.5	9.3
Alaska	0.0*	0.3**	0.0**	1.0	0.0
Arizona	0.7	0.7**	0.0**	0.8	2.6
Arkansas	3.0	3.6	0.7	3.0	2.6
California	1.8	2.1	1.1	2.5	1.6
Colorado	0.8	1.0	1.4	1.0	1.1
Connecticut	1.2	0.9	1.3	2.1	1.2
Delaware	3.9	3.7	0.0	3.2	1.1
Florida	3.1	3.8	2.1	4.0	3.3
Georgia	5.2	3.6	9.2	5.4	10.7
Idaho	0.0	0.0	0.0	0.2	0.0
Illinois	2.4	2.5	1.1	2.8	1.7
Indiana	0.9	0.8	0.8	1.1	0.9
Iowa	0.7	0.6	0.5	1.1	0.4
Kansas	0.5	0.7	0.1	0.7	0.2
Kentucky	1.7	1.6	0.1	1.9	1.3
Louisiana	5.4	5.9	12.0	5.7	20.2
Maine	0.3	0.3	0.8	0.1	0.8
Maryland	4.6	4.1	0.9	0.0***	5.0
Massachusetts	1.6	2.0	1.2	1.8	1.7
Michigan	2.0	2.3	1.2	2.7	2.2
Minnesota	0.6	0.8	0.4	0.9	0.5
Mississippi	5.0	7.8	8.2	7.3	9.0
Missouri	2.0	1.1	1.0	1.4	1.7
Montana	1.0	0.9	0.0	0.2	0.0
Nebraska	0.5	0.6	0.6	1.1	0.9
Nevada	0.0*	0.0*	0.0*	1.1	4.0
New Hampshire	0.7	0.3	0.8	0.2	0.8
New Jersey	2.6	3.2	1.6	3.3	1.4
New Mexico	0.7	0.4	0.2	0.4**	0.0**
New York	2.1	2.3	1.8	2.9	1.5
North Carolina	3.4	5.5	4.5	5.7	3.9
North Dakota	0.0	0.2	0.8	0.1	0.0
Ohio	1.7	1.6	1.3	2.6	1.8
Oklahoma	1.4	0.8	1.8	1.7	0.7
Oregon	0.7	0.7	0.3	0.6	0.4
Pennsylvania	1.7	2.2	0.9	2.8	1.3
Rhode Island	1.2	0.9	1.0	1.2	1.4
South Carolina	3.8	4.6	4.5	3.9	4.4
South Dakota	0.3	0.3	0.0	0.2	0.0
Tennessee	4.6	3.1	3.0	4.1	2.8
Texas	2.2	2.1	4.3	2.6	0.0
Utah	0.2	0.2	0.0	0.2**	0.0**
Vermont	0.9	0.7	0.0	1.2	0.0
Virginia	3.6	3.6	4.0	4.4	0.0
Washington	1.1	0.9	0.6	1.1	0.0***
West Virginia	1.1	1.1	0.3	1.5	0.0
Wisconsin	0.7	0.8	0.9	1.3	1.9
Wyoming	0.4	0.3**	0.0**	0.6**	0.0**

Appendix 2. Participation Rates: Black Female Faculty

State	1979 Combined	1983 Public	Private	1991 Public	Private
Alabama	6.8	4.5	6.0	6.2	8.0
Alaska	0.0*	0.9**	0.0**	0.7	0.0
Arizona	0.5	0.4**	0.0**	1.2	2.1
Arkansas	3.1	3.5	1.3	3.8	2.1
California	1.3	1.4	0.7	1.7	2.8
Colorado	0.6	0.5	0.2	0.8	0.8
Connecticut	0.6	0.6	0.6	1.3	0.6
Delaware	4.4	6.0	0.0	3.4	2.2
Florida	3.6	3.7	1.4	4.2	1.8
Georgia	5.3	4.5	9.4	4.7	10.1
Idaho	0.1	0.3	0.0	0.1	0.0
Illinois	2.5	2.7	0.5	3.4	1.1
Indiana	0.7	0.8	0.7	1.1	0.5
Iowa	0.3	0.3	0.1	0.7	0.4
Kansas	0.6	0.6	0.3	0.7	0.2
Kentucky	1.2	1.2	0.7	1.4	1.5
Louisiana	6.2	6.6	11.9	6.4	17.5
Maine	0.1	0.0	0.6	0.1	0.4
Maryland	3.7	4.1	0.4	0.0***	4.3
Massachusetts	0.8	1.2	0.6	1.2	0.9
Michigan	1.9	2.3	2.0	2.0	3.1
Minnesota	0.3	0.3	0.2	0.4	0.6
Mississippi	4.1	7.1	7.7	7.2	10.5
Missouri	2.5	1.5	0.7	1.4	1.8
Montana	0.2	0.2	0.0	0.1	0.0
Nebraska	0.5	0.4	0.5	0.4	0.3
Nevada	0.0*	0.0*	0.0*	0.6	8.0
New Hampshire	0.1	0.1	0.5	0.1	0.1
New Jersey	2.0	2.0	0.9	2.8	0.8
New Mexico	0.4	0.2	0.5	0.2**	0.0**
New York	1.7	2.1	1.6	2.7	0.9
North Carolina	3.6	5.6	4.1	5.1	3.7
North Dakota	0.3	0.0	0.0	0.2	0.0
Ohio	1.4	1.5	1.2	2.1	1.6
Oklahoma	1.7	1.2	1.8	1.9	1.7
Oregon	0.4	0.3	0.1	0.4	0.2
Pennsylvania	1.1	1.6	0.8	1.9	0.7
Rhode Island	0.4	0.3	0.3	0.6	0.9
South Carolina	3.6	3.9	3.9	5.0	4.1
South Dakota	1.1	0.0	0.2	0.0	0.0
Tennessee	4.5	3.9	2.1	4.8	1.5
Texas	2.1	1.8	2.9	2.3	2.3
Utah	0.1	0.2	0.1	0.1**	0.0**
Vermont	0.2	0.2	0.0	0.4	0.0
Virginia	4.1	4.1	6.1	4.2	0.0
Washington	0.8	0.6	0.4	0.7	0.0***
West Virginia	1.0	1.4	0.5	1.4	0.0
Wisconsin	0.6	0.8	0.2	1.1	0.0
Wyoming	0.0	0.1**	0.0**	0.1**	0.0**

Appendix 3. Participation Rates: Black Male Administrators

State	1979 Combined	1983 Public	1983 Private	1991 Public	1991 Private
Alabama	12.3	6.6	10.7	6.9	19.4
Alaska	0.0*	1.5**	0.0**	0.0	1.8
Arizona	1.1	1.4**	0.0**	2.1	1.9
Arkansas	7.0	7.2	0.9	6.1	4.8
California	3.4	3.9	1.9	4.3	2.9
Colorado	1.5	2.6	1.7	2.2	0.9
Connecticut	3.7	4.0	1.9	4.4	2.3
Delaware	8.8	9.8	5.3	5.6	2.1
Florida	7.0	7.0	3.0	3.9	1.9
Georgia	7.7	6.8	8.9	6.2	11.9
Idaho	0.3	0.4	0.0	0.0	0.0
Illinois	4.4	5.2	3.2	5.8	2.8
Indiana	2.0	2.2	1.1	1.4	2.0
Iowa	1.1	1.7	0.8	1.8	1.1
Kansas	1.3	1.6	0.6	1.8	0.4
Kentucky	3.8	4.2	0.9	3.7	0.6
Louisiana	10.1	6.9	12.3	7.4	9.2
Maine	1.1	0.6	1.1	0.0	2.2
Maryland	9.6	8.9	2.1	0.0***	9.4
Massachusetts	3.0	5.7	2.1	4.2	2.2
Michigan	3.5	3.9	1.1	4.3	4.0
Minnesota	1.4	1.3	1.0	1.7	0.7
Mississippi	10.6	12.8	18.4	10.6	12.2
Missouri	3.4	2.7	1.5	2.4	3.6
Montana	1.3	0.6	0.0	0.0	0.0
Nebraska	1.1	0.3	1.0	0.6	1.3
Nevada	0.0*	0.0*	0.0*	2.8	3.3
New Hampshire	1.7	0.0	1.6	0.0	1.2
New Jersey	6.4	8.5	4.5	8.5	3.3
New Mexico	2.5	0.7	2.1	1.2**	0.0**
New York	3.1	4.1	3.1	4.9	3.5
North Carolina	6.8	9.0	6.3	7.6	6.2
North Dakota	0.4	0.0	0.0	0.0	0.0
Ohio	3.8	3.5	3.6	4.1	3.1
Oklahoma	4.3	2.3	2.2	2.6	1.1
Oregon	1.3	1.2	0.6	0.8	0.7
Pennsylvania	4.3	5.4	2.4	5.0	2.4
Rhode Island	3.0	6.0	2.3	6.6	2.4
South Carolina	5.6	5.7	3.4	4.8	5.7
South Dakota	0.9	0.6	0.0	0.4	0.8
Tennessee	7.6	5.9	8.1	6.3	5.8
Texas	4.2	2.9	4.6	3.4	2.8
Utah	0.3	0.6	0.0	0.4**	0.0**
Vermont	1.5	1.2	0.9	0.7	0.0
Virginia	7.2	6.1	5.2	5.5	1.2
Washington	2.2	2.0	0.8	2.1	0.0***
West Virginia	2.5	2.9	1.8	2.9	2.9
Wisconsin	1.7	1.5	1.6	2.0	3.8
Wyoming	0.0	0.0**	0.0**	0.5**	0.0**

Appendix 4. Participation Rates: Black Female Administrators

State	1979 Combined	1983 Public	1983 Private	1991 Public	1991 Private
Alabama	0.3	1.9	5.6	5.2	13.4
Alaska	0.0*	0.0**	0.0**	0.7	1.8
Arizona	0.0	0.3**	0.0**	1.3	1.0
Arkansas	0.0	3.8	1.7	4.2	5.7
California	0.0	2.2	1.9	3.5	3.5
Colorado	0.0	1.0	1.1	1.6	1.4
Connecticut	0.0	1.8	3.0	4.0	3.6
Delaware	0.8	6.1	0.0	4.6	2.1
Florida	0.2	4.0	2.3	4.0	3.7
Georgia	0.2	3.8	10.4	5.8	12.9
Idaho	0.0	0.0	0.0	0.0	0.0
Illinois	0.5	3.9	4.0	7.2	5.9
Indiana	0.0	1.4	2.5	1.6	1.5
Iowa	0.0	0.6	0.5	1.0	0.8
Kansas	0.1	1.3	0.0	1.9	1.6
Kentucky	0.0	1.2	0.7	3.0	1.1
Louisiana	0.1	4.8	12.4	5.6	12.4
Maine	0.1	0.6	0.0	0.3	1.4
Maryland	0.0	5.4	1.6	0.0***	7.4
Massachusetts	0.0	2.8	1.4	2.9	2.7
Michigan	0.0	4.3	1.8	4.4	4.0
Minnesota	0.1	1.3	0.5	1.8	0.7
Mississippi	0.1	5.3	11.0	6.9	16.6
Missouri	0.1	2.2	2.4	2.0	4.9
Montana	0.0	0.0	0.0	0.0	0.0
Nebraska	0.0	0.5	1.0	0.9	0.7
Nevada	0.0*	0.0*	0.0*	1.8	0.0
New Hampshire	0.2	0.0	0.2	0.4	1.1
New Jersey	0.1	6.2	2.9	11.5	3.7
New Mexico	0.0	0.0	0.5	1.0**	0.0**
New York	0.1	2.8	4.2	5.9	4.5
North Carolina	0.1	4.1	5.3	5.4	7.6
North Dakota	0.0	0.0	0.0	0.0	0.0
Ohio	0.0	2.2	2.8	4.0	5.1
Oklahoma	0.0	2.3	0.9	2.2	0.6
Oregon	0.0	0.4	0.0	0.7	0.2
Pennsylvania	0.0	4.7	4.4	4.7	3.9
Rhode Island	0.0	1.0	0.5	0.9	2.2
South Carolina	0.1	2.7	2.3	2.9	5.3
South Dakota	0.2	0.0	0.3	0.4	0.0
Tennessee	0.3	3.7	9.3	4.8	4.3
Texas	0.2	1.4	4.3	3.0	5.6
Utah	0.0	0.0	0.0	0.0**	0.0**
Vermont	0.0	0.0	0.3	0.6	0.0
Virginia	0.2	6.2	3.4	5.0	4.7
Washington	0.1	1.2	0.3	1.8	0.0***
West Virginia	0.1	1.2	0.9	1.5	0.0
Wisconsin	0.0	1.4	1.2	2.2	0.0
Wyoming	0.0	0.0**	0.0**	0.0**	0.0**

Appendix 5. Participation Rates: White Female Faculty

State	1979 Combined	1983 Public	1983 Private	1991 Public	1991 Private
Alabama	24.5	28.4	41.1	29.3	29.2
Alaska	0.0*	28.8**	0.0**	30.6	35.6
Arizona	21.8	19.3**	0.0**	29.6	32.3
Arkansas	23.4	27.0	29.4	32.9	29.8
California	20.8	22.3	21.2	25.5	26.7
Colorado	20.7	20.8	26.8	26.4	27.6
Connecticut	23.1	25.2	22.9	27.3	26.9
Delaware	26.6	24.9	49.3	32.9	42.2
Florida	22.9	23.7	19.1	28.1	23.9
Georgia	23.7	26.7	23.9	31.5	25.5
Idaho	21.6	18.8	20.2	29.1	15.5
Illinois	23.0	25.1	24.2	28.2	27.6
Indiana	21.6	24.7	24.8	32.5	24.6
Iowa	22.3	24.6	27.5	30.7	29.2
Kansas	26.7	24.1	32.0	29.4	36.9
Kentucky	27.6	29.9	34.2	28.1	42.8
Louisiana	22.5	26.7	20.6	30.0	22.8
Maine	24.8	22.3	23.5	28.5	37.9
Maryland	26.1	29.0	28.4	0.0***	30.4
Massachusetts	24.3	27.5	25.5	31.5	28.7
Michigan	22.6	21.6	28.1	24.3	31.2
Minnesota	21.3	24.1	29.2	29.5	34.2
Mississippi	26.4	32.4	34.5	35.4	33.3
Missouri	26.4	25.1	29.3	25.9	33.1
Montana	16.7	21.5	21.4	24.7	30.1
Nebraska	24.5	23.2	32.0	28.1	35.4
Nevada	0.0*	0.0*	0.0*	27.3	36.0
New Hampshire	22.2	21.7	26.2	31.9	29.4
New Jersey	25.2	29.6	23.7	29.3	25.3
New Mexico	20.2	20.2	21.9	25.4**	0.0**
New York	23.6	25.0	26.0	27.0	29.9
North Carolina	24.6	26.4	24.2	28.8	28.5
North Dakota	21.2	24.0	36.1	26.9	41.2
Ohio	23.0	24.7	22.8	27.7	29.8
Oklahoma	24.5	23.6	26.3	29.6	29.1
Oregon	25.7	26.6	22.6	35.3	27.8
Pennsylvania	21.7	23.1	24.3	28.0	26.9
Rhode Island	25.1	32.3	22.6	36.0	27.5
South Carolina	25.4	26.0	26.6	30.9	29.7
South Dakota	23.0	22.8	34.7	27.5	51.6
Tennessee	23.5	24.0	25.9	28.4	27.7
Texas	23.4	26.0	25.7	29.1	42.7
Utah	17.5	19.4	13.7	23.8**	0.0**
Vermont	24.6	23.4	20.1	30.2	57.1
Virginia	22.0	23.1	27.7	26.1	32.2
Washington	23.2	23.7	27.3	29.1	0.0***
West Virginia	25.8	28.5	34.7	32.5	34.1
Wisconsin	23.4	26.3	25.9	30.3	24.1
Wyoming	22.4	22.7**	0.0**	33.4**	0.0**

Appendix 6. Participation Rates: White Male Faculty

State	1979 Combined	1983 Public	1983 Private	1991 Public	1991 Private
Alabama	58.0	60.0	47.8	55.0	47.4
Alaska	0.0*	64.0**	0.0**	59.6	55.6
Arizona	71.0	72.7**	0.0**	58.0	47.6
Arkansas	68.0	62.7	67.4	55.9	63.4
California	67.5	64.9	69.8	56.7	59.6
Colorado	73.0	72.6	66.9	64.0	63.5
Connecticut	71.4	69.3	70.6	62.5	65.0
Delaware	61.5	61.1	45.3	53.3	47.8
Florida	66.2	64.7	71.5	55.8	62.8
Georgia	62.7	62.5	54.5	53.7	48.7
Idaho	76.3	76.2	78.4	67.0	83.8
Illinois	67.2	64.3	69.4	58.3	63.8
Indiana	71.9	68.4	70.1	58.1	69.3
Iowa	73.2	69.8	69.6	61.0	66.4
Kansas	68.5	70.3	62.2	63.6	60.0
Kentucky	66.6	64.5	62.2	62.8	51.7
Louisiana	61.7	56.3	51.0	50.8	31.8
Maine	74.7	75.2	73.6	69.6	56.8
Maryland	60.6	57.9	65.9	0.0***	54.0
Massachusetts	69.8	64.2	68.3	59.7	62.9
Michigan	69.4	69.1	65.1	62.1	60.4
Minnesota	74.5	70.0	68.0	63.5	60.0
Mississippi	62.2	50.6	44.0	45.9	40.9
Missouri	65.5	69.0	65.9	64.8	58.2
Montana	78.7	74.1	77.9	70.4	64.7
Nebraska	71.7	72.2	65.1	65.5	59.3
Nevada	0.0*	0.0*	0.0*	61.0	52.0
New Hampshire	73.6	74.5	69.4	64.1	66.9
New Jersey	64.8	59.4	67.9	56.4	63.4
New Mexico	70.3	62.3	68.9	57.2**	0.0**
New York	67.2	65.2	64.9	59.9	61.2
North Carolina	65.9	58.6	64.1	55.2	59.0
North Dakota	75.1	72.5	54.1	65.6	58.8
Ohio	70.7	67.9	70.2	60.6	62.5
Oklahoma	67.4	68.2	65.3	59.3	62.6
Oregon	69.8	69.6	74.3	59.3	67.8
Pennsylvania	71.6	69.2	70.2	61.5	65.0
Rhode Island	70.5	62.4	72.2	55.9	65.6
South Carolina	64.1	62.8	62.0	56.3	57.8
South Dakota	72.8	73.2	62.7	66.4	45.7
Tennessee	64.5	65.1	67.1	57.6	63.2
Texas	65.8	62.2	62.7	56.5	48.5
Utah	77.9	76.4	83.7	71.6**	0.0**
Vermont	72.9	74.1	71.3	63.9	42.9
Virginia	67.1	65.2	59.7	60.3	64.5
Washington	69.8	69.6	69.1	62.3	0.0***
West Virginia	68.1	64.9	62.0	58.7	61.0
Wisconsin	72.1	68.8	68.6	61.6	70.4
Wyoming	75.2	75.3**	0.0**	62.7**	0.0**

Appendix 7. Participation Rates: White Female Administrators

State	1979 Combined	1983 Public	1983 Private	1991 Public	1991 Private
Alabama	15.4	15.6	17.8	24.0	19.1
Alaska	0.0*	27.2**	0.0**	29.5	36.8
Arizona	13.9	23.4**	0.0**	28.9	42.3
Arkansas	19.8	22.2	29.3	31.3	24.4
California	22.0	21.3	31.6	33.2	29.4
Colorado	21.0	21.9	39.3	30.0	38.4
Connecticut	22.4	22.5	39.7	33.0	48.8
Delaware	13.7	12.1	31.6	30.9	51.1
Florida	18.3	20.3	35.3	27.6	37.5
Georgia	17.4	18.5	21.4	26.3	25.9
Idaho	14.7	17.4	15.6	22.7	14.9
Illinois	23.9	23.9	29.4	30.2	37.9
Indiana	28.6	28.2	27.7	19.5	36.1
Iowa	23.1	20.1	32.9	25.9	37.9
Kansas	19.1	27.8	28.8	35.1	31.9
Kentucky	19.8	18.1	36.1	27.6	32.5
Louisiana	23.6	27.6	38.9	30.1	40.5
Maine	24.8	21.6	33.3	28.5	38.8
Maryland	16.7	23.5	28.8	0.0***	29.9
Massachusetts	32.3	26.2	41.2	34.5	42.3
Michigan	22.7	24.1	28.0	34.4	34.8
Minnesota	27.7	31.2	31.4	48.6	36.6
Mississippi	14.5	15.2	18.4	28.1	24.3
Missouri	19.7	24.9	38.0	32.2	45.8
Montana	29.3	15.7	27.3	27.7	23.8
Nebraska	20.1	19.3	32.3	23.1	42.6
Nevada	0.0*	0.0*	0.0*	33.0	29.5
New Hampshire	23.9	16.9	35.8	41.0	46.0
New Jersey	26.0	22.3	35.0	30.2	47.0
New Mexico	21.3	18.0	14.5	21.6**	0.0**
New York	31.4	24.7	41.2	33.5	42.9
North Carolina	21.9	21.0	32.6	30.0	31.9
North Dakota	16.7	16.6	26.2	15.9	35.0
Ohio	24.1	23.1	33.3	30.4	41.3
Oklahoma	21.1	20.8	26.5	33.9	22.3
Oregon	24.9	23.5	29.0	33.6	41.4
Pennsylvania	29.7	24.9	42.4	30.5	41.7
Rhode Island	29.4	24.4	39.6	27.9	44.3
South Carolina	21.1	17.0	26.1	21.1	25.2
South Dakota	24.0	14.5	31.1	21.9	45.1
Tennessee	20.3	21.4	24.2	27.2	35.0
Texas	23.9	23.9	32.3	32.0	27.0
Utah	23.8	25.5	2.2	14.9**	0.0**
Vermont	27.9	27.5	37.6	43.9	23.8
Virginia	26.3	27.1	29.3	31.9	38.4
Washington	31.6	34.8	31.4	38.1	0.0***
West Virginia	30.8	34.0	27.2	36.7	31.4
Wisconsin	24.0	28.0	31.9	30.1	46.2
Wyoming	12.7	11.4**	0.0**	18.6**	0.0**

Appendix 8. Participation Rates: White Male Administrators

State	1979 Combined	1983 Public	1983 Private	1991 Public	1991 Private
Alabama	65.0	75.5	65.0	63.1	47.0
Alaska	0.0*	63.1**	0.0**	61.0	56.1
Arizona	79.7	69.8**	0.0**	56.7	51.9
Arkansas	68.9	65.3	66.8	56.9	63.6
California	66.0	62.3	58.7	45.8	52.7
Colorado	70.0	66.7	54.6	56.8	55.1
Connecticut	70.6	69.2	53.6	55.7	42.5
Delaware	70.3	67.8	57.9	58.0	42.6
Florida	68.7	66.2	48.8	59.1	39.1
Georgia	70.0	70.2	58.8	60.9	48.3
Idaho	83.8	77.9	84.4	75.0	85.1
Illinois	66.2	63.9	60.9	52.1	49.6
Indiana	66.3	66.4	67.5	75.7	59.1
Iowa	74.4	76.5	65.2	69.0	59.2
Kansas	76.8	67.4	68.1	59.1	65.4
Kentucky	75.4	75.2	62.3	64.9	65.4
Louisiana	60.2	59.8	34.9	55.3	35.5
Maine	73.1	76.5	65.5	70.8	57.2
Maryland	65.0	60.0	66.6	0.0***	51.4
Massachusetts	61.0	63.5	54.1	55.6	50.1
Michigan	69.4	65.5	67.7	54.5	54.6
Minnesota	68.3	64.7	67.0	44.6	60.7
Mississippi	68.3	66.5	51.5	54.1	46.4
Missouri	74.2	68.2	56.6	62.2	44.3
Montana	65.6	80.0	63.6	69.2	42.9
Nebraska	77.0	78.4	65.0	72.9	54.3
Nevada	0.0*	0.0*	0.0*	58.2	67.2
New Hampshire	73.2	82.6	61.4	57.9	50.3
New Jersey	61.2	58.9	55.1	43.8	43.0
New Mexico	60.5	42.4	72.5	48.2**	0.0**
New York	59.0	65.4	47.0	49.5	43.5
North Carolina	66.3	64.1	55.7	55.5	53.9
North Dakota	80.2	81.0	64.3	73.8	62.5
Ohio	69.3	69.5	59.2	59.8	49.4
Oklahoma	67.5	71.5	64.9	55.5	71.5
Oregon	70.4	72.9	69.6	62.1	53.6
Pennsylvania	61.1	63.7	49.5	57.8	50.2
Rhode Island	65.3	66.9	56.7	62.0	48.5
South Carolina	69.5	73.7	67.8	69.9	63.3
South Dakota	71.6	72.7	63.6	74.9	50.4
Tennessee	65.5	68.5	57.5	61.0	53.9
Texas	63.9	64.9	54.3	53.6	54.5
Utah	66.7	70.1	94.6	83.3**	0.0**
Vermont	69.6	70.1	60.6	53.3	71.4
Virginia	61.0	57.5	61.3	56.4	55.8
Washington	59.4	56.6	61.8	51.6	0.0***
West Virginia	64.7	61.0	70.2	57.8	65.7
Wisconsin	71.3	67.3	63.6	63.1	50.0
Wyoming	86.7	87.6**	0.0**	77.8**	0.0**

Appendix 9. Participation Rates: Hispanic Male Faculty

State	1979 Combined	1983 Public	1983 Private	1991 Public	1991 Private
Alabama	0.6	0.5	0.0	0.5	0.3
Alaska	0.0*	0.5**	0.0**	0.8	0.0
Arizona	2.5	2.3**	0.0**	3.2	4.8
Arkansas	0.5	0.4	0.0	0.4	0.4
California	2.5	2.8	1.7	3.7	1.9
Colorado	1.9	2.2	1.6	2.8	3.1
Connecticut	0.9	0.8	0.7	1.3	1.0
Delaware	0.6	0.4	0.0	0.8	0.0
Florida	1.7	1.3	2.9	2.4	3.3
Georgia	0.7	0.4	0.7	0.5	0.8
Idaho	0.2	0.3	0.8	0.5	0.3
Illinois	0.7	0.7	0.6	0.9	0.9
Indiana	0.6	0.7	0.7	0.8	1.0
Iowa	0.5	0.8	0.2	0.8	0.5
Kansas	0.7	0.6	0.4	0.8	0.7
Kentucky	0.4	0.3	0.2	0.6	0.2
Louisiana	0.9	0.8	0.9	0.8	0.4
Maine	0.3	0.4	0.4	0.0	0.6
Maryland	0.5	0.5	1.1	0.0***	0.8
Massachusetts	0.7	0.7	0.9	0.9	1.0
Michigan	0.5	0.6	0.3	1.0	0.4
Minnesota	0.6	0.6	0.6	0.8	0.8
Mississippi	0.5	0.3	0.2	0.3	0.2
Missouri	0.6	0.5	0.5	0.5	0.7
Montana	0.8	0.4	0.0	0.4	0.0
Nebraska	0.5	0.6	0.2	0.7	0.9
Nevada	0.0*	0.0*	0.0*	1.1	0.0
New Hampshire	1.0	0.8	0.8	0.6	0.8
New Jersey	1.2	1.2	1.0	1.5	1.6
New Mexico	4.8	9.3	4.1	7.8**	0.0**
New York	1.2	1.3	1.3	1.6	1.0
North Carolina	0.5	0.6	0.4	0.8	0.8
North Dakota	0.3	0.1	0.8	0.4	0.0
Ohio	0.5	0.5	0.7	0.8	0.6
Oklahoma	0.5	1.0	0.5	0.5	0.3
Oregon	0.5	0.6	0.6	0.8	0.8
Pennsylvania	0.6	0.5	0.6	0.7	1.0
Rhode Island	0.7	0.6	0.9	0.7	0.8
South Carolina	0.5	0.4	0.7	0.5	0.5
South Dakota	0.7	0.3	0.2	0.9	0.0
Tennessee	0.5	0.5	0.4	0.6	1.4
Texas	2.6	3.0	1.5	3.3	1.8
Utah	0.9	0.9	0.6	1.0**	0.0**
Vermont	0.7	0.5	1.2	0.7	0.0
Virginia	0.4	0.5	0.6	0.6	0.4
Washington	0.7	0.7	0.4	1.1	0.0***
West Virginia	0.5	0.4	0.0	0.3	0.0
Wisconsin	0.6	0.6	0.6	1.0	1.9
Wyoming	1.0	0.7**	0.0**	0.3**	0.0**

Appendix 10 . Participation Rates: Hispanic Female Faculty

State	1979 Combined	1983 Public	1983 Private	1991 Public	1991 Private
Alabama	0.1	0.1	0.0	0.2	0.2
Alaska	0.0*	0.3**	0.0**	0.5	2.2
Arizona	0.8	0.8**	0.0**	2.5	4.8
Arkansas	0.1	0.1	0.0	0.1	0.5
California	1.0	1.1	0.6	2.1	1.5
Colorado	0.6	0.8	0.9	1.3	1.9
Connecticut	0.3	0.4	0.2	0.8	0.5
Delaware	0.1	0.3	0.0	1.1	0.0
Florida	0.9	0.5	0.9	1.6	1.5
Georgia	0.1	0.1	0.3	0.2	0.6
Idaho	0.1	0.3	0.0	0.4	0.3
Illinois	0.4	0.4	0.4	0.7	0.4
Indiana	0.1	0.3	0.2	0.4	0.3
Iowa	0.1	0.1	0.3	0.4	0.5
Kansas	0.2	0.2	0.6	0.3	0.8
Kentucky	0.0	0.0	0.2	0.1	0.2
Louisiana	0.3	0.3	0.5	0.4	1.0
Maine	0.1	0.4	0.0	0.1	0.4
Maryland	0.3	0.4	0.7	0.0***	0.6
Massachusetts	0.3	0.3	0.2	0.6	0.6
Michigan	0.3	0.2	0.3	0.6	0.3
Minnesota	0.1	0.1	0.2	0.3	0.6
Mississippi	0.0	0.1	0.2	0.1	0.0
Missouri	0.2	0.2	0.3	0.5	0.3
Montana	0.1	0.1	0.0	0.2	0.0
Nebraska	0.2	0.4	0.0	0.4	0.3
Nevada	0.0*	0.0*	0.0*	0.6	0.0
New Hampshire	0.2	0.0	0.4	0.2	0.5
New Jersey	0.7	0.8	0.6	1.3	0.7
New Mexico	1.2	5.0	1.7	3.7**	0.0**
New York	0.7	0.7	0.9	1.1	0.7
North Carolina	0.2	0.3	0.4	0.4	0.4
North Dakota	0.1	0.0	0.0	0.3	0.0
Ohio	0.2	0.2	0.2	0.3	0.4
Oklahoma	0.1	0.4	0.2	0.5	0.3
Oregon	0.2	0.2	0.1	0.5	0.3
Pennsylvania	0.2	0.2	0.2	0.5	0.4
Rhode Island	0.1	0.2	0.0	0.2	0.2
South Carolina	0.2	0.1	0.2	0.3	0.2
South Dakota	0.1	0.0	0.2	0.0	0.5
Tennessee	0.1	0.1	0.2	0.3	0.3
Texas	1.2	1.6	0.6	2.1	2.9
Utah	0.4	0.1	0.5	0.4**	0.0**
Vermont	0.1	0.2	0.6	0.4	0.0
Virginia	0.2	0.2	0.3	0.3	0.0
Washington	0.2	0.3	0.2	0.5	0.0***
West Virginia	0.2	0.1	0.8	0.2	0.0
Wisconsin	0.2	0.2	0.3	0.5	0.0
Wyoming	0.0	0.1**	0.0**	0.5**	0.0**

Appendix 11. Participation Rates: Hispanic Male Administrators

State	1979 Combined	1983 Public	1983 Private	1991 Public	1991 Private
Alabama	0.1	0.1	0.0	0.1	0.0
Alaska	0.0*	2.1**	0.0**	0.7	0.0
Arizona	3.3	2.7**	0.0**	5.2	1.9
Arkansas	0.1	0.3	0.4	0.3	0.0
California	3.3	5.6	2.5	4.5	5.3
Colorado	4.2	5.0	1.7	4.9	2.5
Connecticut	0.6	1.2	0.3	1.3	0.6
Delaware	0.4	0.5	0.0	0.3	0.0
Florida	1.0	0.9	4.4	1.9	4.7
Georgia	0.2	0.1	0.3	0.0	0.4
Idaho	0.3	0.4	0.0	0.5	0.0
Illinois	0.5	0.8	0.5	1.3	0.8
Indiana	0.4	0.5	0.3	0.4	0.3
Iowa	0.1	0.0	0.3	0.2	0.7
Kansas	0.6	0.5	0.0	0.4	0.0
Kentucky	0.1	0.6	0.0	0.2	0.0
Louisiana	0.8	0.4	0.6	0.3	1.1
Maine	0.0	0.0	0.0	0.5	0.0
Maryland	0.2	0.3	0.0	0.0***	0.4
Massachusetts	0.5	0.4	0.3	0.6	0.4
Michigan	0.4	0.3	0.3	0.4	0.9
Minnesota	0.4	0.4	0.0	0.9	0.3
Mississippi	0.1	0.0	0.0	0.0	0.0
Missouri	0.3	0.3	0.6	0.6	0.2
Montana	0.1	0.9	0.0	0.3	0.0
Nebraska	0.4	0.6	0.3	0.6	0.0
Nevada	0.0*	0.0*	0.0*	2.1	0.0
New Hampshire	0.3	0.0	0.4	0.0	0.0
New Jersey	1.2	1.9	0.8	1.4	0.8
New Mexico	9.9	30.2	5.2	17.5**	0.0**
New York	1.2	0.8	1.6	2.0	1.8
North Carolina	0.1	0.1	0.1	0.2	0.1
North Dakota	0.0	0.0	0.0	0.0	0.0
Ohio	0.2	0.2	0.0	0.6	0.2
Oklahoma	0.0	0.0	0.4	0.5	0.6
Oregon	0.5	0.7	0.0	0.9	0.5
Pennsylvania	0.2	0.3	0.2	0.4	0.4
Rhode Island	0.2	0.7	0.0	0.0	0.8
South Carolina	0.1	0.1	0.4	0.3	0.2
South Dakota	0.0	0.6	0.0	0.0	0.0
Tennessee	0.2	0.1	0.3	0.2	0.1
Texas	3.1	4.1	1.7	4.0	1.7
Utah	1.8	1.8	1.1	1.1**	0.0**
Vermont	0.3	0.6	0.6	0.0	0.0
Virginia	0.0	0.1	0.1	0.1	0.0
Washington	1.4	1.2	3.4	1.3	0.0***
West Virginia	0.1	0.0	0.0	0.1	0.0
Wisconsin	0.4	0.4	0.5	0.8	0.0
Wyoming	0.0	0.5**	0.0**	0.9**	0.0**

Appendix 12. Participation Rates: Hispanic Female Administrators

State	1979 Combined	1983 Public	1983 Private	1991 Public	1991 Private
Alabama	0.0	0.0	0.0	0.1	0.0
Alaska	0.0*	0.0**	0.0**	0.0	3.5
Arizona	0.6	0.9**	0.0**	2.1	1.0
Arkansas	0.0	0.2	0.0	0.1	1.0
California	0.8	1.3	0.9	2.7	2.7
Colorado	1.0	1.2	0.0	2.6	0.9
Connecticut	0.4	0.3	0.2	1.1	0.6
Delaware	0.0	0.0	0.0	0.3	0.0
Florida	0.8	1.0	5.2	2.2	8.3
Georgia	0.1	0.0	0.0	0.0	0.1
Idaho	0.3	0.4	0.0	0.0	0.0
Illinois	0.4	0.6	0.5	1.1	0.9
Indiana	0.2	0.2	0.1	0.0	0.6
Iowa	0.1	0.2	0.0	0.1	0.1
Kansas	0.2	0.2	0.0	0.4	0.8
Kentucky	0.1	0.0	0.0	0.0	0.0
Louisiana	0.2	0.1	0.2	0.2	0.6
Maine	0.1	0.3	0.0	0.0	0.4
Maryland	0.2	0.3	0.2	0.0***	0.1
Massachusetts	0.1	0.4	0.2	1.0	0.8
Michigan	0.1	0.3	0.2	0.4	0.4
Minnesota	0.1	0.1	0.0	0.1	0.0
Mississippi	0.0	0.0	0.0	0.0	0.0
Missouri	0.0	0.1	0.1	0.1	0.3
Montana	0.1	0.9	0.0	0.3	0.0
Nebraska	0.2	0.3	0.3	0.2	0.4
Nevada	0.0*	0.0*	0.0*	1.1	0.0
New Hampshire	0.0	0.0	0.4	0.0	0.2
New Jersey	0.7	0.4	0.7	2.0	0.4
New Mexico	2.2	6.5	3.1	7.2**	0.0**
New York	0.8	0.6	1.3	2.2	1.4
North Carolina	0.1	0.1	0.0	0.1	0.1
North Dakota	0.4	0.0	0.0	0.0	0.0
Ohio	0.1	0.2	0.1	0.1	0.2
Oklahoma	0.2	0.3	0.2	0.6	0.0
Oregon	0.4	0.2	0.0	0.3	0.3
Pennsylvania	0.1	0.2	0.1	0.3	0.4
Rhode Island	0.0	0.0	0.0	0.0	0.3
South Carolina	0.0	0.0	0.0	0.1	0.0
South Dakota	0.0	0.0	0.0	0.0	0.0
Tennessee	0.1	0.0	0.1	0.1	0.0
Texas	1.3	1.7	1.8	2.4	7.9
Utah	0.5	0.6	0.0	0.0**	0.0**
Vermont	0.0	0.0	0.0	0.3	0.0
Virginia	0.0	0.1	0.0	0.2	0.0
Washington	0.3	0.6	0.3	0.6	0.0***
West Virginia	0.1	0.0	0.0	0.0	0.0
Wisconsin	0.1	0.2	0.1	0.6	0.0
Wyoming	0.0	0.0**	0.0**	0.0**	0.0**

Appendix 13. Participation Rates: Asian Male Faculty

State	1979 Combined	1983 Public	1983 Private	1991 Public	1991 Private
Alabama	2.0	2.5	0.9	3.7	4.8
Alaska	0.0*	1.9**	0.0**	3.3	4.4
Arizona	1.4	2.7**	0.0**	2.2	3.2
Arkansas	1.4	1.7	0.9	2.9	1.1
California	3.6	3.6	3.2	5.0	4.2
Colorado	1.6	1.5	1.4	2.6	1.3
Connecticut	2.0	2.3	3.0	3.8	3.3
Delaware	2.3	2.7	1.3	4.1	5.6
Florida	1.3	1.9	1.9	3.0	2.9
Georgia	1.9	1.8	1.6	3.4	3.3
Idaho	1.1	1.5	0.6	1.8	0.0
Illinois	2.9	3.1	3.3	4.3	3.9
Indiana	3.5	3.6	2.3	5.0	2.8
Iowa	2.4	3.4	1.4	4.4	1.7
Kansas	2.1	2.7	1.5	3.8	1.0
Kentucky	2.1	2.2	2.1	4.0	1.9
Louisiana	2.3	2.7	2.7	5.0	5.1
Maine	0.8	1.2	0.9	1.3	1.4
Maryland	3.2	3.2	2.1	0.0***	3.7
Massachusetts	1.8	2.6	2.5	3.0	2.9
Michigan	2.6	3.2	2.4	6.0	1.6
Minnesota	2.0	2.8	0.7	3.2	1.5
Mississippi	1.6	1.3	4.6	3.1	5.2
Missouri	2.1	2.2	1.7	4.5	3.1
Montana	1.9	1.8	0.7	1.9	0.7
Nebraska	1.6	2.4	1.3	3.1	2.3
Nevada	0.0*	0.0*	0.0*	5.8	0.0
New Hampshire	1.6	2.1	1.2	2.1	1.1
New Jersey	2.7	2.9	3.4	4.2	5.5
New Mexico	1.4	1.2	1.4	3.1**	0.0**
New York	2.6	2.7	2.7	3.6	3.7
North Carolina	1.3	2.4	1.9	3.2	2.8
North Dakota	2.5	2.9	3.3	4.3	0.0
Ohio	2.1	3.2	2.8	4.9	2.4
Oklahoma	1.9	2.2	1.5	2.9	2.1
Oregon	1.7	1.3	1.5	1.8	2.0
Pennsylvania	2.5	2.5	2.3	3.7	3.8
Rhode Island	1.8	3.0	2.4	4.8	2.8
South Carolina	1.8	1.9	1.7	2.5	2.6
South Dakota	1.3	2.1	1.0	3.5	1.1
Tennessee	1.9	2.8	1.2	3.4	2.7
Texas	1.9	2.5	1.8	3.0	0.6
Utah	2.1	1.7	1.0	2.1**	0.0**
Vermont	0.6	0.9	0.6	2.1	0.0
Virginia	2.1	2.7	1.1	3.1	2.5
Washington	2.6	2.5	1.3	3.2	0.0***
West Virginia	2.7	3.1	1.5	4.4	4.9
Wisconsin	2.0	1.9	2.8	3.1	0.0
Wyoming	0.8	0.5**	0.0**	2.0**	0.0**

Appendix 14 . Participation Rates: Asian Female Faculty

State	1979 Combined	1983 Public	1983 Private	1991 Public	1991 Private
Alabama	0.3	0.2	0.3	0.5	0.8
Alaska	0.0*	0.2**	0.0**	0.8	0.0
Arizona	0.5	0.5**	0.0**	1.3	2.6
Arkansas	0.2	0.3	0.0	0.4	0.1
California	1.2	1.3	1.3	2.3	1.6
Colorado	0.4	0.3	0.5	0.6	0.4
Connecticut	0.5	0.5	0.7	0.8	1.3
Delaware	0.4	0.5	4.0	0.9	1.1
Florida	0.2	0.2	0.2	0.6	0.5
Georgia	0.2	0.2	0.3	0.5	0.3
Idaho	0.3	0.2	0.0	0.3	0.0
Illinois	0.8	1.0	0.4	1.1	0.7
Indiana	0.5	0.6	0.3	0.9	0.6
Iowa	0.4	0.3	0.3	0.7	0.6
Kansas	0.3	0.3	0.0	0.5	0.2
Kentucky	0.3	0.3	0.1	0.9	0.3
Louisiana	0.5	0.4	0.2	0.8	1.1
Maine	0.2	0.1	0.2	0.2	1.6
Maryland	0.8	0.7	0.6	0.0***	1.1
Massachusetts	0.4	0.6	0.7	1.2	1.2
Michigan	0.6	0.5	0.4	1.0	0.6
Minnesota	0.3	0.6	0.3	0.8	1.1
Mississippi	0.3	0.3	0.5	0.6	1.0
Missouri	0.6	0.3	0.3	0.6	0.8
Montana	0.5	0.4	0.0	0.6	0.0
Nebraska	0.2	0.0*	0.0*	1.7	0.0
Nevada	0.0*	0.0*	0.0*	1.7	0.0
New Hampshire	0.3	0.2	0.4	0.8	0.3
New Jersey	0.8	0.7	0.8	1.1	1.1
New Mexico	0.5	0.4	0.5	0.4**	0.0**
New York	0.8	0.5	0.6	1.2	1.0
North Carolina	0.2	0.3	0.2	0.5	0.8
North Dakota	0.1	0.0	0.0	0.4	0.0
Ohio	0.3	0.4	0.4	0.9	0.9
Oklahoma	0.4	0.4	0.3	0.7	0.7
Oregon	0.5	0.5	0.3	0.9	0.7
Pennsylvania	0.5	0.6	0.3	0.8	0.7
Rhode Island	0.2	0.2	0.5	0.4	0.8
South Carolina	0.4	0.2	0.2	0.5	0.6
South Dakota	0.2	0.2	0.0	0.7	1.1
Tennessee	0.0	0.5	0.2	0.6	0.6
Texas	0.4	0.4	0.3	0.6	0.0
Utah	0.5	0.6	0.1	0.5**	0.0**
Vermont	0.0	0.0	0.6	0.9	0.0
Virginia	0.3	0.5	0.3	0.8	0.4
Washington	0.9	0.8	0.8	1.2	0.0***
West Virginia	0.4	0.3	0.0	0.6	0.0
Wisconsin	0.3	0.4	0.4	0.7	0.0
Wyoming	0.1	0.0**	0.0**	0.2**	0.0**

Appendix 15. Participation Rates: Asian Male Administrators

State	1979 Combined	1983 Public	1983 Private	1991 Public	1991 Private
Alabama	0.3	0.2	0.5	0.3	1.1
Alaska	0.0*	1.5**	0.0**	2.1	0.0
Arizona	0.3	0.5**	0.0**	1.0	0.0
Arkansas	0.4	0.5	0.4	0.3	0.0
California	1.7	1.7	1.2	2.5	1.5
Colorado	0.7	0.4	0.6	0.5	0.2
Connecticut	0.4	0.3	0.5	0.4	0.9
Delaware	0.0	0.0	5.3	0.3	0.0
Florida	0.4	0.3	0.5	0.9	3.4
Georgia	0.3	0.6	0.1	0.6	0.1
Idaho	0.3	0.7	0.0	1.4	0.0
Illinois	0.8	0.9	1.0	1.4	1.0
Indiana	0.6	0.6	0.7	1.2	0.4
Iowa	0.2	0.5	0.1	1.8	0.1
Kansas	0.4	0.6	0.0	0.6	0.0
Kentucky	0.1	0.6	0.0	0.5	0.2
Louisiana	0.4	0.3	0.6	0.8	0.6
Maine	0.0	0.0	0.0	0.0	0.0
Maryland	0.6	1.0	0.5	0.0***	0.9
Massachusetts	0.4	0.4	0.4	0.5	0.6
Michigan	1.0	1.0	0.3	1.1	0.7
Minnesota	0.7	0.5	0.0	0.5	0.4
Mississippi	0.3	0.1	0.6	0.2	0.0
Missouri	0.3	0.2	0.3	0.2	0.5
Montana	0.7	0.0	0.0	0.0	0.0
Nebraska	0.4	0.0*	0.0*	0.4	0.0
Nevada	0.0*	0.0*	0.0*	0.4	0.0
New Hampshire	0.0	0.5	0.2	0.4	0.5
New Jersey	0.8	1.2	0.3	1.7	0.6
New Mexico	0.6	0.7	0.0	0.4**	0.0**
New York	0.6	0.8	0.8	1.1	1.1
North Carolina	0.5	0.6	0.0	0.4	0.0
North Dakota	0.4	1.0	0.0	0.9	0.0
Ohio	0.5	0.8	0.6	0.6	0.4
Oklahoma	0.4	0.6	0.6	1.0	0.6
Oregon	0.6	0.7	0.6	0.8	1.6
Pennsylvania	0.4	0.4	0.5	0.7	0.4
Rhode Island	0.6	0.7	0.6	1.7	0.8
South Carolina	0.4	0.6	0.0	0.4	0.2
South Dakota	0.9	0.6	0.3	0.4	0.0
Tennessee	0.2	0.2	0.0	0.2	0.7
Texas	0.5	0.6	0.5	0.7	0.0
Utah	1.3	0.6	0.0	0.2**	0.0**
Vermont	0.0	0.6	0.0	0.6	0.0
Virginia	0.4	1.7	0.5	0.4	0.0
Washington	2.1	1.6	0.8	1.9	0.0***
West Virginia	0.3	0.6	0.0	0.5	0.0
Wisconsin	0.4	0.4	0.3	0.6	0.0
Wyoming	0.0	0.0**	0.0**	1.8**	0.0**

Appendix 16. Participation Rates: Asian Female Administrators

State	1979 Combined	1983 Public	1983 Private	1991 Public	1991 Private
Alabama	0.1	0.0	0.0	0.1	0.0
Alaska	0.0*	0.0**	0.0**	0.7	0.0
Arizona	0.2	0.4**	0.0**	0.8	0.0
Arkansas	0.0	0.0	0.0	0.1	0.0
California	0.9	1.0	1.0	2.5	1.4
Colorado	0.2	0.3	0.6	0.6	0.0
Connecticut	0.4	0.4	0.8	0.2	0.8
Delaware	0.0	0.9	0.0	0.0	2.1
Florida	0.0	0.1	0.2	0.2	1.2
Georgia	0.2	0.1	0.1	0.2	0.2
Idaho	0.3	0.4	0.0	0.0	0.0
Illinois	0.4	0.6	0.4	0.6	1.0
Indiana	0.3	0.3	0.1	0.1	0.1
Iowa	0.0	0.0	0.0	0.1	0.1
Kansas	0.1	0.2	0.0	0.3	0.0
Kentucky	0.0	0.1	0.0	0.1	0.2
Louisiana	0.1	0.1	0.0	0.1	0.2
Maine	0.0	0.0	0.0	0.0	0.0
Maryland	0.1	0.3	0.2	0.0***	0.3
Massachusetts	0.3	0.4	0.3	0.6	0.8
Michigan	0.4	0.4	0.1	0.3	0.3
Minnesota	0.3	0.4	0.2	0.5	0.2
Mississippi	0.0	0.0	0.0	0.0	0.6
Missouri	0.1	0.2	0.3	0.2	0.3
Montana	0.1	0.3	0.0	0.3	0.0
Nebraska	0.0	0.2	0.0	0.2	0.4
Nevada	0.0*	0.0*	0.0*	0.7	0.0
New Hampshire	0.0	0.0	0.0	0.0	0.4
New Jersey	0.3	0.5	0.5	1.0	1.1
New Mexico	0.1	0.0	0.0	0.2**	0.0**
New York	0.6	0.5	0.7	0.9	1.1
North Carolina	0.1	0.0	0.0	0.0	0.2
North Dakota	0.0	0.0	0.0	0.0	0.0
Ohio	0.3	0.3	0.3	0.3	0.2
Oklahoma	0.3	0.0	0.2	0.3	0.0
Oregon	0.3	0.2	0.3	0.1	1.6
Pennsylvania	0.3	0.3	0.4	0.4	0.4
Rhode Island	0.2	0.3	0.3	0.0	0.5
South Carolina	0.1	0.0	0.0	0.1	0.0
South Dakota	0.0	0.0	0.0	0.4	0.0
Tennessee	0.1	0.0	0.1	0.1	0.0
Texas	0.3	0.3	0.6	0.5	0.0
Utah	0.4	0.6	0.0	0.2**	0.0**
Vermont	0.0	0.0	0.0	0.3	4.8
Virginia	0.2	0.3	0.1	0.4	0.0
Washington	0.7	1.1	0.6	1.3	0.0***
West Virginia	0.1	0.2	0.0	0.3	0.0
Wisconsin	0.3	0.2	0.3	0.3	0.0
Wyoming	0.0	0.0**	0.0**	0.0**	0.0**

Appendix 17 . Participation Rates: Native American Male
Faculty

	1979	1983		1991	
State	Combined	Public	Private	Public	Private
Alabama	0.1	0.1	0.0	0.2	0.0
Alaska	0.0*	2.6**	0.0**	1.4	2.2
Arizona	0.8	0.5**	0.0**	0.7	0.0
Arkansas	0.2	0.4	0.0	0.6	0.0
California	0.3	0.3	0.4	0.4	0.1
Colorado	0.3	0.3	0.0	0.3	0.3
Connecticut	0.1	0.1	0.0	0.1	0.1
Delaware	0.2	0.1	0.0	0.1	0.0
Florida	0.1	0.1	0.1	0.2	0.1
Georgia	0.2	0.0	0.1	0.1	0.0
Idaho	0.1	2.4	0.0	0.3	0.0
Illinois	0.1	0.1	0.1	0.2	0.0
Indiana	0.1	0.1	0.0	0.1	0.0
Iowa	0.1	0.1	0.1	0.2	0.1
Kansas	0.2	0.3	2.0	0.3	0.2
Kentucky	0.0	0.1	0.0	0.1	0.1
Louisiana	0.2	0.2	0.0	0.1	0.0
Maine	0.0	0.1	0.0	0.1	0.0
Maryland	0.1	0.1	0.0	0.0***	0.1
Massachusetts	0.2	0.6	0.1	0.1	0.1
Michigan	0.2	0.1	0.1	0.2	0.1
Minnesota	0.3	0.3	0.3	0.3	0.4
Mississippi	0.0	0.0	0.0	0.1	0.0
Missouri	0.1	0.2	0.3	0.3	0.2
Montana	0.2	0.3	0.0	0.9	3.7
Nebraska	0.3	0.3	0.2	0.2	0.3
Nevada	0.0*	0.0*	0.0*	0.5	0.0
New Hampshire	0.2	0.2	0.1	0.0	0.1
New Jersey	0.0	0.1	0.1	0.1	0.1
New Mexico	0.2	0.6	0.3	0.9**	0.0**
New York	0.1	0.1	0.1	0.1	0.1
North Carolina	0.1	0.2	0.1	0.2	0.1
North Dakota	0.2	0.2	1.6	0.9	0.0
Ohio	0.1	0.1	0.2	0.1	0.1
Oklahoma	1.4	1.6	1.6	1.7	0.7
Oregon	0.3	0.1	0.0	0.3	0.1
Pennsylvania	0.1	0.1	0.2	0.1	0.1
Rhode Island	0.0	0.1	0.0	0.2	0.0
South Carolina	0.0	0.1	0.1	0.1	0.1
South Dakota	0.3	0.8	1.0	0.7	0.0
Tennessee	0.1	0.1	0.0	0.2	0.1
Texas	0.3	0.3	0.2	0.2	0.6
Utah	0.3	0.3	0.0	0.1**	0.0**
Vermont	0.0	0.0	5.5	0.0	0.0
Virginia	0.1	0.1	0.3	0.1	0.0
Washington	0.5	0.5	0.0	0.5	0.0***
West Virginia	0.2	0.1	0.3	0.2	0.0
Wisconsin	0.1	0.1	0.1	0.2	1.9
Wyoming	0.0	0.0**	0.0**	0.0**	0.0**

Appendix 18 . Participation Rates: Native American Female
Faculty

State	1979 Combined	1983 Public	1983 Private	1991 Public	1991 Private
Alabama	0.0	0.0	0.0	0.0	0.0
Alaska	0.0*	0.5**	0.0**	1.4	0.0
Arizona	0.1	0.1**	0.0**	0.5	0.0
Arkansas	0.2	0.2	0.2	0.2	0.0
California	0.1	0.2	0.0	0.2	0.0
Colorado	0.1	0.1	0.2	0.2	0.0
Connecticut	0.0	0.0	0.1	0.0	0.0
Delaware	0.0	0.2	0.0	0.2	0.0
Florida	0.1	0.1	0.0	0.1	0.0
Georgia	0.0	0.0	0.0	0.0	0.1
Idaho	0.1	0.1	0.0	0.3	0.0
Illinois	0.0	0.1	0.0	0.1	0.0
Indiana	0.0	0.1	0.0	0.1	0.0
Iowa	0.0	0.0	0.0	0.0	0.1
Kansas	0.1	0.1	0.9	0.1	0.0
Kentucky	0.0	0.0	0.0	0.0	0.0
Louisiana	0.0	0.0	0.1	0.0	0.0
Maine	0.0	0.2	0.0	0.1	0.0
Maryland	0.0	0.0	0.0	0.0***	0.0
Massachusetts	0.0	0.3	0.0	0.1	0.0
Michigan	0.1	0.0	0.1	0.1	0.1
Minnesota	0.0	0.1	0.1	0.3	0.4
Mississippi	0.0	0.0	0.0	0.0	0.0
Missouri	0.1	0.0	0.1	0.1	0.0
Montana	0.1	0.3	0.0	0.8	0.7
Nebraska	0.1	0.1	0.0	0.1	0.2
Nevada	0.0*	0.0*	0.0*	0.2	0.0
New Hampshire	0.1	0.0	0.2	0.1	0.0
New Jersey	0.0	0.0	0.0	0.1	0.1
New Mexico	0.3	0.4	0.3	0.9**	0.0**
New York	0.0	0.0	0.1	0.0	0.0
North Carolina	0.1	0.1	0.1	0.1	0.0
North Dakota	0.1	0.1	3.3	1.0	0.0
Ohio	0.0	0.0	0.0	0.0	0.0
Oklahoma	0.6	0.7	0.8	1.2	1.7
Oregon	0.2	0.1	0.1	0.2	0.0
Pennsylvania	0.0	0.0	0.0	0.1	0.0
Rhode Island	0.0	0.0	0.0	0.0	0.2
South Carolina	0.1	0.1	0.0	0.0	0.2
South Dakota	0.1	0.5	0.0	0.2	0.0
Tennessee	0.0	0.1	0.0	0.1	0.0
Texas	0.1	0.1	0.0	0.2	0.6
Utah	0.2	0.2	0.3	0.2**	0.0**
Vermont	0.0	0.0	0.0	0.1	0.0
Virginia	0.0	0.0	0.0	0.0	0.0
Washington	0.2	0.2	0.0	0.4	0.0***
West Virginia	0.1	0.0	0.0	0.2	0.0
Wisconsin	0.1	0.1	0.2	0.2	0.0
Wyoming	0.1	0.2**	0.0**	0.1**	0.0**

Appendix 19. Participation Rates: Native American Male
Administrators

State	1979 Combined	1983 Public	1983 Private	1991 Public	1991 Private
Alabama	0.2	0.1	0.5	0.1	0.0
Alaska	0.0*	4.1**	0.0**	4.1	0.0
Arizona	0.2	0.5**	0.0**	1.1	0.0
Arkansas	0.2	0.5	0.0	0.4	0.0
California	0.4	0.5	0.2	0.4	0.3
Colorado	0.1	0.3	0.3	0.4	0.5
Connecticut	0.2	0.4	0.0	0.0	0.1
Delaware	0.0	2.8	0.0	0.3	0.0
Florida	0.1	0.1	0.1	0.1	0.1
Georgia	0.1	0.0	0.0	0.0	0.0
Idaho	0.0	2.5	0.0	0.0	0.0
Illinois	0.1	0.1	0.1	0.1	0.1
Indiana	0.1	0.0	0.0	0.1	0.0
Iowa	0.0	0.2	0.0	0.1	0.0
Kansas	0.3	0.3	2.2	0.1	0.0
Kentucky	0.0	0.0	0.0	0.0	0.0
Louisiana	0.0	0.0	0.0	0.0	0.0
Maine	0.3	0.3	0.0	0.0	0.0
Maryland	1.0	0.3	0.0	0.0***	0.2
Massachusetts	0.0	0.1	0.0	0.0	0.1
Michigan	0.1	0.2	0.3	0.2	0.2
Minnesota	0.1	0.1	0.0	0.5	0.3
Mississippi	0.1	0.0	0.0	0.0	0.0
Missouri	0.3	1.1	0.1	0.1	0.1
Montana	0.4	0.3	4.5	0.8	16.7
Nebraska	0.0	0.2	0.0	0.2	0.0
Nevada	0.0*	0.0*	0.0*	0.0	0.0
New Hampshire	0.0	0.0	0.0	0.0	0.2
New Jersey	0.1	0.0	0.1	0.0	0.1
New Mexico	1.0	1.4	1.6	1.2**	0.0**
New York	0.1	0.1	0.1	0.0	0.0
North Carolina	0.3	0.8	0.1	0.6	0.0
North Dakota	0.8	1.0	2.4	5.6	2.5
Ohio	0.0	0.1	0.0	0.1	0.0
Oklahoma	2.0	1.4	2.5	1.9	1.7
Oregon	0.7	0.3	0.0	0.7	0.2
Pennsylvania	0.0	0.1	0.0	0.1	0.1
Rhode Island	0.2	0.0	0.0	0.4	0.2
South Carolina	0.1	0.2	0.0	0.2	0.0
South Dakota	2.1	6.7	3.4	1.2	2.3
Tennessee	0.1	0.2	0.4	0.1	0.0
Texas	0.1	0.1	0.1	0.2	0.0
Utah	0.2	0.1	2.2	0.0**	0.0**
Vermont	0.0	0.0	0.0	0.1	0.0
Virginia	0.0	0.9	0.0	0.0	0.0
Washington	0.7	0.6	0.3	0.8	0.0***
West Virginia	0.2	0.1	0.0	0.2	0.0
Wisconsin	0.3	0.3	0.3	0.0	0.0
Wyoming	0.7	0.5**	0.0**	0.5**	0.0**

Appendix 20. Participation Rates: Native American Female
Administrators

State	1979 Combined	1983 Public	1983 Private	1991 Public	1991 Private
Alabama	0.1	0.0	0.0	0.1	0.0
Alaska	0.0*	0.5**	0.0**	1.4	0.0
Arizona	0.1	0.1**	0.0**	0.9	0.0
Arkansas	0.1	0.0	0.4	0.4	0.5
California	0.1	0.2	0.1	0.4	0.2
Colorado	0.1	0.4	0.3	0.4	0.0
Connecticut	0.0	0.0	0.0	0.0	0.0
Delaware	0.0	0.0	0.0	0.0	0.0
Florida	0.0	0.0	0.2	0.0	0.1
Georgia	0.0	0.0	0.0	0.0	0.1
Idaho	0.0	0.0	0.0	0.5	0.0
Illinois	0.0	0.1	0.1	0.1	0.0
Indiana	0.1	0.0	0.0	0.0	0.0
Iowa	0.0	0.1	0.1	0.1	0.0
Kansas	0.0	0.2	0.3	0.2	0.0
Kentucky	0.0	0.0	0.0	0.0	0.0
Louisiana	0.0	0.1	0.0	0.1	0.0
Maine	0.0	0.0	0.0	0.0	0.0
Maryland	0.0	0.0	0.0	0.0***	0.0
Massachusetts	0.0	0.1	0.0	0.0	0.0
Michigan	0.1	0.0	0.0	0.1	0.1
Minnesota	0.1	0.0	0.0	0.9	0.1
Mississippi	0.0	0.0	0.0	0.0	0.0
Missouri	0.1	0.0	0.1	0.0	0.1
Montana	0.4	1.4	4.5	1.5	16.7
Nebraska	0.0	0.0	0.0	0.0	0.0
Nevada	0.0*	0.0*	0.0*	0.0	0.0
New Hampshire	0.0	0.0	0.0	0.4	0.2
New Jersey	0.0	0.0	0.0	0.0	0.0
New Mexico	0.1	0.0	0.5	1.2**	0.0**
New York	0.0	0.1	0.1	0.0	0.1
North Carolina	0.0	0.2	0.0	0.2	0.0
North Dakota	0.0	0.5	7.1	3.7	0.0
Ohio	0.0	0.0	0.0	0.1	0.0
Oklahoma	1.0	0.8	1.6	1.5	1.7
Oregon	0.4	0.0	0.0	0.2	0.0
Pennsylvania	0.0	0.0	0.0	0.1	0.0
Rhode Island	0.0	0.0	0.0	0.4	0.0
South Carolina	0.0	0.0	0.0	0.0	0.0
South Dakota	0.0	4.2	1.4	0.4	1.0
Tennessee	0.1	0.0	0.0	0.0	0.1
Texas	0.1	0.1	0.0	0.2	0.6
Utah	0.2	0.1	0.0	0.0**	0.0**
Vermont	0.3	0.0	0.0	0.1	0.0
Virginia	0.0	0.1	0.0	0.0	0.0
Washington	0.2	0.3	0.3	0.5	0.0***
West Virginia	0.1	0.0	0.0	0.0	0.0
Wisconsin	0.2	0.1	0.2	0.2	0.0
Wyoming	0.0	0.0**	0.0**	0.0**	0.0**

Appendix 21. Representation Ratios: Black Male Faculty

State	1979 Combined	1983 Public	1983 Private	1991 Public	1991 Private
Alabama	0.65	0.31	0.34	0.39	0.80
Alaska	0.00*	0.16**	0.00**	0.45	0.00
Arizona	0.49	0.49**	0.00**	0.51	1.66
Arkansas	0.39	0.47	0.09	0.41	0.35
California	0.48	0.56	0.29	0.68	0.43
Colorado	0.44	0.55	0.78	0.48	0.53
Connecticut	0.37	0.27	0.40	0.53	0.30
Delaware	0.52	0.49	0.00	0.40	0.14
Florida	0.47	0.58	0.32	0.62	0.51
Georgia	0.41	0.29	0.73	0.43	0.85
Idaho	0.00	0.00	0.00	1.00	0.00
Illinois	0.35	0.37	0.16	0.40	0.25
Indiana	0.25	0.22	0.22	0.30	0.25
Iowa	0.98	0.84	0.70	1.27	0.46
Kansas	0.19	0.26	0.04	0.24	0.07
Kentucky	0.49	0.46	0.03	0.56	0.38
Louisiana	0.39	0.43	0.87	0.40	1.41
Maine	1.77	1.77	4.72	0.40	3.16
Maryland	0.43	0.38	0.08	0.00***	0.43
Massachusetts	0.87	1.09	0.66	0.75	0.71
Michigan	0.33	0.37	0.20	0.42	0.34
Minnesota	0.90	1.20	0.60	0.80	0.45
Mississippi	0.30	0.47	0.50	0.44	0.55
Missouri	0.41	0.22	0.20	0.28	0.34
Montana	6.91	6.22	0.00	1.12	0.00
Nebraska	0.33	0.40	0.40	0.62	0.51
Nevada	0.00*	0.00*	0.00*	0.33	1.20
New Hampshire	2.83	1.21	3.24	0.55	2.21
New Jersey	0.44	0.55	0.27	0.52	0.22
New Mexico	0.73	0.42	0.21	0.38**	0.00**
New York	0.34	0.37	0.29	0.40	0.20
North Carolina	0.32	0.52	0.42	0.55	0.38
North Dakota	0.00	0.78	3.13	0.31	0.00
Ohio	0.36	0.34	0.28	0.52	0.36
Oklahoma	0.43	0.24	0.55	0.47	0.19
Oregon	0.96	0.96	0.41	0.71	0.47
Pennsylvania	0.42	0.54	0.22	0.66	0.30
Rhode Island	0.85	0.64	0.71	0.62	0.72
South Carolina	0.26	0.32	0.31	0.28	0.32
South Dakota	1.47	1.47	0.00	0.70	0.00
Tennessee	0.62	0.42	0.41	0.55	0.38
Texas	0.38	0.36	0.74	0.45	0.00
Utah	0.54	0.54	0.00	0.50**	0.00**
Vermont	7.14	5.55	0.00	6.02	0.00
Virginia	0.40	0.40	0.44	0.49	0.00
Washington	0.80	0.65	0.43	0.67	0.00***
West Virginia	0.70	0.70	0.19	1.02	0.00
Wisconsin	0.38	0.43	0.49	0.55	0.80
Wyoming	1.00	0.75**	0.00**	1.37**	0.00**

Appendix 22. Representation Ratios: Black Female Faculty

State	1979 Combined	1983 Public	1983 Private	1991 Public	1991 Private
Alabama	0.50	0.33	0.44	0.45	0.59
Alaska	0.00*	0.61**	0.00**	0.38	0.00
Arizona	0.38	0.30**	0.00**	0.83	1.45
Arkansas	0.36	0.40	0.15	0.45	0.25
California	0.33	0.36	0.18	0.45	0.75
Colorado	0.35	0.29	0.12	0.41	0.41
Connecticut	0.16	0.16	0.16	0.30	0.14
Delaware	0.51	0.70	0.00	0.38	0.25
Florida	0.50	0.51	0.19	0.59	0.25
Georgia	0.37	0.32	0.66	0.33	0.70
Idaho	0.88	2.65	0.00	0.75	0.00
Illinois	0.32	0.35	0.06	0.43	0.14
Indiana	0.18	0.20	0.18	0.27	0.12
Iowa	0.42	0.42	0.14	0.81	0.46
Kansas	0.23	0.23	0.11	0.24	0.07
Kentucky	0.33	0.33	0.19	0.37	0.40
Louisiana	0.40	0.42	0.76	0.39	1.06
Maine	0.92	0.00	5.52	0.60	2.42
Maryland	0.31	0.34	0.03	0.00***	0.33
Massachusetts	0.39	0.59	0.30	0.46	0.35
Michigan	0.28	0.34	0.29	0.27	0.42
Minnesota	0.47	0.47	0.31	0.38	0.57
Mississippi	0.22	0.38	0.41	0.38	0.55
Missouri	0.45	0.27	0.13	0.24	0.31
Montana	2.43	2.43	0.00	0.83	0.00
Nebraska	0.32	0.25	0.32	0.21	0.16
Nevada	0.00*	0.00*	0.00*	0.19	2.49
New Hampshire	0.54	0.54	2.68	0.35	0.35
New Jersey	0.30	0.30	0.13	0.40	0.11
New Mexico	0.45	0.23	0.57	0.21**	0.00**
New York	0.23	0.28	0.21	0.32	0.11
North Carolina	0.31	0.48	0.35	0.44	0.32
North Dakota	2.18	0.00	0.00	0.89	0.00
Ohio	0.26	0.28	0.23	0.37	0.28
Oklahoma	0.49	0.34	0.52	0.50	0.45
Oregon	0.59	0.44	0.15	0.51	0.26
Pennsylvania	0.23	0.34	0.17	0.39	0.14
Rhode Island	0.27	0.20	0.20	0.31	0.47
South Carolina	0.22	0.24	0.24	0.31	0.26
South Dakota	10.31	0.00	1.87	0.00	0.00
Tennessee	0.53	0.46	0.25	0.56	0.18
Texas	0.34	0.29	0.47	0.37	0.37
Utah	0.38	0.76	0.38	0.36**	0.00**
Vermont	2.09	2.09	0.00	2.71	0.00
Virginia	0.42	0.42	0.62	0.43	0.00
Washington	0.68	0.51	0.34	0.49	0.00***
West Virginia	0.56	0.79	0.28	0.84	0.00
Wisconsin	0.30	0.40	0.10	0.42	0.00
Wyoming	0.00	0.32**	0.00**	0.28**	0.00**

Appendix 23. Representation Ratios: Black Male Administrators

State	1979 Combined	1983 Public	1983 Private	1991 Public	1991 Private
Alabama	1.03	0.56	0.90	0.59	1.67
Alaska	0.00*	0.79**	0.00**	0.00	.80
Arizona	0.77	0.98**	0.00**	1.34	1.21
Arkansas	0.92	0.94	0.12	0.83	0.65
California	0.90	1.04	0.51	1.17	0.79
Colorado	0.83	1.44	0.94	1.06	0.44
Connecticut	1.13	1.22	0.58	1.11	0.58
Delaware	1.16	1.29	0.70	0.70	0.26
Florida	1.07	1.07	0.46	0.60	0.29
Georgia	0.61	0.54	0.71	0.49	0.95
Idaho	1.72	2.29	0.00	0.00	0.00
Illinois	0.64	0.76	0.47	0.84	0.40
Indiana	0.56	0.61	0.31	0.38	0.55
Iowa	1.54	2.38	1.12	2.08	1.27
Kansas	0.49	0.60	0.22	0.62	0.14
Kentucky	1.10	1.22	0.26	1.09	0.18
Louisiana	0.73	0.50	0.89	0.52	0.64
Maine	6.49	3.54	6.49	0.00	8.70
Maryland	0.89	0.83	0.20	0.00***	0.80
Massachusetts	1.64	3.11	1.15	1.75	0.91
Michigan	0.57	0.63	0.18	0.66	0.62
Minnesota	2.09	1.94	1.50	1.52	0.63
Mississippi	0.64	0.77	1.11	0.64	0.74
Missouri	0.69	0.55	0.31	0.48	0.72
Montana	8.98	4.14	0.00	0.00	0.00
Nebraska	0.74	0.20	0.67	0.34	0.73
Nevada	0.00*	0.00*	0.00*	0.84	0.99
New Hampshire	6.88	0.00	6.47	0.00	3.32
New Jersey	1.09	1.45	0.77	1.34	0.52
New Mexico	2.60	0.73	2.18	1.14**	0.00**
New York	0.50	0.66	0.50	0.67	0.48
North Carolina	0.64	0.85	0.59	0.74	0.60
North Dakota	1.56	0.00	0.00	0.00	0.00
Ohio	0.81	0.75	0.77	0.82	0.62
Oklahoma	1.31	0.70	0.67	0.72	0.30
Oregon	1.79	1.65	0.83	0.95	0.83
Pennsylvania	1.05	1.32	0.59	1.17	0.56
Rhode Island	2.13	4.26	1.63	3.41	1.24
South Carolina	0.39	0.40	0.24	0.34	0.41
South Dakota	4.42	2.95	0.00	1.41	2.82
Tennessee	1.03	0.80	1.10	0.85	0.78
Texas	0.73	0.50	0.80	0.59	0.49
Utah	0.81	1.63	0.00	1.01**	0.00**
Vermont	11.89	9.52	7.14	3.51	0.00
Virginia	0.79	0.67	0.57	0.61	0.13
Washington	1.59	1.45	0.58	1.28	0.00***
West Virginia	1.60	1.86	1.15	1.98	1.98
Wisconsin	0.92	0.81	0.86	0.84	1.60
Wyoming	0.00	0.00**	0.00**	1.14**	0.00**

Appendix 24. Representation Ratios: Black Female Administrators

State	1979 Combined	1983 Public	1983 Private	1991 Public	1991 Private
Alabama	0.02	0.14	0.41	0.38	0.98
Alaska	0.00*	0.00**	0.00**	0.38	0.98
Arizona	0.00	0.23**	0.00**	0.90	0.69
Arkansas	0.00	0.44	0.20	0.49	0.67
California	0.01	0.56	0.48	0.93	0.93
Colorado	0.00	0.58	0.64	0.81	0.71
Connecticut	0.00	0.49	0.81	0.91	0.82
Delaware	0.09	0.71	0.00	0.52	0.24
Florida	0.03	0.55	0.32	0.56	0.52
Georgia	0.01	0.27	0.73	0.40	0.90
Idaho	0.00	0.00	0.00	0.00	0.00
Illinois	0.06	0.50	0.51	0.91	0.75
Indiana	0.01	0.35	0.63	0.39	0.36
Iowa	0.00	0.84	0.70	1.16	0.92
Kansas	0.04	0.49	0.00	0.66	0.56
Kentucky	0.00	0.33	0.19	0.80	0.29
Louisiana	0.01	0.31	0.79	0.34	0.75
Maine	0.92	5.52	0.00	1.81	8.46
Maryland	0.00	0.45	0.13	0.00***	0.56
Massachusetts	0.02	1.38	0.69	1.12	1.05
Michigan	0.00	0.63	0.26	0.59	0.54
Minnesota	0.16	2.03	0.78	1.71	0.67
Mississippi	0.01	0.28	0.59	0.36	0.87
Missouri	0.02	0.40	0.43	0.35	0.85
Montana	0.00	0.00	0.00	0.00	0.00
Nebraska	0.00	0.32	0.63	0.48	0.38
Nevada	0.00*	0.00*	0.00*	0.56	0.00
New Hampshire	1.07	0.00	1.07	1.39	3.83
New Jersey	0.01	0.92	0.43	1.63	0.52
New Mexico	0.00	0.00	0.57	1.06**	0.00**
New York	0.01	0.38	0.56	0.69	0.53
North Carolina	0.01	0.35	0.45	0.46	0.65
North Dakota	0.00	0.00	0.00	0.00	0.00
Ohio	0.00	0.42	0.53	0.70	0.90
Oklahoma	0.00	0.66	0.26	0.58	0.16
Oregon	0.00	0.59	0.00	0.90	0.26
Pennsylvania	0.00	0.99	0.93	0.96	0.80
Rhode Island	0.00	0.67	0.33	0.47	1.14
South Carolina	0.01	0.17	0.14	0.18	0.33
South Dakota	1.87	0.00	2.81	2.17	0.00
Tennessee	0.04	0.44	1.10	0.56	0.50
Texas	0.03	0.22	0.69	0.49	0.91
Utah	0.00	0.00	0.00	0.00**	0.00**
Vermont	0.00	0.00	3.13	4.07	0.00
Virginia	0.02	0.63	0.35	0.51	0.48
Washington	0.04	1.02	0.26	1.26	0.00***
West Virginia	0.06	0.68	0.51	0.90	0.00
Wisconsin	0.02	0.69	0.59	0.84	0.00
Wyoming	0.00	0.00**	0.00**	0.00**	0.00**

Appendix 25. Representation Ratios: White Female Faculty

State	1979 Combined	1983 Public	1983 Private	1991 Public	1991 Private
Alabama	0.65	0.75	1.08	0.78	0.77
Alaska	0.00*	0.80**	0.00**	0.89	1.03
Arizona	0.52	0.46**	0.00**	0.81	0.89
Arkansas	0.55	0.64	0.69	0.78	0.70
California	0.54	0.57	0.55	0.88	0.92
Colorado	0.46	0.46	0.60	0.65	0.68
Connecticut	0.50	0.54	0.49	0.63	0.62
Delaware	0.63	0.59	1.17	0.81	1.04
Florida	0.52	0.54	0.44	0.74	0.63
Georgia	0.64	0.72	0.65	0.88	0.71
Idaho	0.45	0.39	0.42	0.62	0.33
Illinois	0.55	0.60	0.58	0.73	0.72
Indiana	0.46	0.53	0.53	0.71	0.53
Iowa	0.44	0.49	0.55	0.62	0.59
Kansas	0.57	0.51	0.68	0.65	0.82
Kentucky	0.58	0.63	0.72	0.60	0.91
Louisiana	0.64	0.76	0.58	0.89	0.68
Maine	0.49	0.44	0.46	0.57	0.75
Maryland	0.68	0.76	0.74	0.00***	0.86
Massachusetts	0.50	0.56	0.52	0.69	0.63
Michigan	0.52	0.50	0.65	0.58	0.74
Minnesota	0.43	0.49	0.59	0.62	0.71
Mississippi	0.81	0.99	1.05	1.09	1.03
Missouri	0.58	0.55	0.64	0.58	0.74
Montana	0.35	0.46	0.45	0.53	0.65
Nebraska	0.50	0.48	0.66	0.59	0.75
Nevada	0.00*	0.00*	0.00*	0.71	0.93
New Hampshire	0.44	0.43	0.52	0.64	0.59
New Jersey	0.58	0.69	0.55	0.77	0.66
New Mexico	0.53	0.53	0.58	0.99**	0.00**
New York	0.57	0.60	0.63	0.75	0.83
North Carolina	0.63	0.68	0.62	0.75	0.74
North Dakota	0.44	0.50	0.76	0.57	0.87
Ohio	0.50	0.54	0.50	0.62	0.66
Oklahoma	0.56	0.54	0.60	0.71	0.70
Oregon	0.53	0.55	0.47	0.76	0.60
Pennsylvania	0.47	0.50	0.52	0.61	0.59
Rhode Island	0.51	0.65	0.46	0.77	0.59
South Carolina	0.73	0.74	0.76	0.89	0.85
South Dakota	0.49	0.49	0.74	0.59	1.11
Tennessee	0.55	0.56	0.60	0.67	0.65
Texas	0.58	0.65	0.64	0.94	1.38
Utah	0.37	0.41	0.29	0.52**	0.00**
Vermont	0.48	0.46	0.40	0.60	1.14
Virginia	0.55	0.57	0.69	0.68	0.84
Washington	0.50	0.51	0.59	0.66	0.00***
West Virginia	0.52	0.58	0.70	0.65	0.69
Wisconsin	0.49	0.55	0.54	0.65	0.52
Wyoming	0.48	0.49**	0.00**	0.73**	0.00**

Appendix 26. Representation Ratios: White Male Faculty

State	1979 Combined	1983 Public	1983 Private	1991 Public	1991 Private
Alabama	1.62	1.67	1.33	1.55	1.33
Alaska	0.00*	1.55**	0.00**	1.51	1.41
Arizona	1.76	1.80**	0.00**	1.65	1.35
Arkansas	1.69	1.56	1.68	1.40	1.59
California	1.81	1.74	1.87	2.00	2.11
Colorado	1.66	1.65	1.52	1.61	1.59
Connecticut	1.64	1.59	1.62	1.54	1.60
Delaware	1.55	1.54	1.14	1.38	1.24
Florida	1.64	1.61	1.77	1.57	1.77
Georgia	1.78	1.77	1.54	1.56	1.42
Idaho	1.61	1.60	1.65	1.47	1.84
Illinois	1.71	1.64	1.77	1.61	1.76
Indiana	1.62	1.54	1.58	1.34	1.59
Iowa	1.55	1.47	1.47	1.32	1.43
Kansas	1.53	1.57	1.39	1.47	1.39
Kentucky	1.48	1.43	1.38	1.41	1.16
Louisiana	1.81	1.66	1.50	1.58	0.99
Maine	1.56	1.57	1.54	1.46	1.19
Maryland	1.66	1.59	1.80	0.00***	1.59
Massachusetts	1.57	1.44	1.54	1.42	1.50
Michigan	1.67	1.66	1.57	1.55	1.50
Minnesota	1.58	1.48	1.44	1.38	1.31
Mississippi	1.99	1.62	1.41	1.49	1.33
Missouri	1.54	1.62	1.55	1.54	1.39
Montana	1.68	1.58	1.66	1.55	1.42
Nebraska	1.55	1.56	1.41	1.45	1.32
Nevada	0.00*	0.00*	0.00*	1.52	1.30
New Hampshire	1.53	1.55	1.44	1.35	1.40
New Jersey	1.62	1.48	1.70	1.58	1.78
New Mexico	1.90	1.68	1.86	2.31**	0.00**
New York	1.77	1.72	1.71	1.80	1.84
North Carolina	1.78	1.58	1.73	1.51	1.61
North Dakota	1.56	1.50	1.12	1.40	1.25
Ohio	1.64	1.58	1.63	1.44	1.49
Oklahoma	1.61	1.63	1.56	1.51	1.59
Oregon	1.50	1.50	1.60	1.34	1.53
Pennsylvania	1.66	1.60	1.63	1.46	1.54
Rhode Island	1.57	1.39	1.60	1.31	1.54
South Carolina	1.89	1.85	1.83	1.67	1.72
South Dakota	1.59	1.60	1.37	1.48	1.02
Tennessee	1.59	1.60	1.65	1.44	1.58
Texas	1.70	1.61	1.62	1.90	1.63
Utah	1.66	1.63	1.79	1.58**	0.00**
Vermont	1.51	1.54	1.48	1.33	0.89
Virginia	1.72	1.68	1.53	1.61	1.72
Washington	1.54	1.54	1.53	1.45	0.00***
West Virginia	1.46	1.39	1.33	1.27	1.32
Wisconsin	1.56	1.49	1.48	1.38	1.58
Wyoming	1.55	1.55**	0.00**	1.38**	0.00**

Appendix 27. Representation Ratios: White Female Administrators

State	1979 Combined	1983 Public	1983 Private	1991 Public	1991 Private
Alabama	0.41	0.41	0.47	0.64	0.51
Alaska	0.00*	0.76**	0.00**	0.85	1.07
Arizona	0.33	0.56**	0.00**	0.79	1.16
Arkansas	0.47	0.52	0.69	0.74	0.58
California	0.57	0.55	0.81	1.15	1.02
Colorado	0.47	0.49	0.87	0.73	0.94
Connecticut	0.48	0.48	0.85	0.76	1.13
Delaware	0.32	0.29	0.75	0.76	1.25
Florida	0.42	0.46	0.81	0.73	0.99
Georgia	0.47	0.50	0.58	0.74	0.73
Idaho	0.31	0.36	0.32	0.49	0.32
Illinois	0.58	0.58	0.71	0.78	0.98
Indiana	0.61	0.60	0.59	0.42	0.78
Iowa	0.46	0.40	0.66	0.52	0.76
Kansas	0.41	0.59	0.61	0.78	0.70
Kentucky	0.42	0.38	0.76	0.58	0.69
Louisiana	0.67	0.78	1.10	0.89	1.20
Maine	0.49	0.43	0.66	0.57	0.77
Maryland	0.43	0.61	0.75	0.00***	0.84
Massachusetts	0.66	0.53	0.84	0.75	0.92
Michigan	0.52	0.56	0.65	0.82	0.83
Minnesota	0.56	0.63	0.64	1.02	0.76
Mississippi	0.44	0.32	0.39	0.87	0.75
Missouri	0.43	0.76	1.16	0.72	1.02
Montana	0.62	0.34	0.60	0.60	0.51
Nebraska	0.41	0.40	0.66	0.49	0.90
Nevada	0.00*	0.00*	0.00*	0.85	0.76
New Hampshire	0.47	0.33	0.71	0.82	0.93
New Jersey	0.60	0.52	0.81	0.79	1.23
New Mexico	0.56	0.47	0.38	0.84**	0.00**
New York	0.76	0.59	0.99	0.93	1.19
North Carolina	0.56	0.54	0.84	0.78	0.83
North Dakota	0.35	0.35	0.55	0.34	0.74
Ohio	0.53	0.50	0.73	0.68	0.92
Oklahoma	0.48	0.47	0.60	0.81	0.53
Oregon	0.52	0.49	0.60	0.72	0.89
Pennsylvania	0.64	0.53	0.91	0.67	0.91
Rhode Island	0.59	0.49	0.80	0.60	0.95
South Carolina	0.60	0.49	0.75	0.61	0.72
South Dakota	0.51	0.31	0.66	0.47	0.97
Tennessee	0.47	0.50	0.56	0.64	0.82
Texas	0.60	0.60	0.81	1.04	0.87
Utah	0.50	0.53	0.05	0.32**	0.00**
Vermont	0.55	0.54	0.74	0.88	0.47
Virginia	0.65	0.67	0.73	0.83	1.00
Washington	0.68	0.75	0.68	0.87	0.00***
West Virginia	0.62	0.69	0.55	0.74	0.63
Wisconsin	0.50	0.58	0.66	0.65	0.99
Wyoming	0.27	0.25**	0.00**	0.41**	0.00**

Appendix 28. Representation Ratios: White Male Administrators

State	1979 Combined	1983 Public	1983 Private	1991 Public	1991 Private
Alabama	1.81	2.11	1.81	1.77	1.32
Alaska	0.00*	1.53**	0.00**	1.55	1.42
Arizona	1.97	1.73**	0.00**	1.61	1.48
Arkansas	1.71	1.62	1.66	1.43	1.59
California	1.77	1.67	1.57	1.62	1.86
Colorado	1.59	1.51	1.24	1.43	1.38
Connecticut	1.62	1.59	1.23	1.37	1.05
Delaware	1.77	1.71	1.46	1.50	1.11
Florida	1.70	1.64	1.21	1.67	1.10
Georgia	1.98	1.99	1.67	1.77	1.40
Idaho	1.76	1.64	1.78	1.64	1.86
Illinois	1.69	1.63	1.55	1.44	1.37
Indiana	1.50	1.50	1.52	1.74	1.36
Iowa	1.57	1.62	1.38	1.49	1.28
Kansas	1.72	1.51	1.52	1.37	1.52
Kentucky	1.67	1.67	1.38	1.46	1.47
Louisiana	1.77	1.76	1.03	1.72	1.11
Maine	1.53	1.60	1.37	1.49	1.20
Maryland	1.78	1.64	1.82	0.00***	1.51
Massachusetts	1.37	1.43	1.22	1.32	1.19
Michigan	1.67	1.58	1.63	1.36	1.36
Minnesota	1.44	1.37	1.42	0.97	1.32
Mississippi	2.18	2.13	1.65	1.76	1.51
Missouri	1.74	1.60	1.33	1.48	1.05
Montana	1.40	1.70	1.35	1.52	0.94
Nebraska	1.66	1.69	1.40	1.62	1.21
Nevada	0.00*	0.00*	0.00*	1.45	1.68
New Hampshire	1.52	1.72	1.28	1.22	1.06
New Jersey	1.53	1.47	1.38	1.23	1.20
New Mexico	1.64	1.15	1.96	1.95**	0.00**
New York	1.55	1.72	1.24	1.49	1.31
North Carolina	1.79	1.73	1.51	1.51	1.47
North Dakota	1.66	1.68	1.33	1.57	1.33
Ohio	1.61	1.61	1.37	1.42	1.17
Oklahoma	1.61	1.71	1.55	1.41	1.82
Oregon	1.52	1.57	1.50	1.40	1.21
Pennsylvania	1.42	1.48	1.15	1.37	1.19
Rhode Island	1.45	1.49	1.26	1.45	1.14
South Carolina	2.05	2.18	2.00	2.07	1.88
South Dakota	1.57	1.59	1.39	1.67	1.12
Tennessee	1.61	1.69	1.42	1.52	1.35
Texas	1.65	1.68	1.40	1.80	1.83
Utah	1.42	1.50	2.02	1.84**	0.00**
Vermont	1.44	1.45	1.26	1.11	1.49
Virginia	1.57	1.48	1.58	1.51	1.49
Washington	1.31	1.25	1.37	1.20	0.00***
West Virginia	1.39	1.31	1.50	1.25	1.43
Wisconsin	1.54	1.45	1.37	1.41	1.12
Wyoming	1.78	1.80**	0.00**	1.71**	0.00**

Appendix 29. Representation Ratios: Hispanic
Male and Female Faculty Combined****

State	1979	1983 Public	Private
Alabama	0.78	0.67	0.00
Alaska	0.00*	0.33**	0.00**
Arizona	0.20	0.19**	0.00**
Arkansas	0.75	0.63	0.00
California	0.18	0.20	0.12
Colorado	0.21	0.25	0.21
Connecticut	0.30	0.30	0.22
Delaware	0.44	0.44	0.00
Florida	0.30	0.20	0.43
Georgia	0.73	0.45	0.91
Idaho	0.08	0.15	0.21
Illinois	0.20	0.20	0.18
Indiana	0.44	0.63	0.56
Iowa	0.67	1.00	0.56
Kansas	0.33	0.30	0.37
Kentucky	0.61	0.43	0.57
Louisiana	0.50	0.46	0.58
Maine	1.00	2.00	1.00
Maryland	0.53	0.60	1.20
Massachusetts	0.40	0.40	0.44
Michigan	0.44	0.44	0.33
Minnesota	0.88	0.88	1.00
Mississippi	0.49	0.36	0.36
Missouri	0.73	0.64	0.73
Montana	0.69	0.38	0.00
Nebraska	0.39	0.56	0.11
Nevada	0.00*	0.00*	0.00*
New Hampshire	2.00	1.33	2.00
New Jersey	0.28	0.30	0.24
New Mexico	0.16	0.39	0.16
New York	0.20	0.21	0.23
North Carolina	0.70	0.90	0.80
North Dakota	0.67	0.17	1.33
Ohio	0.64	0.64	0.82
Oklahoma	0.32	0.74	0.37
Oregon	0.28	0.32	0.28
Pennsylvania	0.62	0.54	0.62
Rhode Island	0.38	0.38	0.43
South Carolina	0.64	0.45	0.82
South Dakota	1.33	0.50	0.67
Tennessee	0.86	0.79	0.86
Texas	0.18	0.22	0.10
Utah	0.32	0.24	0.27
Vermont	1.33	1.17	3.00
Virginia	0.40	0.47	0.60
Washington	0.31	0.34	0.21
West Virginia	1.00	0.71	1.14
Wisconsin	0.62	0.62	0.69
Wyoming	0.19	0.15**	0.00**

Appendix 30. Representation Ratios: Hispanic Faculty,
1991

State	Public		Private	
	Male	Female	Male	Female
Alabama	1.59	0.68	0.95	0.68
Alaska	0.46	0.33	0.00	1.47
Arizona	0.34	0.27	0.51	0.52
Arkansas	0.90	0.25	0.90	1.25
California	0.27	0.17	0.14	0.12
Colorado	0.43	0.20	0.48	0.30
Connecticut	0.41	0.24	0.31	0.15
Delaware	0.64	0.98	0.00	0.00
Florida	0.40	0.26	0.55	0.24
Georgia	0.53	0.27	0.85	0.81
Idaho	0.18	0.17	0.11	0.12
Illinois	0.22	0.19	0.22	0.11
Indiana	0.88	0.46	1.10	0.34
Iowa	1.32	0.70	0.83	0.88
Kansas	0.40	0.17	0.35	0.45
Kentucky	1.90	0.36	0.63	0.71
Louisiana	0.73	0.36	0.37	0.90
Maine	0.00	0.36	2.15	1.45
Maryland	0.00***	0.00***	0.60	0.46
Massachusetts	0.38	0.25	0.42	0.25
Michigan	0.91	0.56	0.37	0.28
Minnesota	1.26	0.50	1.26	1.01
Mississippi	0.98	0.32	0.65	0.00
Missouri	0.82	0.84	1.14	0.51
Montana	0.51	0.27	0.00	0.00
Nebraska	0.58	0.35	0.74	0.27
Nevada	0.20	0.12	0.00	0.00
New Hampshire	1.14	0.40	1.52	1.01
New Jersey	0.31	0.27	0.33	0.15
New Mexico	0.41**	0.19**	0.00**	0.00**
New York	0.27	0.17	0.17	0.11
North Carolina	1.22	0.80	1.22	0.80
North Dakota	1.07	0.84	0.00	0.00
Ohio	1.24	0.47	0.93	0.62
Oklahoma	0.35	0.38	0.21	0.23
Oregon	0.37	0.28	0.37	0.17
Pennsylvania	0.71	0.52	1.01	0.41
Rhode Island	0.31	0.09	0.35	0.09
South Carolina	1.07	0.73	1.07	0.49
South Dakota	2.39	0.00	0.00	1.32
Tennessee	1.71	0.94	3.99	0.94
Texas	0.26	0.17	0.14	0.23
Utah	0.40**	0.17**	0.00**	0.00**
Vermont	2.15	1.23	0.00	0.00
Virginia	0.44	0.24	0.29	0.00
Washington	0.47	0.24	0.00***	0.00***
West Virginia	1.26	0.85	0.00	0.00
Wisconsin	1.01	0.55	1.92	0.00
Wyoming	0.10**	0.18**	0.00**	0.00**

Appendix 31. Representation Ratios:
Hispanic Male and Female Administrators
Combined****

State	1979	1983 Public	Private
Alabama	0.11	0.11	0.00
Alaska	0.00*	0.87**	0.00**
Arizona	0.24	0.22**	0.00**
Arkansas	0.13	0.63	0.50
California	0.21	0.36	0.18
Colorado	0.44	0.53	0.14
Connecticut	0.25	0.38	0.13
Delaware	0.25	0.31	0.00
Florida	0.20	0.22	1.09
Georgia	0.27	0.05	0.27
Idaho	0.15	0.21	0.00
Illinois	0.16	0.25	0.18
Indiana	0.38	0.44	0.25
Iowa	0.22	0.22	0.33
Kansas	0.30	0.26	0.00
Kentucky	0.29	0.86	0.00
Louisiana	0.42	0.21	0.33
Maine	0.25	0.75	0.00
Maryland	0.27	0.40	0.13
Massachusetts	0.24	0.32	0.20
Michigan	0.28	0.33	0.28
Minnesota	0.63	0.63	0.00
Mississippi	0.09	0.00	0.00
Missouri	0.27	0.36	0.64
Montana	0.15	1.38	0.00
Nebraska	0.33	0.50	0.33
Nevada	0.00*	0.00*	0.00*
New Hampshire	0.50	0.00	1.33
New Jersey	0.28	0.34	0.22
New Mexico	0.33	1.00	0.23
New York	0.21	0.15	0.31
North Carolina	0.20	0.20	0.10
North Dakota	0.67	0.00	0.00
Ohio	0.27	0.36	0.13
Oklahoma	0.11	0.16	0.32
Oregon	0.36	0.36	0.00
Pennsylvania	0.23	0.38	0.23
Rhode Island	0.10	0.33	0.00
South Carolina	0.09	0.09	0.36
South Dakota	0.00	1.00	0.00
Tennessee	0.36	0.14	0.57
Texas	0.21	0.28	0.17
Utah	0.56	0.59	0.27
Vermont	0.50	1.00	1.00
Virginia	0.05	0.10	0.07
Washington	0.59	0.62	1.28
West Virginia	0.29	0.00	0.00
Wisconsin	0.38	0.46	0.46
Wyoming	0.00	0.10**	0.00**

Appendix 32. Representation Ratios: Hispanic
Administrators, 1991

State	Public Male	Public Female	Private Male	Private Female
Alabama	0.32	0.34	0.00	0.00
Alaska	0.40	0.00	0.00	2.34
Arizona	0.55	0.23	0.20	0.11
Arkansas	0.67	0.25	0.00	2.50
California	0.33	0.22	0.39	0.22
Colorado	0.76	0.41	0.39	0.14
Connecticut	0.41	0.33	0.19	0.18
Delaware	0.24	0.27	0.00	0.00
Florida	0.32	0.36	0.78	1.35
Georgia	0.04	0.05	0.42	0.14
Idaho	0.18	0.00	0.00	0.00
Illinois	0.31	0.30	0.19	0.24
Indiana	0.44	0.00	0.33	0.69
Iowa	0.33	0.18	1.16	0.18
Kansas	0.20	0.22	0.00	0.45
Kentucky	0.63	0.00	0.00	0.00
Louisiana	0.27	0.18	1.01	0.54
Maine	1.79	0.00	0.00	1.45
Maryland	0.00***	0.00***	0.30	0.08
Massachusetts	0.25	0.41	0.17	0.33
Michigan	0.37	0.37	0.82	0.37
Minnesota	1.41	0.17	0.47	0.00
Mississippi	0.00	0.00	0.00	0.00
Missouri	0.98	0.17	0.33	0.51
Montana	0.38	0.41	0.00	0.00
Nebraska	0.49	0.18	0.00	0.35
Nevada	0.38	0.23	0.00	0.00
New Hampshire	0.00	0.00	0.00	0.40
New Jersey	0.29	0.42	0.17	0.08
New Mexico	0.92**	0.37**	0.00**	0.00**
New York	0.33	0.35	0.30	0.22
North Carolina	0.31	0.20	0.15	0.20
North Dakota	0.00	0.00	0.00	0.00
Ohio	0.93	0.16	0.31	0.31
Oklahoma	0.35	0.46	0.42	0.00
Oregon	0.41	0.17	0.23	0.17
Pennsylvania	0.41	0.31	0.41	0.41
Rhode Island	0.00	0.00	0.35	0.13
South Carolina	0.64	0.24	0.43	0.00
South Dakota	0.00	0.00	0.00	0.00
Tennessee	0.57	0.31	0.29	0.00
Texas	0.31	0.19	0.13	0.62
Utah	0.44**	0.00**	0.00**	0.00**
Vermont	0.00	0.92	0.00	0.00
Virginia	0.07	0.16	0.00	0.00
Washington	0.55	0.29	0.00***	0.00***
West Virginia	0.42	0.00	0.00	0.00
Wisconsin	0.81	0.65	0.00	0.00
Wyoming	0.31**	0.00**	0.00**	0.00**

Appendix 33. Representation Ratios: Asian Male Faculty

State	1979 Combined	1983 Public	1983 Private	1991 Public	1991 Private
Alabama	19.30	24.12	8.68	14.66	19.02
Alaska	0.00*	1.98**	0.00**	1.94	2.59
Arizona	3.85	7.42**	0.00**	3.05	4.44
Arkansas	10.83	13.15	6.96	11.63	4.41
California	1.39	1.39	1.23	1.07	0.90
Colorado	3.38	3.17	2.95	3.03	1.52
Connecticut	6.74	7.75	10.11	4.91	4.26
Delaware	7.26	8.52	4.10	6.26	8.55
Florida	5.01	7.33	7.33	5.36	5.18
Georgia	9.71	9.20	8.17	6.01	5.84
Idaho	3.72	5.07	2.03	4.04	0.00
Illinois	4.26	4.56	4.85	3.49	3.16
Indiana	20.50	21.08	13.47	15.09	8.45
Iowa	13.07	18.51	7.62	9.47	3.66
Kansas	7.07	9.09	5.05	6.01	1.58
Kentucky	18.23	19.10	18.23	17.84	8.47
Louisiana	8.31	9.75	9.75	10.31	10.52
Maine	7.00	10.50	7.88	5.05	5.44
Maryland	4.37	4.37	2.87	0.00***	2.62
Massachusetts	4.23	6.10	5.87	2.54	2.45
Michigan	8.93	10.99	8.25	10.80	2.88
Minnesota	6.60	9.24	2.31	3.73	1.75
Mississippi	12.36	10.04	35.52	12.83	21.52
Missouri	9.90	10.37	8.02	11.53	7.94
Montana	14.01	13.27	5.16	8.19	3.02
Nebraska	7.84	11.76	6.37	8.30	6.16
Nevada	0.00*	0.00*	0.00*	4.03	0.00
New Hampshire	11.98	15.72	8.98	5.17	2.71
New Jersey	3.94	4.23	4.96	2.42	3.16
New Mexico	6.13	5.26	6.13	7.34**	0.00**
New York	2.96	3.07	3.07	1.85	1.90
North Carolina	8.38	15.48	12.25	8.67	7.58
North Dakota	19.24	22.32	25.40	16.71	0.00
Ohio	10.12	15.43	13.50	11.87	5.81
Oklahoma	7.46	8.64	5.89	5.58	4.04
Oregon	2.70	2.06	2.38	1.53	1.70
Pennsylvania	9.51	9.51	8.75	6.44	6.61
Rhode Island	6.58	10.96	8.77	5.24	3.06
South Carolina	10.54	11.12	9.95	8.68	9.03
South Dakota	12.47	20.15	9.59	17.22	5.41
Tennessee	13.90	20.49	8.78	10.82	8.60
Texas	4.71	6.20	4.46	3.22	0.64
Utah	4.24	3.43	2.02	2.21**	0.00**
Vermont	5.32	7.98	5.32	7.87	0.00
Virginia	3.63	4.67	1.90	2.53	2.04
Washington	2.21	2.13	1.11	1.58	0.00***
West Virginia	22.37	25.69	12.43	22.37	24.91
Wisconsin	11.08	10.52	15.51	5.73	0.00
Wyoming	4.38	2.74**	0.00**	7.29**	0.00**

Appendix 34. Representation Ratios: Asian Female Faculty

State	1979 Combined	1983 Public	1983 Private	1991 Public	1991 Private
Alabama	2.05	1.37	2.05	1.74	2.79
Alaska	0.00*	0.19**	0.00**	0.42	0.00
Arizona	1.12	1.12**	0.00**	1.66	3.31
Arkansas	1.21	1.82	0.00	1.41	0.35
California	0.44	0.48	0.48	0.47	0.33
Colorado	0.71	0.53	0.89	0.63	0.42
Connecticut	1.59	1.59	2.23	1.04	1.69
Delaware	1.07	1.34	10.69	1.28	1.56
Florida	0.62	0.62	0.62	0.95	0.79
Georgia	0.79	0.79	1.19	0.83	0.50
Idaho	0.90	0.60	0.00	0.62	0.00
Illinois	1.27	1.59	0.64	0.87	0.55
Indiana	2.45	2.95	1.47	2.59	1.73
Iowa	1.87	1.40	1.40	1.55	1.33
Kansas	0.88	0.88	0.00	0.77	0.31
Kentucky	1.91	1.91	0.64	3.47	1.16
Louisiana	1.73	1.39	0.69	1.64	2.25
Maine	1.35	0.68	1.35	0.70	5.58
Maryland	1.01	0.88	0.76	0.00***	0.73
Massachusetts	0.92	1.37	1.60	1.00	1.00
Michigan	1.86	1.55	1.24	1.74	1.05
Minnesota	0.86	1.72	0.86	0.87	1.19
Mississippi	1.82	1.82	3.04	2.27	3.79
Missouri	2.33	1.16	1.16	1.44	1.92
Montana	2.74	2.19	0.00	1.99	0.00
Nebraska	0.79	0.39	0.79	1.21	0.48
Nevada	0.00*	0.00*	0.00*	0.98	0.00
New Hampshire	1.65	1.10	2.20	1.83	0.69
New Jersey	1.10	0.97	1.10	0.62	0.62
New Mexico	1.69	1.35	1.69	0.78**	0.00**
New York	0.90	0.56	0.67	0.63	0.52
North Carolina	0.98	1.46	0.98	1.20	1.91
North Dakota	0.58	0.00	0.00	1.41	0.00
Ohio	1.32	1.75	1.75	2.10	2.10
Oklahoma	1.26	1.26	0.95	1.28	1.28
Oregon	0.72	0.72	0.43	0.72	0.56
Pennsylvania	1.79	2.14	1.07	1.38	1.20
Rhode Island	0.70	0.70	1.76	0.44	0.88
South Carolina	1.92	0.96	0.96	1.41	1.70
South Dakota	1.36	1.36	0.00	2.85	4.48
Tennessee	0.00	2.99	1.19	1.77	1.77
Texas	0.90	0.90	0.68	0.63	0.00
Utah	0.93	1.12	0.19	0.51**	0.00**
Vermont	0.00	0.00	4.06	2.95	0.00
Virginia	0.45	0.76	0.45	0.60	0.30
Washington	0.69	0.61	0.61	0.52	0.00***
West Virginia	2.76	2.07	0.00	2.74	0.00
Wisconsin	1.46	1.95	1.95	1.26	0.00
Wyoming	0.42	0.00**	0.00**	0.58**	0.00**

Appendix 35. Representation Ratios: Asian Male Administrators

State	1979 Combined	1983 Public	1983 Private	1991 Public	1991 Private
Alabama	2.89	1.93	4.82	1.19	4.36
Alaska	0.00*	1.56**	0.00**	1.23	0.00
Arizona	0.82	1.37**	0.00**	1.39	0.00
Arkansas	3.09	3.87	3.09	1.20	0.00
California	0.66	0.66	0.46	0.53	0.32
Colorado	1.48	0.84	1.27	0.58	0.23
Connecticut	1.35	1.01	1.69	0.52	1.16
Delaware	0.00	0.00	16.73	0.46	0.00
Florida	1.54	1.16	1.93	1.61	6.08
Georgia	1.53	3.07	0.51	1.06	0.18
Idaho	1.01	2.36	0.00	3.14	0.00
Illinois	1.18	1.32	1.47	1.14	0.81
Indiana	3.51	3.51	4.10	3.62	1.21
Iowa	1.09	2.72	0.54	3.87	0.22
Kansas	1.35	2.02	0.00	0.95	0.00
Kentucky	0.87	5.21	0.00	2.23	0.89
Louisiana	1.44	1.08	2.17	1.65	1.24
Maine	0.00	0.00	0.00	0.00	0.00
Maryland	0.82	1.37	0.68	0.00***	0.64
Massachusetts	0.94	0.94	0.94	0.42	0.51
Michigan	3.44	3.44	1.03	1.98	1.26
Minnesota	2.31	1.65	0.00	0.58	0.47
Mississippi	2.32	0.77	4.63	0.83	0.00
Missouri	1.41	0.94	1.41	0.51	1.28
Montana	5.16	0.00	0.00	0.00	0.00
Nebraska	1.96	1.47	0.00	3.48	0.54
Nevada	0.00*	0.00*	0.00*	0.28	0.00
New Hampshire	0.00	3.74	1.50	0.98	1.23
New Jersey	1.17	1.75	0.44	0.98	0.35
New Mexico	2.63	3.07	0.00	0.95**	0.00**
New York	0.68	0.91	0.91	0.57	0.57
North Carolina	3.22	3.87	0.00	1.08	0.00
North Dakota	3.08	7.70	0.00	3.50	0.00
Ohio	2.41	3.86	2.89	1.45	0.97
Oklahoma	1.57	2.36	2.36	1.92	1.15
Oregon	0.95	1.11	0.95	0.68	1.36
Pennsylvania	1.52	1.52	1.90	1.22	0.70
Rhode Island	2.19	2.56	2.19	1.86	0.87
South Carolina	2.34	3.51	0.00	1.39	0.69
South Dakota	8.63	5.76	2.88	1.97	0.00
Tennessee	1.46	1.46	0.00	0.64	2.23
Texas	1.24	1.49	1.24	0.75	0.00
Utah	2.62	1.21	0.00	0.21**	0.00**
Vermont	0.00	5.32	0.00	2.25	0.00
Virginia	0.69	2.94	0.87	0.33	0.00
Washington	1.79	1.36	0.68	0.94	0.00***
West Virginia	2.49	4.97	0.00	2.54	0.00
Wisconsin	2.22	2.22	1.66	1.11	0.00
Wyoming	0.00	0.00**	0.00**	6.56**	0.00**

Appendix 36. Representation Ratios: Asian Female Administrators

State	1979 Combined	1983 Public	1983 Private	1991 Public	1991 Private
Alabama	0.68	0.00	0.00	0.35	0.00
Alaska	0.00*	0.00**	0.00**	0.37	0.00
Arizona	0.45	0.90**	0.00**	1.02	0.00
Arkansas	0.00	0.00	0.00	0.35	0.00
California	0.33	0.37	0.37	0.51	0.29
Colorado	0.36	0.53	1.07	0.63	0.00
Connecticut	1.27	1.70	2.55	0.26	1.04
Delaware	0.00	2.41	0.00	0.00	2.98
Florida	0.09	0.31	0.62	0.32	1.90
Georgia	0.79	0.40	0.40	0.33	0.33
Idaho	0.90	1.20	0.00	0.00	0.00
Illinois	0.64	0.95	0.64	0.47	0.79
Indiana	1.47	1.47	0.49	0.29	0.29
Iowa	0.00	0.00	0.00	0.22	0.22
Kansas	0.29	0.59	0.00	0.46	0.00
Kentucky	0.00	0.64	0.00	0.39	0.77
Louisiana	0.35	0.35	0.00	0.20	0.41
Maine	0.00	0.00	0.00	0.00	0.00
Maryland	0.13	0.38	0.25	0.00***	0.20
Massachusetts	0.69	0.92	0.69	0.50	0.67
Michigan	1.24	1.24	0.31	0.52	0.52
Minnesota	0.86	1.15	0.57	0.54	0.22
Mississippi	0.00	0.00	0.00	0.00	2.27
Missouri	0.39	0.78	1.16	0.48	0.72
Montana	0.55	1.64	0.00	1.00	0.00
Nebraska	0.00	0.79	0.00	0.48	0.97
Nevada	0.00*	0.00*	0.00*	0.40	0.00
New Hampshire	0.00	0.00	0.00	0.00	0.92
New Jersey	0.41	0.69	0.69	0.56	0.62
New Mexico	0.34	0.00	0.00	0.39**	0.00**
New York	0.67	0.56	0.79	0.47	0.58
North Carolina	0.49	0.00	0.00	0.10	0.48
North Dakota	0.00	0.00	0.00	0.00	0.00
Ohio	1.32	1.32	1.32	0.70	0.47
Oklahoma	0.95	0.00	0.63	0.55	0.00
Oregon	0.43	0.29	0.43	0.08	1.27
Pennsylvania	1.07	1.07	1.43	0.69	0.69
Rhode Island	0.70	1.05	1.05	0.00	0.55
South Carolina	0.48	0.00	0.00	0.28	0.00
South Dakota	0.00	0.00	0.00	1.63	0.00
Tennessee	0.60	0.00	0.60	0.30	0.00
Texas	0.68	0.68	1.36	0.53	0.00
Utah	0.75	1.12	0.00	0.20**	0.00**
Vermont	0.00	0.00	0.00	0.98	15.76
Virginia	0.30	0.45	0.15	0.30	0.00
Washington	0.54	0.84	0.46	0.56	0.00***
West Virginia	0.69	1.38	0.00	1.37	0.00
Wisconsin	1.46	0.97	1.46	0.54	0.00
Wyoming	0.00	0.00**	0.00**	0.00**	0.00**

Appendix 37. Representation Ratios: Native American Male
Faculty

State	1979 Combined	1983 Public	Private	1991 Public	Private
Alabama	1.02	1.02	0.00	0.99	0.00
Alaska	0.00*	0.32**	0.00**	0.18	0.28
Arizona	0.29	0.18**	0.00**	0.26	0.00
Arkansas	0.99	1.98	0.00	2.24	0.00
California	0.71	0.71	0.95	0.99	0.25
Colorado	0.94	0.94	0.00	0.72	0.72
Connecticut	0.69	1.39	0.00	0.97	0.97
Delaware	1.85	0.93	0.00	0.66	0.00
Florida	0.99	0.99	0.99	1.40	0.70
Georgia	2.68	0.27	1.34	0.93	0.00
Idaho	0.18	4.35	0.00	0.44	0.00
Illinois	1.41	1.41	1.41	2.07	0.21
Indiana	1.40	1.40	0.00	0.87	0.00
Iowa	1.08	1.08	1.08	1.54	0.77
Kansas	0.61	0.92	6.12	0.68	0.46
Kentucky	0.57	1.90	0.00	1.25	1.25
Louisiana	1.35	1.35	0.00	0.45	0.00
Maine	0.22	0.55	0.00	0.42	0.00
Maryland	1.05	1.05	0.00	0.00***	0.73
Massachusetts	3.02	9.07	1.51	1.00	1.00
Michigan	0.93	0.47	0.47	0.68	0.34
Minnesota	0.71	0.71	0.71	0.53	0.71
Mississippi	0.00	0.00	0.00	0.61	0.00
Missouri	0.80	1.59	2.39	1.52	1.02
Montana	0.09	0.13	0.00	0.30	1.25
Nebraska	1.04	1.04	0.69	0.52	0.78
Nevada	0.00*	0.00*	0.00*	0.61	0.00
New Hampshire	2.60	2.60	1.30	0.00	1.00
New Jersey	0.35	1.77	1.77	1.05	0.53
New Mexico	0.05	0.15	0.08	0.21**	0.00**
New York	0.92	0.92	0.92	0.59	0.59
North Carolina	0.18	0.37	0.18	0.34	0.17
North Dakota	0.13	0.13	1.05	0.45	0.00
Ohio	1.78	1.78	3.56	1.06	1.06
Oklahoma	0.51	0.58	0.58	0.43	0.18
Oregon	0.58	0.19	0.00	0.45	0.15
Pennsylvania	2.53	2.53	5.06	1.62	1.62
Rhode Island	0.28	0.69	0.00	1.02	0.00
South Carolina	0.32	1.06	1.06	0.82	0.82
South Dakota	0.09	0.25	0.31	0.20	0.00
Tennessee	1.75	1.75	0.00	1.92	0.48
Texas	2.07	2.07	1.38	1.02	3.05
Utah	0.47	0.47	0.00	0.15**	0.00**
Vermont	0.00	0.00	59.72	0.00	0.00
Virginia	1.06	1.06	3.19	0.79	0.00
Washington	0.68	0.68	0.00	0.60	0.00***
West Virginia	4.95	2.48	7.43	2.94	0.00
Wisconsin	0.32	0.32	0.32	0.50	4.78
Wyoming	0.00	0.00**	0.00**	0.00**	0.00**

Appendix 38. Representation Ratios: Native American Female
Faculty

State	1979 Combined	1983 Public	1983 Private	1991 Public	1991 Private
Alabama	0.10	0.00	0.00	0.10	0.00
Alaska	0.00*	0.06**	0.00**	0.18	0.00
Arizona	0.03	0.03**	0.00**	0.18	0.00
Arkansas	0.95	0.95	0.95	0.73	0.00
California	0.23	0.46	0.05	0.49	0.05
Colorado	0.33	0.16	0.65	0.47	0.00
Connecticut	0.27	0.00	0.68	0.00	0.00
Delaware	0.00	1.78	0.00	1.31	0.00
Florida	0.52	1.04	0.00	0.73	0.00
Georgia	0.15	0.00	0.00	0.20	1.02
Idaho	0.18	0.18	0.00	0.44	0.00
Illinois	0.42	1.40	0.00	1.06	0.00
Indiana	0.14	1.40	0.42	0.44	0.35
Iowa	0.00	0.00	0.00	0.22	0.37
Kansas	0.31	0.31	2.78	0.22	0.00
Kentucky	0.65	0.00	0.00	0.39	0.00
Louisiana	0.22	0.29	0.72	0.09	0.00
Maine	0.00	1.11	0.00	0.40	0.00
Maryland	0.21	0.00	0.00	0.00***	0.15
Massachusetts	0.29	4.36	0.15	0.97	0.39
Michigan	0.46	0.09	0.23	0.16	0.33
Minnesota	0.07	0.23	0.23	0.52	0.69
Mississippi	0.00	0.24	0.00	0.00	0.00
Missouri	0.80	0.00	0.80	0.52	0.00
Montana	0.04	0.13	0.00	0.27	0.23
Nebraska	0.34	0.34	0.00	0.12	0.50
Nevada	0.00*	0.00*	0.00*	0.24	0.00
New Hampshire	1.46	0.00	2.93	1.08	0.00
New Jersey	0.69	0.69	0.00	1.01	0.51
New Mexico	0.07	0.09	0.07	0.20**	0.00**
New York	0.26	0.17	0.43	0.17	0.22
North Carolina	0.18	0.18	0.18	0.16	0.00
North Dakota	0.06	0.06	2.11	0.48	0.00
Ohio	0.35	0.18	0.35	0.43	0.21
Oklahoma	0.21	0.24	0.28	0.29	0.41
Oregon	0.38	0.19	0.19	0.29	0.00
Pennsylvania	0.25	0.25	0.25	1.60	0.32
Rhode Island	0.00	0.00	0.00	0.00	0.95
South Carolina	0.56	1.11	0.00	0.35	1.75
South Dakota	0.03	0.15	0.00	0.05	0.00
Tennessee	0.00	1.85	0.00	0.98	0.00
Texas	0.73	0.73	0.00	1.05	3.14
Utah	0.30	0.30	0.44	0.28**	0.00**
Vermont	0.00	0.00	0.00	0.69	0.00
Virginia	0.48	0.48	0.00	0.33	0.00
Washington	0.27	0.27	0.00	0.47	0.00***
West Virginia	1.18	0.00	0.00	2.90	0.00
Wisconsin	0.32	0.32	0.63	0.49	0.00
Wyoming	0.13	0.26**	0.00**	0.10**	0.00**

Appendix 39. Representation Ratios: Native American Male
Administrators

State	1979 Combined	1983 Public	Private	1991 Public	Private
Alabama	2.03	1.02	5.09	0.49	0.00
Alaska	0.00*	0.51**	0.00**	0.52	0.00
Arizona	0.07	0.18**	0.00**	0.41	0.00
Arkansas	0.99	2.48	0.00	1.49	0.00
California	0.95	1.19	0.48	0.99	0.75
Colorado	0.31	0.94	0.94	0.95	1.19
Connecticut	2.77	5.54	0.00	0.00	0.97
Delaware	0.00	25.96	0.00	1.99	0.00
Florida	0.99	0.99	0.99	0.70	0.70
Georgia	1.34	0.00	0.00	0.37	0.00
Idaho	0.00	4.53	0.00	0.00	0.00
Illinois	1.41	1.41	1.41	1.04	1.04
Indiana	1.40	0.56	0.00	0.87	0.00
Iowa	0.00	2.17	0.00	0.77	0.00
Kansas	0.92	0.92	6.74	0.23	0.00
Kentucky	0.00	0.00	0.00	0.00	0.00
Louisiana	0.00	0.00	0.00	0.00	0.00
Maine	1.65	1.65	0.00	0.00	0.00
Maryland	10.54	3.16	0.00	0.00***	1.47
Massachusetts	0.60	1.51	0.30	0.00	1.00
Michigan	0.47	0.93	1.40	0.68	0.68
Minnesota	0.24	0.24	0.00	0.89	0.53
Mississippi	0.82	0.00	0.00	0.00	0.00
Missouri	2.39	8.77	0.80	0.51	0.51
Montana	0.17	0.13	1.92	0.27	5.66
Nebraska	0.00	0.69	0.00	0.52	0.00
Nevada	0.00*	0.00*	0.00*	0.00	0.00
New Hampshire	0.00	0.00	0.00	0.00	2.00
New Jersey	1.77	0.00	1.77	0.42	1.05
New Mexico	0.26	0.36	0.41	0.28**	0.00**
New York	0.92	0.92	0.92	0.00	0.24
North Carolina	0.55	1.47	0.18	1.01	0.00
North Dakota	0.52	0.66	1.57	2.82	1.26
Ohio	0.53	1.78	0.71	1.06	0.42
Oklahoma	0.73	0.51	0.91	0.49	0.43
Oregon	1.36	0.58	0.00	1.04	0.30
Pennsylvania	0.76	2.53	0.00	1.62	1.62
Rhode Island	1.39	0.00	0.00	2.04	1.02
South Carolina	1.06	2.11	0.00	1.64	0.00
South Dakota	0.66	2.10	1.07	0.34	0.64
Tennessee	1.75	3.50	7.01	0.96	0.00
Texas	0.69	0.69	0.34	1.02	0.00
Utah	0.31	0.16	3.42	0.00**	0.00**
Vermont	0.00	0.00	0.00	0.64	0.00
Virginia	0.43	9.57	0.00	0.31	0.00
Washington	0.96	0.82	0.41	0.97	0.00***
West Virginia	4.95	2.48	0.00	2.94	0.00
Wisconsin	0.97	0.97	0.97	0.10	0.00
Wyoming	0.93	0.67**	0.00**	0.48**	0.00**

Appendix 40. Representation Ratios: Native American Female
Administrators

State	1979 Combined	1983 Public	1983 Private	1991 Public	1991 Private
Alabama	1.04	0.00	0.00	0.49	0.00
Alaska	0.00*	0.06**	0.00**	0.18	0.00
Arizona	0.03	0.03**	0.00**	0.32	0.00
Arkansas	0.48	0.00	1.90	1.45	1.82
California	0.23	0.46	0.23	0.97	0.49
Colorado	0.33	1.31	0.98	0.94	0.00
Connecticut	0.00	0.00	0.00	0.00	0.00
Delaware	0.00	0.00	0.00	0.00	0.00
Florida	0.31	0.41	2.07	0.00	0.73
Georgia	0.00	0.00	0.00	0.00	1.02
Idaho	0.00	0.00	0.00	0.73	0.00
Illinois	0.42	1.40	1.40	1.06	0.00
Indiana	1.40	0.56	0.00	0.00	0.00
Iowa	0.00	1.05	1.05	0.74	0.00
Kansas	0.00	0.62	0.93	0.45	0.00
Kentucky	0.00	0.00	0.00	0.00	0.00
Louisiana	0.00	0.72	0.00	0.46	0.00
Maine	0.00	0.00	0.00	0.00	0.00
Maryland	0.00	0.00	0.00	0.00***	0.00
Massachusetts	0.29	1.45	0.00	0.00	0.19
Michigan	0.23	0.14	0.00	0.33	0.33
Minnesota	0.23	0.00	0.00	1.56	0.17
Mississippi	0.00	0.00	0.00	0.00	0.00
Missouri	0.80	0.00	0.80	0.00	0.52
Montana	0.17	0.59	1.88	0.50	5.54
Nebraska	0.00	0.00	0.00	0.00	0.00
Nevada	0.00*	0.00*	0.00*	0.00	0.00
New Hampshire	0.00	0.00	0.00	4.34	2.17
New Jersey	0.00	0.00	0.00	0.00	0.00
New Mexico	0.02	0.00	0.12	0.26**	0.00**
New York	0.34	0.86	0.86	0.22	0.56
North Carolina	0.00	0.36	0.00	0.33	0.00
North Dakota	0.00	0.32	4.55	1.78	0.00
Ohio	0.00	0.00	0.00	1.07	0.43
Oklahoma	0.35	0.28	0.56	0.37	0.41
Oregon	0.77	0.00	0.00	0.29	0.00
Pennsylvania	0.25	0.74	0.50	1.60	0.64
Rhode Island	0.00	0.00	0.00	1.91	0.00
South Carolina	0.00	0.00	0.00	1.91	0.00
South Dakota	0.00	1.26	0.42	0.11	0.41
Tennessee	0.92	0.00	0.00	0.00	0.98
Texas	0.73	0.73	0.00	1.05	3.14
Utah	0.30	0.15	0.00	0.00**	0.00**
Vermont	3.09	0.00	0.00	0.69	0.00
Virginia	0.48	0.60	0.00	0.33	0.00
Washington	0.27	0.41	0.41	0.59	0.00***
West Virginia	2.37	0.00	0.00	0.00	0.00
Wisconsin	0.63	0.32	0.63	0.49	0.00
Wyoming	0.00	0.00**	0.00**	0.00**	0.00**

Notes

INTRODUCTION

1. For debates on affirmative action, see Nicolaus Mills, ed., *Debating Affirmative Action: Race, Gender, Ethnicity, and the Politics of Inclusion* (New York: Delta Books, 1994).

2. Cited in Reynolds Farley and Walter R. Allen, *The Color Line and the Quality of Life in America* (New York: Russell Sage Foundation, 1987), 3.

3. Gunnar Myrdal with the assistance of Richard Sterner and Arnold Rose, *An American Dilemma: The Negro Problem and Modern Democracy* (New York: Harper and Brothers, 1944), xlvii, 4, 1009–10.

4. Liah Greenfeld, *Nationalism: Five Roads to Modernity* (Cambridge MA: Harvard University Press, 1992), 460.

5. See Andrew Hacker, *Two Nations: Black and White, Separate, Hostile, Unequal* (New York: Ballantine Books, 1992), 14; and Alexis de Tocqueville, *Democracy in America*, ed. J. P. Mayer, trans. George Lawrence (New York: HarperPerennial, 1988), 360.

6. Tocqueville, *Democracy in America*, 342.

7. Myrdal, *American Dilemma*, 87.

8. Tocqueville, *Democracy in America*, 343.

9. Richard Delgado, "Introduction," in Richard Delgado, ed., *Critical Race Theory: The Cutting Edge* (Philadelphia: Temple University Press, 1995), xiv.

10. Cited in Derrick Bell, *And We Are Not Saved: The Elusive Quest for Racial Justice* (New York: Basic Books, 1987), 4–5.

11. Thomas Ross, "Innocence and Affirmative Action," in Delgado, *Critical Race Theory*, 557–58.

12. See Derrick Bell, *Race, Racism, and American Law*, 3d ed. (Boston: Little, Brown, 1992), 8.

13. Derrick Bell, "Racial Realism – After We're Gone: Prudent Speculations on America in a Post-Racial Epoch," in Delgado, *Critical Race Theory*, 7. Also see Bell, *And We Are Not Saved*, and Derrick Bell, *Faces at the Bottom of the Well: The Permanence of Racism* (New York: Basic Books, 1992).

14. Derrick Bell, "Property Rights in Whiteness – Their Legal Legacy, Their Economic Cost," in Delgado, *Critical Race Theory*, 79–81.

15. Ian F. Haney López, *White by Law: The Legal Construction of Race* (New York: New York University Press, 1996), 9–19, 25, 58. Feminist legal theorists among others have examined the legal and social construction of the human body and its relationship to gen-

der discrimination. For a discussion of feminist legal theory, see Katharine T. Bartlett and Rosanne Kennedy, "Introduction," 1–11; Wendy W. Williams, "The Equality Crisis: Some Reflections on Culture, Courts, and Feminism," 15–34; and Catharine A. MacKinnon, "Difference and Dominance: On Sex Discrimination," 81–94; all in Katharine T. Bartlett and Rosanne Kennedy, eds., *Feminist Legal Theory: Readings in Law and Gender* (Boulder CO: Westview Press, 1991).

16. See, for example, the various chapters in Delgado, *Critical Race Theory*, on Asian Americans, Hispanic Americans, and Native Americans. Also see Haney López, *White by Law*, for an examination of various legal decisions concerning Asians and race. On race and gender, see Angela P. Harris, "Race and Essentialism in Feminist Legal Theory," in Delgado, *Critical Race Theory*, 253–66; and Kimberlè Crenshaw, "Demarginalizing the Intersection of Race and Sex: A Black Feminist Critique of Antidiscrimination Doctrine, Feminist Theory, and Antiracist Politics," in Bartlett and Kennedy, *Feminist Legal Theory*, 57–80.

17. See, e.g. Glenn C. Loury, "Why Should We Care about Group Inequality?" in Steven Shulman and William Darity Jr., eds., *The Question of Discrimination: Racial Inequality in the U.S. Labor Market* (Middletown: Wesleyan University Press, 1989), 281.

18. Myrdal, *American Dilemma*, 216.

19. See, for example, the discussion by Albert D. Freeman, a critical race theorist, in "Derrick Bell – Race and Class: The Dilemma of Liberal Reform," in Delgado, *Critical Race Theory*, 458–63, in which he questions how a law professor might use Bell's legal textbook on American racism and race relations, given its pessimistic tone.

20. Rodney E. Hero, *Latinos and the U.S. Political System: Two-Tiered Pluralism* (Philadelphia: Temple University Press, 1992), 32–33.

21. On Manifest Destiny, see Thomas R. Hietala, *Manifest Design: Anxious Aggrandizement in Late Jacksonian America* (Ithaca NY: Cornell University Press, 1985); and Reginald Horsman, *Race and Manifest Destiny: The Origins of American Racial Anglo-Saxonism* (Cambridge MA: Harvard University Press, 1981).

22. Myrdal, *American Dilemma*, 53–54.

23. Myrdal, *American Dilemma*, 53–55.

24. John Chester Miller, *The Wolf by the Ears: Thomas Jefferson and Slavery* (New York: Free Press, 1977), 47, 65–71.

25. See Myrdal, *American Dilemma*, 1073–78.

26. Betty Friedan, "Our Revolution Is Unique," in Michael B. Levy, ed., *Political Thought in America: An Anthology*, 2d ed. (Chicago: Dorsey Press, 1988), 467–68.

27. Tocqueville, *Democracy in America*, 593. For Tocqueville's views on women, see especially 592–603.

28. Paul M. Sniderman and Thomas Piazza, *The Scar of Race* (Cambridge MA: Harvard University Press, 1993), 103, 109, 177.

29. Thomas Sowell, *Preferential Policies: An International Perspective* (New York: Quill, 1990), 14, 177.

30. See Howard Schuman, Charlotte Steeh, and Lawrence Bobo, *Racial Attitudes in America: Trends and Interpretations* (Cambridge MA: Harvard University Press, 1985); and Sniderman and Piazza, *Scar of Race*.

31. William A. Kelso, *Poverty and the Underclass: Changing Perceptions of the Poor in America* (New York: New York University Press, 1994), 205.

32. See such works as J. Donald Kingsley, *Representative Bureaucracy: An Interpretation of the British Civil Service* (Yellow Springs OH: Antioch Press, 1944); Samuel Kirslov, *Representative Bureaucracy* (Englewood Cliffs NJ: Prentice–Hall, 1974); Harry Kranz, *The Participatory Bureaucracy: Women and Minorities in a More Representative Public Service* (Lexington MA: Lexington Books, 1976); and Frederick Mosher, *Democracy and the Public Service* (New York: Oxford University Press, 1968).

33. Department of Education, National Center for Education Statistics CNCES), *Fall Staff in Postsecondary Institutions, 1995* (Washington DC: U.S. Government Printing Office, 1998), xviii, xvii, C–8.

34. Sowell, *Preferential Policies*, 156–58.

1. HISTORY OF AFFIRMATIVE ACTION

1. For a discussion of the relationship between affirmative action and liberalism, see W. R. Newell, "Affirmative Action and the Dilemmas of Liberalism," in Michael W. Cowles and John Gruhl, eds., *Affirmative Action: Theory, Analysis, and Prospects* (Jefferson NC: McFarland, 1986), 44–60.

2. For a discussion of these laws, see Eric Foner, *Reconstruction: America's Unfinished Revolution, 1863–1877* (New York: Harper and Row, 1988), 243–47, 553–56.

3. William Gillette, *Retreat from Reconstruction, 1869–1879* (Baton Rouge: Louisiana State University Press, 1979), 191. See also Melvin I. Urofsky, *A Conflict of Rights: The Supreme Court and Affirmative Action* (New York: Charles Scribner's Sons, 1991), 15–16.

4. Edward S. Greenberg and Benjamin I. Page, *The Struggle for Democracy*, 3d ed. (New York: Longman, 1997), 580.

5. Urofsky, *Conflict of Rights*, 16.

6. Herman Belz, *Equality Transformed: A Quarter-Century of Affirmative Action* (New Brunswick NJ: Transaction, 1991), 12.

7. Charles V. Hamilton, "Affirmative Action and the Clash of Experiential Realities," *Annals of the American Academy of Political and Social Science*, no. 523 (September 1992): 16.

8. George T. Felkenes and Peter Charles Unsinger, eds., *Diversity, Affirmative Action and Law Enforcement* (Springfield IL: Charles C. Thomas, 1992), 4–5.

9. Belz, *Equality Transformed*, 13.

10. For the importance of this executive order in the history of federal equal employment opportunity policy, see J. Edward Kellough, *Federal Equal Employment Opportunity Policy and Numerical Goals and Timetables: An Impact Assessment* (New York: Praeger, 1989), 13–26.

11. Nijole V. Benokraitis and Joe R. Feagin, *Affirmative Action and Equal Opportunity: Action, Inaction, Reaction* (Boulder CO: Westview Press, 1978), 8.

12. Hugh Davis Graham, "The Origins of Affirmative Action: Civil Rights and the Regulatory State," *Annals of the American Academy of Political and Social Science*, no. 523 (September 1992): 53.

13. See Kellough, *Federal Equal Employment Opportunity Policy*, 16.

14. John Edwards, *When Race Counts: The Morality of Racial Preference in Britain and America* (London: Routledge, 1995), 94.

15. Kenneth C. McGuiness, ed., *Preferential Treatment in Employment: Affirmative Action or Reverse Discrimination* (Washington DC: Equal Employment Advisory Council, 1977), 120. Authors of different chapters are not listed separately.

16. For a discussion of these executive orders, see McGuiness, *Preferential Treatment in Employment*, 13–16; Benokraitis and Feagan, *Affirmative Action and Equal Opportunity*, 8–9; and Kellough, *Federal Equal Employment Opportunity Policy*, 17–18.

17. Benokraitis and Feagin, *Affirmative Action and Equal Opportunity*, 8.

18. Ronald D. Sylvia, *Critical Issues in Public Personnel Policy* (Pacific Grove CA: Brooks/Cole, 1989), 55.

19. Urofsky, *Conflict of Rights*, 17.

20. See, for example, Graham, "Origins of Affirmative Action," 54. See also William Bradford Reynolds, "Affirmative Action and Its Negative Repercussions," *Annals of the American Academy of Political and Social Science*, no. 523 (September 1992): 39.

21. Edwards, *When Race Counts*, 96.

22. Felkenes and Unsinger, *Diversity, Affirmative Action and Law Enforcement*, 5.

23. See Charles Whalen and Barbara Whalen, *The Longest Debate: A Legislative History of the 1964 Civil Rights Act* (Cabin John MD: Seven Locks Press, 1985), 1–2.

24. For a summary of the political battle on this bill, see Hugh Davis Graham, *Civil Rights and the Presidency: Race and Gender in American Politics, 1960–1972* (New York: Oxford University Press, 1992), 67–86. For a detailed history of the law, see Whalen and Whalen, *Longest Debate*, and Robert D. Loevy, *To End All Segregation: The Politics of the Passage of the Civil Rights Act of 1964* (Lanham MD: University Press of America, 1990).

25. Quoted in Carl M. Brauer, *John F. Kennedy and the Second Reconstruction* (New York: Columbia University Press, 1977), 11.

26. Whalen and Whalen, *Longest Debate*, 232–33.

27. *Congressional Record*, 88th Cong., 2d sess., 1964 (May 9, 1964–June 3, 1964), 110, pt. 9:11848. See also Reynolds, "Affirmative Action," 40–41; Nicolaus Mills, "Introduction:

To Look like America," in Nicolaus Mills, ed., *Debating Affirmative Action: Race, Gender, Ethnicity, and the Politics of Inclusion* (New York: Delta, 1994), 6–7; and Graham, "Origins of Affirmative Action," 54–55.

28. Quoted in Reynolds, "Origins of Affirmative Action," 41.

29. Reynolds, "Origins of Affirmative Action," 41. *Anderson v. Martin* (1964) involved "a state statute requiring that the race of each candidate for public office be accurately designated on each ballot."

30. Graham, "Origins of Affirmative Action," 56.

31. The race/ethnic groups now used are white, black, Hispanic, Asian or Pacific Islands, and American Indian or Alaskan natives. The occupational categories included in affirmative action reports are official/administrator, professional, protective service, technician/para-professional, secretarial/clerical, skilled craft, and service/maintenance.

32. See Mills, "Introduction," 8–9.

33. *U.S. Code of Federal Regulations*, 41 (July 1, 1994), FR 60–2.12. For detailed discussions of these orders, see Edwards, *When Race Counts*, 108–15, and Benokraitis and Feagin, *Affirmative Action and Equal Opportunity*, 12–15.

34. See Sylvia, *Critical Issues in Public Personnel Policy*, 59–60. Also see Kellough, *Federal Equal Employment Opportunity Policy*, 1.

35. Felkenes and Unsinger, *Diversity, Affirmative Action and Law Enforcement*, 11.

36. Mills, "Introduction," 10.

37. Belz, *Equality Transformed*, 35.

38. Graham, "Origins of Affirmative Action," 59.

39. See James P. Turner, "The Fairest Cure," *New York Times*, April 16, 1995, E11.

40. See Belz, *Equality Transformed*, 41.

41. For a discussion of some of these cases, see Benokraitis and Feagin, *Affirmative Action and Equal Opportunity*, 18–19.

42. Benokraitis and Feagin, *Affirmative Action and Equal Opportunity*, 21.

43. Turner, "Fairest Cure," E11.

44. Mills, *Debating Affirmative Action*, 20.

45. Edwards, *When Race Counts*, 122.

46. See Mills, *Debating Affirmative Action*, 21.

47. *New York Times*, June 13, 1995, D25.

48. See *New York Times*, July 2, 1996, A12.

49. See *New York Times*, August 10, 1996, A1.

50. White and minority college faculty also view affirmative action differently. For differences between the views of the black and white faculty, see Stephanie L. Witt, *The Pursuit of Race and Gender Equity in American Academe* (New York: Praeger, 1990), 64.

51. *New York Times*, July 21, 1995, A1.

52. *Hartford Courant*, April 5, 1995, A3.

53. See Kul B. Rai and John W. Critzer, "Exclude the Privileged Classes from Affirmative Action," *Hartford Courant*, October 15, 1993, C11. For some other opinions on affirmative action benefits to middle classes, see Graham, "Origins of Affirmative Action," 61–62; and Thomas Sewell, "Black Progress Can't Be Legislated," *Washington Post*, August 12, 1984. See also Lance Morrow, "An Essay on the Unfairness of Life," *Horizon* 20 (December 1977): 34–37; and Nathan Glazer, *Affirmative Discrimination: Ethnic Inequality and Public Policy* (New York: Basic Books, 1975).

54. Rai and Critzer, "Exclude the Privileged Classes."

55. Kul B. Rai and John W. Critzer, "The Case Against Affirmative Action," an op-ed piece wired on June 23, 1995, by the Scripps Howard News Service to 360 American newspapers, many of which ran it within the next few weeks.

56. Shelby Steele, "Affirmative Action Must Go," *New York Times*, March 1, 1995, A19.

57. See *New York Times*, June 18, 1995, sec. 4, 1, 4.

58. Cited in a Knight-Ridder Tribune release, March 16, 1995.

59. *New York Times*, March 17, 1995, A28. Women and minorities do much better in the managerial categories in public administration than in the private sector. See Federal Glass Ceiling Commission, "Good for Business: Making Full Use of the Nation's Human Capital – The Environmental Scan: A Fact-Finding Report of the Federal Glass Ceiling Commission" (Washington DC: U.S. Government Printing Office, 1995), 13.

60. *New York Times*, March 17, 1995, A28.

61. See *New York Times*, March 31, 1995, A23.

62. See Kingsley R. Browne, "Lawsuits Don't Tell Affirmative Action Story," *New York Times*, April 4, 1995, A24.

63. *New York Times*, May 31, 1995, A1.

64. *New York Times*, July 20, 1995, A1.

65. *Washington Post*, July 28, 1995, A10. "A stripped-down version" of this bill was introduced in 1996, thus killing the 1995 proposal. See *New York Times*, July 13, 1996, A1.

2. INEQUALITY AND REPRESENTATION

1. Samuel Krislov, *The Negro in Federal Employment: The Quest for Equal Opportunity* (Minneapolis: University of Minnesota Press, 1967), 8–9, 19–21.

2. See James E. Kellough and Susan Ann Kay, "Affirmative Action in the Federal Bureaucracy: An Impact Assessment," *Review of Public Personnel Administration* 6 (spring 1986): 1–13; and David H. Rosenbloom, "The Federal Affirmative Action Policy," in David Nachmias, ed., *The Practice of Policy Evaluation* (New York: St. Martin's Press, 1980), 169–86.

3. J. Edward Kellough, "Integration in the Public Workplace: Determinants of Minority and Female Employment in Federal Agencies," *Public Administration Review* 50 (September/October 1990): 557–66.

4. On black male and female gains, see Gregory B. Lewis, "Progress toward Racial and Sexual Equality in the Federal Civil Service?" *Public Administration Review* 48 (May/June 1988): 701–2.

5. Paul Page, "African-Americans in Executive Branch Agencies," *Review of Public Personnel Administration* 14 (winter 1994): 24–51.

6. Nelson C. Domitrius and Lee Sigelman, "Assessing Progress toward Affirmative Action Goals in State and Local Government: A New Benchmark," *Public Administration Review* 44 (May/June 1984): 241–46.

7. Thomas R. Dye and James Renick, "Political Power and City Jobs: Determinants of Minority Employment," *Social Science Quarterly* 62 (September 1981): 475–86.

8. U.S. Equal Employment Opportunity Commission (EEOC), *Job Patterns for Minorities and Women in State and Local Government, 1991* (Washington DC: EEOC, 1992), 1, 4–11.

9. Norma M. Riccuci and David H. Rosenbloom, "Equity in Federal Employment in the United States," in Krishna K. Tummala, ed., *Equity in Public Employment across Nations* (Lanham MD: University Press of America, 1989), 25.

10. Kellough, "Integration in the Public Workplace," 560.

11. On the comparison between white male and white female employment and earnings in the federal service, see Lewis, "Progress toward Racial and Sexual Equality," 701–3. For his earnings model, see 704–5.

12. See Lewis, "Progress toward Racial and Sexual Equality," 703, table 3.

13. Katherine C. Naff, "Through the Glass Ceiling: Prospects for the Advancement of Women in the Federal Civil Service," *Public Administration Review* 54 (November/December 1994): 509.

14. N. Joseph Cayer and Lee Sigelman, "Minorities and Women in State and Local Government: 1973–1975," *Public Administration Review* 40 (September/October 1980): 443–50.

15. See Dometrius and Sigelman, "Assessing Progress toward Affirmative Action," 244, table 1, for data on women in state and local government managerial positions.

16. Rita Mae Kelly, Mary E. Guy, et al., "Public Managers in the States: A Comparison of Career Advancement by Sex," *Public Administration Review* 51 (September/October 1991): 411.

17. EEOC, *Job Patterns for Minorities and Women.*

18. Antonio Sisneros, "Hispanics in the Public Service in the Late Twentieth Century," *Public Administration Review* 15 (January/February 1993): 1–7.

19. Kellough, "Integration in the Public Workplace," 560.

20. Pan Suk Kim, "Racial Integration in the American Federal Government: With Special Reference to Asian-Americans," *Review of Public Personnel Administration* 13 (winter 1993): 55.

21. Sisneros, "Hispanics in the Public Service," 2.

22. Lewis, "Progress toward Racial and Sexual Equality," 703.

23. Sisneros, "Hispanics in the Public Service," 3.

24. Kenneth J. Meier and Joseph Stewart Jr., *The Politics of Hispanic Education: Un paso pa'lante y dos pa'tras* (Albany: State University of New York Press, 1991), 105.

25. Sisneros, "Hispanics in the Public Service," 3, see table 2.

26. EEOC, *Job Patterns for Minorities and Women.*

27. For statistics on Asian Americans, see Kim, "Racial Integration in the American Federal Government," 56–59, especially his tables.

28. For these comparative statistics on Asian Americans, see Herbert R. Barringer, Robert W. Gardner, and Michael J. Levin, *Asian and Pacific Islanders in the United States* (New York: Russell Sage Foundation, 1993), 210, table 7.6.

29. For a discussion of Asian-American earnings at the federal level, see Lewis, "Progress toward Racial and Sexual Equality," 702–5; on gender differences, see table 3 on page 703; and for a comparison of Asian-American earnings with white males, see 704–5.

30. Pan Suk Kim and Gregory B. Lewis, "Asian Americans in the Public Service: Success, Diversity, and Discrimination," *Public Administration Review* 54 (May/June 1994): 288–89.

31. See Cayer and Sigelman, "Minorities and Women," 445, table 2.

32. See Barringer, Gardner, and Levin, *Asian and Pacific Islanders*, 210–11, table 7.6 for data on Asian-American employment at the state and local level for 1980.

33. Data on Asian-American earnings in 1975 are found in Cayer and Sigelman, "Minorities and Women," 446, table 3.

34. EEOC, *Job Patterns for Minorities and Women.*

35. Kim and Lewis, "Asian Americans in the Public Service."

36. See Walter C. Fleming, "Equal Opportunity and the American Indian," in Tummala, *Equity in Public Employment*, 201–7, for a discussion of such government policies as the Buy Indian Act of 1910, which encouraged the secretary of the interior to buy Indian-made goods, and termination policy and its impact on Native Americans.

37. For a discussion of the Indian Reorganization Act of 1934, see Jerry D. Stubben, "Indian Preference: Racial Discrimination or a Political Right?" in Lyman H. Legters and Fremont J. Lyden, eds., *American Indian Policy: Self-Governance and Economic Development* (Westport CT: Greenwood Press, 1994), 106–8; Howard is quoted on 107.

38. Fleming, "Equal Opportunity," 210.

39. For a discussion of the major court decisions concerning preference for Native Americans, see Stubben, "Indian Preference," 109–11.

40. Fleming, "Equal Opportunity," 212–16.

41. Lewis, "Progress toward Racial and Sexual Equality," 703.

42. Kim, "Racial Integration in the American Federal Government," 56.

43. C. Matthew Snipp, *American Indians: The First of This Land* (New York: Russell Sage Foundation, 1989), 238–39.

44. EEOC, *Job Patterns for Minorities and Women*.

45. Richard J. Stillman II, *The American Bureaucracy* (Chicago: Nelson-Hall, 1987), 3–4.

46. See, for example, Kingsley, *Representative Bureaucracy*; and Kranz, *Participatory Bureaucracy*.

47. Cited in B. Guy Peters, *The Politics of Bureaucracy*, 4th ed. (New York: Longman, 1995), 3.

48. Brian R. Fry, *Mastering Public Administration: From Max Weber to Dwight Waldo* (Chatham NJ: Chatham House, 1989), 27–33.

49. Meier and Stewart, *Politics of Hispanic Education*, 33, 6. For a detailed discussion of the discretionary powers of street-level bureaucrats, see Michael Lipsky, *Street Level Bureaucracy* (New York: Russell Sage Foundation, 1980).

50. Kranz, *Participatory Bureaucracy*, 14.

51. See Samuel Krislov, *Representative Bureaucracy* (Englewood Cliffs NJ: Prentice-Hall, 1974), 10, 13. Although Kingsley is credited with first using the term in a narrow sense, Krislov argues that Kingsley's examination of discrimination toward women in bureaucracy provides a much broader view of representative bureaucracy. See Kingsley, *Representative Bureaucracy*, especially 185, 273, 282–83.

52. David H. Rosenbloom, *Federal Equal Employment Opportunity: Politics and Public Personnel Administration* (New York: Praeger, 1977), 34–35.

53. Frederick Mosher, *Democracy and the Public Service* (New York: Oxford University Press, 1968), 61–63.

54. Mosher, *Democracy and the Public Service*, 11–14.

55. For a discussion about the predictors of bureaucratic attitudes, see Kenneth John Meier, "Representative Bureaucracy: An Empirical Analysis," *American Political Science Review* 69 (June 1975): 526–42. For an analysis of the differences in attitudes between the general population and bureaucrats, see Kenneth J. Meier and Lloyd G. Nigro, "Representative Bureaucracy and Policy Preferences," *Public Administration Review* 36 (July/August 1976): 456–69.

56. Mosher, *Democracy and the Public Service*, 13–14.

57. Krislov, *Representative Bureaucracy*, 129. Also see Rosenbloom, *Federal Equal Employment Opportunity*, 36–37.

58. Krislov, *Negro in Federal Employment*, 5.

59. V. Subramaniam, "Representative Bureaucracy: A Reassessment," *American Political Science Review* 61 (December 1967): 1010.

60. Meier, "Representative Bureaucracy," 528–30.

61. Subramaniam, "Representative Bureaucracy," 1014.

62. Meier, "Representative Bureaucracy," 526.

63. Dennis Daley, "Political and Occupational Barriers to the Implementation of Affirmative Action: Administrative, Executive, and Legislative Attitudes toward Representative Bureaucracy," *Review of Public Personnel Administration* 4 (summer 1994): 5.

64. Rosenbloom, *Federal Equal Employment Opportunity*, 38–42.

65. Daley, "Political and Occupational Barriers," 4.

66. Judith J. Hendricks, "The Prognosis for Affirmative Action at the State Level: A Study of Affirmative Action Implementation in Delaware," *Review of Public Personnel Administration* 4 (summer 1984): 57–58.

67. Sowell, *Preferential Policies*, 156.

68. John J. Beggs, "The Institutional Environment: Implications for Race and Gender Inequality in the U.S. Labor Market," *American Sociological Review* 60 (August 1995): 612–33; Thomas D. Boston, "Segmented Labor Markets: New Evidence from a Study of Four Race-Gender Groups," *Industrial and Labor Relations Review* 44 (October 1990): 99–115; James E. Coverdill, "The Dual Economy and Sex Differences in Earnings," *Social Forces* 66 (June 1988): 970–93; Thomas N. Daymont, "Pay Premiums for Economic Sector and Race: A Decomposition," *Social Science Research* 9 (September 1980): 245–72; David S. Hachen Jr., "Gender Differences in Job Mobility Rates in the United States," *Social Science Research* 17 (June 1988): 93–116; Robert L. Kaufman, "The Impact of Industrial and Occupational Structure on Black-White Employment Allocation," *American Sociological Review* 51 (June 1986): 310–23; Gordon Lafer, "Minority Unemployment, Labor Market Segmentation, and the Failure of Job-Training Policy in New York," *Urban Affairs Quarterly* 28 (December 1992): 206–35; Shelly A. Smith, "Sources of Earnings Inequality in the Black and White Female Labor Forces," *Sociological Quarterly* 32 (spring 1991): 117–38; and Linda Brewster Stearns and Charlotte Wilkinson Coleman, "Industrial and Local Market Structures and Black Male Employment in the Manufacturing Sector," *Social Science Quarterly* 71 (June 1990): 285–98.

69. There is an enormous literature on dual labor market theory. For a survey of the literature, see Robert P. Althauser, "Internal Labor Markets," *American Review of Sociology* 15 (1989): 143–61; and Randy Hodson and Robert L. Kaufman, "Economic Dualism: A Critical Review," *American Sociological Review* 47 (December 1982): 727–39.

70. See, for example, William Finlay, "One Occupation, Two Labor Markets: The Case of Longshore Crane Operators," *American Sociological Review* 48 (June 1983): 306–15; and Toby L. Parcel and Marie B. Sickmeier, "One Firm, Two Labor Markets: The Case of McDonald's in the Fast-Food Industry," *Sociological Quarterly* 29 (spring 1988): 29–46.

71. Lafer, "Minority Unemployment," 215–19, 221.

3. BLACKS IN HIGHER EDUCATION

1. *Missouri ex rel. Gaines v. Canada*, 305 U.S. 337 (1938). Also see Kenneth J. Meier, Joseph Stewart Jr., and Robert E. England, *Race, Class, and Education: The Politics of Second-Generation Discrimination* (Madison: University of Wisconsin Press, 1989), 44.

2. Julian B. Roebuck and Komanduri S. Murty, *Historically Black Colleges and Universities: Their Place in American Higher Education* (Westport CT: Praeger, 1993), 27.

3. Roebuck and Murty, *Historically Black Colleges and Universities*, 40, 45–49. Also see Carol Olson and Joe Hagy, "Achieving Social Justice: An Examination of Oklahoma's Response to *Adams v. Richardson*," *Journal of Negro Education* 59 (spring 1990): 173–85.

4. Southern Education Foundation, *Redeeming the American Promise* (Alanta: Southern Education Foundation, 1995), 13.

5. See John E. Fleming, Gerald R. Gill, and David H. Swinton, *The Case for Affirmative Action for Blacks in Higher Education* (Washington DC: Howard University Press, 1978), 21–22. On the problems facing black faculty integration in predominantly white universities, see William H. Exum, "Climbing the Crystal Stair: Values, Affirmative Action, and Minority Faculty," *Social Problems* 30 (April 1983): 383–99; and David M. Rafky, "The Black Scholar in the Academic Marketplace," *Teachers College Record* 74 (December 1972): 226–60.

6. Cited in Fleming, Gill, and Swinton, *Case for Affirmative Action*, 29.

7. Exum, "Climbing the Crystal Stair," 384.

8. Kenneth W. Jackson, "Black Faculty in Academia," in Philip G. Altbach and Kofi Lomotey, eds., *The Racial Crisis in American Higher Education* (Albany: State University Press of New York, 1991), 136–37. For a discussion of the early surveys completed in the 1940s and 1960s, see Fleming, Gill, and Swinton, *Case for Affirmative Action*, 35–37. Also see Roslyn Arlin Mickelson and Melvin L. Oliver, "Making the Short List: Black Candidates and the Faculty Recruitment Process," in Altbach and Lootey, 149–66, for an analysis of the problems facing blacks in finding employment as faculty members.

9. Cynthia Fuchs Epstein, "Positive Effects of the Multiple Negative: Explaining the Success of Black Professional Women," *American Journal of Sociology* 78 (January 1973): 912–35.

10. Shirley M. Clark and Mary Corcoran, "Perspectives on the Professional Socialization of Women Faculty: A Case of Accumulative Disadvantage?" *Journal of Higher Education* 57 (January/February 1986): 20–43.

11. Southern Education Foundation, *Redeeming the American Promise*, 40.

12. NCES, *Fall Staff in Postsecondary Institutions, 1995*, tables B–1f, B–7a, B–8a.

13. W. Lee Hansen and Thomas F. Guidugli, "Comparing Salary and Employment Gains for Higher Education Administrators and Faculty Members," *Journal of Higher Education* 61 (March/April 1990): 155–56. See page 156, table 6, for percentages on private higher education employment.

14. NCES, *Fall Staff in Postsecondary Institutions*, table B-1f.

15. The major categories for these other occupations are determined by the Equal Employment Opportunity Commission. See EEOC, *Job Patterns for Minorities and Women*, 7. The professional non-faculty category refers to staff who are neither faculty nor administrators and who do not fit into the four other categories. The secretarial/clerical category refers to office employees such as bookkeepers, stenographers, clerk typists, bookstore salesclerks, and library clerks. The technical/para-professional category includes computer programmers, drafters, licensed nurses, scientific assistants, and electronic technicians, who usually receive their training in two-year colleges or technical schools or through on-the-job programs. The skilled crafts category is based on specialized manual work that involves on-the-job training, apprenticeship, or other types of formalized training and that includes mechanics, electricians, and carpenters. The service/maintenance category refers to the cleaning and care of facilities and includes such positions as cafeteria workers, bus drivers, garage laborers, custodial workers, groundskeepers, and security officers.

16. Given the extensive number of tables required to present this data, we have decided to simply summarize our findings. Data to support these findings are available from the authors upon request.

4. WHITE WOMEN IN HIGHER EDUCATION

1. Barbara Miller Solomon, *In the Company of Educated Women: A History of Women and Higher Education in America* (New Haven CT: Yale University Press, 1985), 15. Much of the historical background on women in education is taken from this book.

2. Solomon, *In the Company of Educated Women*, 135.

3. Betty Friedan, "Our Revolution Is Unique," in Michael B. Levy, ed., *Political Thought in America: An Anthology*, 2d ed. (Chicago: Dorsey Press, 1988), 468.

4. Peggy Elder, "Women in Higher Education: Qualified, Except for Sex," *National Association of Student Personnel Administrators Journal* 13 (fall 1975): 10–17.

5. Susan Astin and Mary Beth Snyder, "Affirmative Action, 1972–1982: A Decade of Response," *Change* 14 (July/August 1982): 27.

6. Kathryn M. Moore and Michael P. Johnson, "The Status of Women and Minorities in the Professoriate: The Role of Affirmative Action and Equity," *New Directions for Institutional Research* 16 (fall 1989): 49.

7. Martin J. Finkelstein, "The State of Academic Women: An Assessment of Five Competing Explanations," *Review of Higher Education* 7 (spring 1984): 223, 225.

8. Shirley M. Clark and Mary Corcoran, "Perspectives on the Professional Socialization of Women Faculty: A Case of Accumulative Disadvantage?" *Journal of Higher Education* 57 (January/February 1986): 39.

9. Linda K. Johnsrud, "Administrative Promotion: The Power of Gender," *Journal of Higher Education* 62 (March/April 1991): 120, 140–42, 139–40, 143–44.

10. Amy S. Wharton, "Gender Segregation in Private-Sector, Public-Sector, and Self-Employed Occupations, 1950–1981," *Social Science Quarterly* 70 (December 1989): 923–40.

11. Rita Mae Kelly, *The Gendered Economy: Work, Careers, and Success* (Newbury Park CA: Sage, 1991), 47–49.

12. Lee Sigelman, "The Curious Case of Women in State and Local Government," *Social Science Quarterly* 57 (March 1976): 591–604.

13. NCES, *Fall Staff in Postsecondary Institutions*, tables B1-f, B-8a, B-7a.

14. NCES, *Fall Staff in Postsecondary Institutions*, table B-1f.

15. As in chapter 3, we summarize our findings without presenting all the data in tables. Data to support these findings are available from the authors upon request.

16. Unpublished data from the EEOC.

5. HISPANICS IN HIGHER EDUCATION

1. Meyer Weinberg, *A Chance to Learn: The History of Race and Education in the United States* (Cambridge: Cambridge University Press, 1977), 337.

2. Weinberg, *Chance to Learn*, 340–42.

3. For statistics on minority college enrollment and graduation rates, see U.S. Department of Education, National Center for Education Statistics, *The Condition of Education, 1994* (Washington DC: U.S. Government Printing Office, 1994); and Deborah J. Carter and Reginald Wilson, *Minorities in Higher Education: 1992* (Washington DC: American Council on Education, 1993).

4. See Adalberto Aguirre Jr. and Ruben O. Martinez, *Chicanos in Higher Education: Issues and Dilemmas for the 21st Century* (Washington DC: George Washington University, 1993), 38, 41, 46.

5. The relationship between the supply of Hispanic doctorates and the number of Hispanic faculty as well as Hispanic new faculty hires is considered in chapter 7.

6. Richard R. Verdugo, "Analysis of Tenure among Hispanic Higher Education Faculty," *Journal of the Association of Mexican-American Educators*, 1992, 25, 27.

7. Hisauro Garza, "The 'Barrioization' of Hispanic Faculty," *Educational Record* 68 (fall 1987–winter 1988): 123, 124.

8. Valora Washington and William Harvey, *Affirmative Rhetoric, Negative Action* (Washington DC: George Washington University, 1989), 75. On the theme of racism against minorities, particularly Hispanics, see also Hisauro Garza, "Second-Class Academics: Chicano/Latino Faculty in U.S. Universities," *New Directions for Teaching and Learning*, no. 53 (spring 1993): 33–41; Michael A. Olivas, "Latino Faculty at the Border,"

in Donald Altschiller, ed., *Affirmative Action* (New York: H. W. Wilson, 1991), 101–8; Maria de la Luz Reyes, "Practices of the Academy: Barriers to Access for Chicano Academics," in Philip G. Altbach and Kofi Lomotey, eds., *The Racial Crisis in American Higher Education* (Albany: State University of New York Press, 1991), 167–86; Maria de la Luz Reyes and John J. Halcon, "Racism in Academia: The Old Wolf Revisited," *Harvard Educational Review* 58 (August 1988): 299–314; and Richard R. Verdugo, "The Segregated Citadel: Some Personal Observations on the Academic Career Not Offered," in Raymond V. Padilla and Rudolfo Chávez Chávez, eds., *The Leaning Ivory Tower: Latino Professors in American Universities* (Albany: State University of New York Press, 1993), 101–9.

9. Garza, "Second-Class Academics," 35.

10. See, for example, Aguirre and Martinez, *Chicanos in Higher Education*, 56; Robert Haro, "Held to a Higher Standard: Latino Executive Selection in Higher Education," 189–207, especially 202–5, in Padilla and Chávez Chávez, *Leaning Ivory Tower*, 101–9; Luz Reyes and Halcon, "Racism in Academia," 299–314; and Yolanda T. Moses, "The Roadblocks Confronting Minority Administrators," *Chronicle of Higher Education*, January 13, 1993, B1–2.

11. Moses, "Roadblocks Confronting Minority Administrators," B1.

12. Haro, "Held to a Higher Standard," 203. Haro defines the term *Latino* to include "men and women of Cuban, Mexican, Puerto Rican, and Central or South American descent, and those from other Spanish-speaking regions of the world," 199, 203, 204, 205.

13. Robert P. Haro, "Latinos and Executive Positions in Higher Education," *Educational Record* 71 (summer 1990): 40.

14. Leonard A. Valverde, "The Missing Element: Hispanics at the Top in Higher Education," *Change* 20 (May/June 1988): 11.

15. As in previous chapters, we summarize our findings without presenting all the data in tables. Data to support these findings are available from the authors upon request.

16. NCES, *Fall Staff in Postsecondary Institutions*, tables B-7a, B-8a, B-1f.

6. ASIANS AND NATIVE AMERICANS IN HIGHER EDUCATION

1. Deborah J. Carter and Reginald Wilson, *Minorities in Higher Education: 1992* (Washington DC: American Council on Education, 1993), 24.

2. Jayjia Hsia, *Asian Americans in Higher Education and at Work* (Hillsdale NJ: Lawrence Erlbaum Associates, 1988), 13.

3. Victor Hao Li, "Asian Discrimination: Fact or Fiction," *College Board Review*, no. 149 (fall 1988): 21.

4. Bill Ong Hing, *Making and Remaking Asian America through Immigration Policy, 1850–1990* (Stanford CA: Stanford University Press, 1993), 147–53.

5. L. Ling-Chi Wang, "Meritocracy and Diversity in Higher Education: Discrimination against Asian Americans in the Post-Bakke Era," *Urban Review* 20 (fall 1988): especially 202, 204–6. Also see Dana Y. Takagi, "From Discrimination to Affirmative Action: Facts in the Asian American Admissions Controversy," *Social Problems* 37 (November 1990): 578–92; and Dana Y. Talago, *The Retreat from Race: Asian-American Admissions and Racial Politics* (New Brunswick NJ: Rutgers University Press, 1992).

6. Hsia, *Asian Americans in Higher Education*, 147–48.

7. Don T. Nakanishi, "Asian Pacific Americans in Higher Education: Faculty and Administrative Representation and Tenure," *New Directions for Teaching and Learning*, no. 53 (spring 1993): 51, 52, 53, 55.

8. Nakanishi, "Asian Pacific Americans in Higher Education," 53.

9. Hsia, *Asian Americans in Higher Education*, 193–94.

10. See S. Chan, "Beyond Affirmative Action: Empowering Asian American Faculty," *Change* 21 (Nov.–Dec. 1989): 48–51; E. Escuetta and E. O'Brien, "Asian Americans in Higher Education: Trends and Issues," *Research Briefs* (American Council on Education) 2, no. 4 (1991): 1–11; D. Minami, "Guerrilla War at UCLA: Political and Legal Dimensions of the Tenure Battle," *Amerasia Journal* 16, no. 10 (1990): 81–107; and Nakanishi, "Asian Pacific Americans in Higher Education."

11. See, in particular, Chan, "Beyond Affirmative Action," 48–51; and Minami, "Guerrilla War at UCLA," 81–107. See also Escuetta and O'Brien, "Asian Americans in Higher Education," 1–11; and Nakanishi, "Asian Pacific Americans in Higher Education," 53.

12. As in previous chapters, we summarize our findings without presenting all the data in tables. Data to support these findings are available from the authors upon request.

13. Kim and Lewis, "Asian Americans in the Public Service," 289.

14. NCES, *Fall Staff in Postsecondary Institutions, 1995*, tables B-7a, B-8a, B-1f.

15. Mary B. Davis, ed., *Native America in the Twentieth Century: An Encyclopedia* (New York: Garland, 1994), 237.

16. See Philip James, "Native Americans and Higher Education," *College Student Affairs Journal* 12 (fall 1992): 56.

17. David H. DeJong, *Promises of the Past: A History of Indian Education in the United States* (Golden CO: North American Press, 1993), 244.

18. See Carnegie Foundation for the Advancement of Teaching, *Tribal Colleges: Shaping the Future of Native America, A Special Report* (Princeton NJ: Carnegie Foundation, 1989), 21. A list of twenty-four tribal colleges is in the appendix, 89–90. In 1996 there were twenty-nine such colleges. For a list of these colleges, see *New York Times*, October 27, 1996, 24.

19. Joe T. Darden, Joshua G. Bagakas, Tracy Armstrong, and Terrence Payne, "Segregation of American Indian Undergraduate Students in Institutions of Higher Education," *Equity and Excellence in Education* 27 (December 1994): 62.

20. See James, "Native Americans and Higher Education," 56–57; and Judith Davis, "Factors Contributing to Post-Secondary Achievement of American Indians," *Tribal College: Journal of American Indian Higher Education* 4 (fall 1992): 24.

21. Wayne J. Stein, "The Survival of American Indian Faculty," *Thought and Action: The NEA Higher Education Journal* 10 (spring 1994): 101.

22. The percentages were computed from the U.S. Bureau of the Census population data for 1980 and 1990.

23. Stein, "Survival of American Indian Faculty," 103.

24. Linda Sue Warner, "A Study of American Indian Females in Higher Education Administration," *Initiatives*, 56, no. 4 (1995): 11–17.

25. As in previous chapters, we summarize our findings without presenting all the data in tables. Data to support these findings are available from the authors upon request.

26. NCES, *Fall Staff in Postsecondary Institutions, 1995*, tables B-7a, B-8a, B-1f.

7. MINORITY AND FEMALE DOCTORATES

1. The data on doctorates discussed in this chapter are from reports prepared by the National Research Council. Doctorate recipients of every race/ethnic group – men or women – are placed in four categories by NRC: U.S. citizens, permanent visa holders, those with temporary visas, and scholars of unknown citizenship. Since many of the foreign students with temporary visas or unknown citizenship seek faculty positions in American colleges and universities, we emphasize total doctorates earned by a group rather than the immigration status of the members of a group.

2. U.S. Department of Education, National Center for Education Statistics, *Projections of Education Statistics to 2005* (Washington DC: U.S. Government Printing Office, 1995), 63.

3. See U.S. Department of Education, National Center for Education Statistics, *Digest of Education Statistics* (Washington DC: U.S. Government Printing Office, 1989); and American Council on Education, *Minorities in Higher Education* (Washington DC: U.S. Government Printing Office, 1991). See also Harold Orlans, "Affirmative Action in Higher Education," *Annals of the American Academy of Political and Social Science*, no. 523 (September 1992): 154.

4. Orlans, "Affirmative Action in Higher Education," 154.

5. Martha S. West, "Women Faculty: Frozen in Time," *Academe* 81 (July/August 1995): 26.

6. The data on faculty and administrative positions reported in this chapter, as in the rest of the book, are from reports prepared by the Equal Employment Opportunity Commission (EEOC). In this chapter we focus on positions in *all* institutions, since the

distinction between private and public institutions is less relevant to our discussion of the relationship between supply and demand of the doctorates.

7. One problem with the data reported by Orlans is that faculty positions are "based on number of different individuals, not full-time equivalents." See Orlans, "Affirmative Action in Higher Education," 154.

8. See Helen Astin and M. B. Snyder, "Affirmative Action, 1972–1982 – A Decade of Response," *Change* 14 (July–August 1982): 26–31, 59; Howard R. Bowen and Jack H. Schuster, *American Professors: A National Resource Imperiled* (New York: Oxford University Press, 1986); Mary Frank Fox, "Women and Higher Education: Sex Differentials in the Status of Students and Scholars," in Jo Freeman, ed., *Women: A Feminist Perspective* (Palo Alto CA: Mayfield, 1984); Judith M. Gappa and Barbara S. Uehling, *Women in Academe: Steps to Greater Equality* (Washington DC: American Association for Higher Education, 1979); Robert J. Menges and William H. Exum, "Barriers to the Progress of Women and Minority Faculty," *Journal of Higher Education* 54 (March–April 1983): 123–44; Orlans, "Affirmative Action in Higher Education"; and Stephanie L. Witt, *The Pursuit of Race and Gender Equity in American Academe* (New York: Praeger, 1990).

9. We cannot derive similar conclusions about administrative positions because a doctorate is generally required for faculty positions, but that is not the case for many of the administrative positions included in our data. For example, deans and academic administrators above the rank of dean are usually required to have doctorates. Administrators such as those in admissions, records, financial aid, and housing, on the other hand, are not required to hold this degree.

10. See, for example, John H. Bunzel, "Exclusive Opportunities," *American Enterprise* 1 (March/April 1990): 46–51.

11. NCES, *Fall Staff in Postsecondary Institutions, 1995,* tables B-7a, B-1f.

12. NCES, *Fall Staff in Postsecondary Institutions, 1995,* table B-8a.

13. Astin and Snyder, "Affirmative Action"; and Bowen and Schuster, *American Professors,* 57.

14. Horace Mann Bond, *Black American Scholars* (Detroit: Balamp, 1972), 29.

15. See Harry Washington Greene, *Holders of Doctorates among American Negroes: An Educational and Social Study of Negroes Who Have Earned Doctoral Degrees in Course, 1876–1943* (Boston: Meador, 1946), 22; and Bond, *Black American Scholars,* 26. According to Bond's research, another black, Father Patrick Francis Healy, S.J., from Georgia, received a doctorate in 1865 from the University of Louvain in Belgium. See Bond, *Black American Scholars,* 26.

16. Greene, *Holders of Doctorates,* 26, table 1.

17. Bond, *Black American Scholars,* 27, table 2–1.

18. See, for example, Bowen and Schuster, *American Professors,* in particular 153 n. 10;

Greene, *Holders of Doctorates*, 40; and Alan Fechter, "A Statistical Portrait of Black Ph.D.'s," in Willie Pearson Jr. and H. Kenneth Bechtel, eds., *Blacks, Science and American Education* (New Brunswick NJ: Rutgers University Press, 1989), 79–101.

19. Greene, *Holders of Doctorates*, 40. Greene listed twenty-six black doctorates in psychology and philosophy. NRC data include psychology in the social sciences and philosophy in the humanities.

20. Fechter, "Statistical Portrait," 80.

21. In our data, the physical sciences include mathematics, computer science, physics and astronomy, chemistry, and earth, atmosphere, and marine science. Engineering is placed in a separate category.

22. H. Kenneth Bechtel, "Introduction," in Pearson and Bechtel, *Blacks, Science and American Education*, 19.

23. See Donald R. Deskins Jr., "Prospects for Minority Doctorates in the Year 2000: Employment Opportunities in a Changing American Society," *National Political Science Review* 4 (1994): 111–17; Pearson and Bechtel, *Blacks, Science and American Education*, 100–101; see also Fred Crossland, *Minority Access to College* (New York: Schocken, 1971); and National Board on Graduate Education, *Minority Group Participation in Graduate Education: A Report with Recommendations* (Washington DC: National Science Foundation, 1976).

24. For a history of blacks in higher education, see Meyer Weinberg, *A Chance to Learn* (Cambridge: Cambridge University Press, 1977), 263–336.

25. See Bowen and Schuster, *American Professors*, 154–55.

26. Fechter, "Statistical Portrait," 100.

27. Deskins, "Prospects for Minority Doctorates," 114.

28. Rosyln Arlin Mickelson and Melvin L. Oliver, "The Demographic Fallacy of the Black Academic: Does Quality Rise to the Top?" in Walter R. Allen, Edgar G. Epps, and Nesha Z. Haniff, eds., *College in Black and White* (Albany: State University of New York Press, 1991), 177.

29. See, for example, Orlans, "Affirmative Action in Higher Education," 153; and a report by Valora Washington and William Harvey, *Affirmative Rhetoric, Negative Action* (Washington DC: George Washington University, 1989), 25.

30. For a study on the rather disappointing advancement of black students in graduate and professional programs, see Gail E. Thomas, "Black Students in U.S. Graduate and Professional Schools in the 1980s: A National and Institutional Assessment," *Harvard Educational Review* 57 (August 1987): 261–82.

31. Weinberg, *Chance to Learn*, 340, 345.

32. The NRC data of 1979 consider all Hispanics in one category; 1983, 1991, and 1995 data are on doctorates awarded to Puerto-Rican, Mexican-Americans, and "other" Hispanics. We placed all three subgroups of Hispanics under the umbrella of "Hispanics."

33. See Deskins, "Prospects for Minority Doctorates," 119.

34. National Science Foundation, *Women, Minorities and Persons with Disabilities in Science and Engineering: 1994* (Arlington VA: NSF, 1994), 98.

35. NSF, *Women, Minorities and Persons with Disabilities*, 98 n. 11.

36. Orlans, "Affirmative Action in Higher Education," 156.

37. See NSF, *Women, Minorities and Persons with Disabilities*, 10, 131.

38. NCES, *Fall Staff in Postsecondary Institutions*, tables B-7a, B-8a.

39. Some sources, however, maintain that there is little prejudice against Asians in faculty positions. See NCES, *Fall Staff in Postsecondary Institutions*, 99–100; see also Orlans, "Affirmative Action in Higher Education," 155.

40. Weinberg, *Chance to Learn*, 338, 337.

41. Theodore Caplow and Reece McGee, *The Academic Marketplace* (New York: Basic Books, 1958).

42. Neil J. Smelser and Robin Content, *The Changing Academic Market* (Berkeley: University of California Press, 1980).

43. Bowen and Schuster, *American Professors*.

44. William J. Bowen and Julie Ann Sosa, *Prospects for Faculty in the Arts and Sciences* (Princeton NJ: Princeton University Press, 1989).

45. Dolores L. Burke, *A New Academic Marketplace* (New York: Greenwood Press, 1988).

46. See, for example, Burke, *New Academic Marketplace*, 56–58; and Bowen and Schuster, *American Professors*, 57–60.

47. Washington and Harvey, *Affirmative Rhetoric, Negative Action*, 24.

48. Bowen and Sosa, *Prospects for Faculty*, 84–89, 128–43.

49. See, for example, Deskins, "Prospects for Minority Doctorates," 117–18.

50. Deskins, "Prospects for Minority Doctorates," 117, 119. These percentages are lower than our percentages because Deskins considered only Ph.D.'s earned by U.S. citizens and then divided these figures by *all* Ph.D.'s, including those earned by foreign students.

51. Deskins, "Prospects for Minority Doctorates," 129, table 8.

52. Deskins, "Prospects for Minority Doctorates," 135.

53. See *New York Times*, February 21, 1995, A1 and B5.

8. POLITICAL AND SOCIOECONOMIC DETERMINANTS

1. See Dennis Daley, "Political and Occupational Barriers to the Implementation of Affirmative Action: Administrative, Executive, and Legislative Attitudes toward Representative Bureaucracy," *Review of Public Personnel Administration* 4 (summer 1984): 4–15; and Judith J. Hendricks, "The Prognosis for Affirmative Action at the State Level: A Study of Affirmative Action Implementation in Delaware," *Review of Public Personnel*

Administration 4 (summer 1984): 57–70. On state higher education, see Kul B. Rai and John W. Critzer, "Black Faculty Employment and Party Control: A Comparative State Analysis," *Western Journal of Black Studies* 17 (December 1993): 211–18; and John W. Critzer and Kul B. Rai, "Blacks and Women in Public Higher Education: Political and Socioeconomic Factors Underlying Diversity at the State Level," *Women & Politics* 19, no. 1 (1998): 19–38.

2. On the influence of city councils, see Thomas R. Dye and James Renick, "Political Power and City Jobs: Determinants of Minority Employment," *Social Science Quarterly* 62 (September 1981): 475–86; and Kenneth R. Mladenka, "Blacks and Hispanics in Urban Politics," *American Political Science Review* 83 (March 1989): 165–91. For the significance of minority mayors, see Peter K. Eisinger, "Black Employment in Municipal Jobs: The Impact of Black Political Power," *American Political Science Review* 76 (June 1982), 380–92; and Lana Stein, "Representative Local Government: Minorities in the Municipal Work Force," *Journal of Politics* 48 (August 1986): 694–713. The role of female mayors is discussed in Grace Hall Saltzstein, "Female Mayors and Women in Municipal Jobs," *American Journal of Political Science* 30 (February 1986), 140–64.

3. Mladenka, "Blacks and Hispanics in Urban Politics," 165–91. On the role of public sector unions, see Kenneth R. Mladenka, "Public Employee Unions, Reformism, and Black Employment in 1,200 American Cities," *Urban Affairs Quarterly* 26 (June 1991): 532–48; and Mladenka, "Barriers to Hispanic Employment Success in 1,200 Cities," *Social Science Quarterly* 70 (June 1989): 391–407.

4. Grace Hall and Alan Saltzstein, "Equal Employment in Urban Governments: The Potential Problem of Interminority Competition," *Public Personnel Management* 4 (November–December 1975), 386–93; Paula D. McClain, "The Changing Dynamics of Urban Politics: Black and Hispanic Municipal Employment – Is There Competition?" *Journal of Politics* 55 (May 1993), 399–414; Albert K. Karnig, Susan Welch, and Richard A. Eribes, "Employment of Women by Cities in the Southwest," *Social Science Journal* 21 (October 1984): 41–48; Susan Welch, Albert K. Karnig, and Richard Eribes, "Correlates of Women's Employment in Local Governments," *Urban Affairs Quarterly* 18 (June 1983): 551–64; and Susan Welch, Albert K. Karnig, and Richard Eribes, "Changes in Hispanic Local Public Employment in the Southwest," *Western Political Science Journal* 36 (December 1983): 660–73.

5. Welch, Karnig, and Eribes, "Changes in Hispanic Local Public Employment."

6. McClain, "Changing Dynamics of Urban Politics."

7. Sigelman, "Curious Case of Women," 591–604.

8. Kellough, "Integration in the Public Workplace," 557–66.

9. See, for example, Dye and Resnick, "Political Power and City Jobs"; Eisinger, "Black Employment in Municipal Jobs"; Mladenka, "Blacks and Hispanics in Urban Politics";

Stein, "Representative Local Government"; and Welch, Karnig, and Eribes, "Changes in Hispanic Local Public Employment."

10. V. O. Key Jr. *Southern Politics in State and Nation* (New York: Random House, 1949), 307.

11. Richard E. Dawson and James A. Robinson, "Inter-Party Competition, Economic Variables, and Welfare Policies in the American States," *Journal of Politics* 25 (May 1963): 265–89.

12. Thomas R. Dye, *Politics, Economics, and the Public* (Chicago: Rand McNally, 1966); Richard I. Hofferbert, "The Relation between Public Policy and Some Structural and Environmental Variables in the American States," *American Political Science Review* 60 (March 1966): 73–82; and Richard Winters, "Party Control and Policy Change," *American Journal of Political Science* 20 (November 1976): 597–636.

13. See Charles F. Cnudde and Donald J. McCrone, "Party Competition and Welfare Policies in the American States," *American Political Science Review* 63 (September 1969): 858–66; Brian R. Fry and Richard F. Winters, "The Politics of Redistribution," *American Political Science Review* 64 (June 1970): 508–22; and Ira Sharkansky and Richard I. Hofferbert, "Dimensions of State Politics, Economics, and Public Policy," *American Political Science Review* 63 (September 1969): 867–79.

14. Sung-Don Hwang and Virginia Gray, "External Limits and Internal Determinants of State Public Policy," *Western Political Quarterly* 44 (June 1991): 277–98.

15. Edward T. Jennings, "Competition, Constituencies, and Welfare Policies in American States," *American Political Science Review* 73 (June 1979): 414–29.

16. See Hwang and Gray, "External Limits and Internal Determinants"; and Thomas R. Dye, "Party and Policy in the States," *Journal of Politics* 46 (November 1984): 1097–116.

17. See Dye, "Party and Policy in the States"; James C. Garand, "Explaining Government Growth in the U.S. States," *American Political Science Review* 82 (September 1988): 837–49; and Winters, "Politics of Redistribution."

18. See Jennings, "Competition, Constituencies, and Welfare Policies"; Dye, "Party and Policy in the States"; and Hwang and Gray, "External Limits and Internal Determinants."

19. Daniel J. Elazar, *American Federalism: A View from the States* (New York: Thomas Y. Crowell, 1972).

20. See for example, Jody L. Fitzpatrick and Rodney E. Hero, "Political Culture and Political Characteristics of the American States: A Consideration of Some Old and New Questions," *Western Political Quarterly* 41 (March 1988): 145–53; Charles A. Johnson, "Political Culture in the American States: Elazar's Formulation Examined," *American Journal of Political Science* 20 (August 1976): 491–509; David Lowery and Lee Sigelman, "Political Culture and State Public Policy: The Missing Link," *Western Political Quar-*

terly 35 (September 1982): 376–84; Peter F. Nardulli, "Political Subcultures in the American States: An Empirical Examination of Elazar's Formulation," *American Politics Quarterly* 18 (July 1990): 287–315; Timothy D. Schiltz and R. Lee Rainey, "The Geographical Distribution of Elazar's Political Subculture among the Mass Population: A Research Note," *Western Political Quarterly* 31 (September 1978): 410–15; and Robert L. Savage, "Looking for Political Subcultures: A Critique of the Rummage-Sale Approach," *Western Political Quarterly* 34 (June 1981): 331–36.

21. Rai and Critzer, "Black Faculty Employment and Party Control."

22. See Jeff Stonecash, review of *Statehouse Democracy*, by Robert Erikson, Gerald C. Wright, and John P. McIver, *American Political Science Review* 89 (March 1995): 200–201.

23. Gerald C. Wright, Robert S. Erikson, and John P. McIver, "Measuring State Partisanship and Ideology with Survey Data," *Journal of Politics* 47 (May 1985): 469–89; Gerald C. Wright Jr., Robert S. Erikson, and John P. McIver, "Public Opinion and Policy Liberalism in the American States," *American Journal of Political Science* 31 (November 1987): 980–1001; and Robert S. Erikson, Gerald C. Wright Jr., and John P. McIver, "Political Parties, Public Opinion, and State Policy in the United States," *American Political Science Review* 83 (September 1989): 729–50.

24. Wright, Erikson, and McIver, "Measuring State Partisanship and Ideology."

25. Thomas M. Holbrook-Provow and Steven C. Poe, "Measuring State Political Ideology," *American Politics Quarterly* 15 (July 1987): 399–416.

26. See Wright, Erikson, and McIver, "Measuring State Partisanship and Ideology."

27. Critzer and Rai, "Blacks and Women in Public Higher Education."

28. Wright, Erikson, and McIver, "Measuring State Partisanship and Ideology." 478–79, 247.

29. Council of State Governments, *Book of the States*, vol. 27 (Lexington KY: Council of State Governments, 1988).

30. Council of State Governments, *Book of the States*, vol. 28 (Lexington KY: Council of State Governments, 1990); U.S. Bureau of the Census, *U.S. Statistical Abstracts* (Washington DC: U.S. Government Printing Office, 1994). For New Jersey and Virginia, 1990 data is used.

31. U.S. Bureau of the Census, *General Population Characteristics in the United States* (Washington DC: U.S. Printing Office, 1990).

32. U.S. Bureau of the Census, *U.S. Statistical Abstracts*; various editions are used in this study.

33. See Kim Quaile Hill and Jan E. Leighley, "The Policy Consequences of Class Bias in State Electorates," *American Journal of Political Science* 36 (May 1992): 351–65; and Robert D. Brown, "Party Cleavages and Welfare Effort in the American States," *American Political Science Review* 89 (March 1995): 23–33. The data used are from U.S. Depart-

ment of Commerce, *County and City Data Book: 1994* (Washington DC: U.S. Government Printing Office, 1994).

34. Michael S. Lewis-Beck, *Applied Regression: An Introduction* (Beverly Hills CA: Sage, 1980).

35. See, for example, Raul Hinojosa-Ojeka, Martin Carnoy, and Hugh Daley, "An Even Greater U-turn: Latinos and the New Inequality," in Edwin Melendez, Clara Rodriguez, and Janis Barry Figueroa, eds., *Hispanics in the Labor Force: Issues and Policies* (New York: Plenum Press, 1991), 25–52.

36. See Hall and Saltzstein, "Equal Employment in Urban Governments"; and Welch, Karnig, and Eribes, "Changes in Hispanic Local Public Employment."

37. Gregory B. Lewis, "Progress toward Racial and Sexual Equality in the Federal Civil Service? *Public Administration Review* 48 (May–June 1988): 705.

38. James N. Baron, Brian S. Mittman, and Andrew E. Newman, "Targets of Opportunity: Organizational and Environmental Determinants of Gender Integration within the California Civil Service, 1979-1985," *American Journal of Sociology* 96 (May 1991): 1396.

9. SUMMARY AND CONCLUSION

1. Sowell, *Preferential Policies.*

APPENDIXES

1. EEOC, *Job Patterns of Minorities and Women,* 7.

2. EEOC, *Job Patterns of Minorities and Women,* 6.

Index